D1564131

LOYALISTS *and* LAYABOUTS

Reparations
Sailors, Slackers and Blind Pigs: Halifax at War
Not Guilty: The Trial of Gerald Regan
Flight 111: The Tragedy of the Swissair Crash
More Than Just Folks
Net Profits

LOYALISTS
and
LAYABOUTS

THE RAPID RISE AND FASTER FALL OF SHELBURNE, NOVA SCOTIA: 1783–1792

STEPHEN KIMBER

DOUBLEDAY CANADA

Doubleday Canada and colophon are trademarks.

Library and Archives Canada Cataloguing in Publication

Kimber, Stephen
    Loyalists and layabouts : the rapid rise and faster fall of Shelburne, Nova Scotia, 1783-1792 / Stephen Kimber.

Includes bibliographical references.
ISBN 978-0-385-66172-0

    1. United Empire loyalists—Nova Scotia—Shelburne—History. 2. Shelburne (N.S.)—History. 3. United Empire Loyalists—Nova Scotia—Shelburne—Biography. I. Title.

FC2349.S55K54 2008   971.6'2502   C2008-900267-9

Jacket image: Sketch by J. E. Woolford, History Collection, Nova Scotia Museum
Text design: Terri Nimmo

Printed and bound in the USA

Published in Canada by Doubleday Canada
a division of Random House of Canada Limited

Visit Random House of Canada Limited's website: www.randomhouse.ca

BVG 10 9 8 7 6 5 4 3 2 1

FOR MY CHILDREN

Matthew
Emily
Michael

In all Canada there is no other community that has a history akin to that of the now modest town of Shelburne, Nova Scotia. Like individuals, some places have greatness thrust upon them—greatness which may grow or recede, and the fluctuating fortunes of this haven on the rugged coast of southern Nova Scotia will here be briefly told.

J. PLIMSOLL EDWARDS
"The Shelburne That Was and Was Not"

The inhabitants of Shelburne from the highest to the lowest, have a pitiable passion for finery, reveling and dancing and every species of sensual gratification. They vie with one another in making an external appearance in the public eye, as being persuaded that the world will judge of them much more by this than from their internal worth.

JAMES FRASER
"A Sketch of Shelburnian Manners"

CONTENTS

SAMUEL BIRCH, British general responsible for the fate of black
Loyalists in New York.

STEPHEN BLUCKE, free black, unofficial leader of Birchtown settlers,
schoolmaster.

WILLIAM BOOTH, captain lieutenant in Royal Corps of Engineers, posted
against his will to Shelburne, 1787–89, with his wife Hannah (Proudfoot).

EDWARD BRINLEY, commissary officer for the settlement at Shelburne,
responsible for distributing king's bounty.

OLIVER BRUFF, prominent New York jeweller before the war, unsuccessful Shelburne tinker afterwards.

MAJOR GENERAL JOHN BURGOYNE, British army officer and politician
who surrendered after the Battle of Saratoga.

CAPTAIN JOHN CAMBEL, commander-in-chief of the Royal Corps of
Engineers in Nova Scotia during the late 1780s, William's Booth's boss
and nemesis.

GENERAL JOHN CAMPBELL, commander-in-chief of British forces in
British North America in the years after the American Revolution, succeeded Guy Carleton.

SIR GUY CARLETON, New York–based commander-in-chief of British
forces in the Americas, 1782–83; later, governor-in-chief of Canada.

THOMAS CLARKSON, British navy lieutenant, abolitionist, Sierra Leone
Company agent in Nova Scotia, 1791–92.

GENERAL HENRY CLINTON, army officer who became commander-in-
chief of British forces after the defeat at Saratoga and served for four
years, led successful assault on Charles Town.

CHARLES CORNWALLIS, British general at the fateful Battle of Yorktown.

GEORGE DRUMMOND, Shelburne settler, doctor, and collector of customs.

JOSEPH DURFEE, Newport sea captain and merchant, original member of
the Port Roseway Associates, gentleman farmer and civic official in
Shelburne.

FREEBORN GARRETTSON, Methodist missionary to Nova Scotia, 1785–87.

DAVID GEORGE, freed slave and prominent black Baptist preacher in
Shelburne and Sierra Leone, married to Phyllis.

GEORGE GERMAIN, British politician, secretary of state during the American Revolution.

LAWRENCE HARTSHORNE, Halifax businessman and Quaker, agent who assisted John Clarkson in compiling list of Halifax-area blacks who wanted to go to Sierra Leone.

ADMIRAL RICHARD HOWE, GENERAL WILLIAM HOWE, British military commanders in America during the revolution.

BOSTON KING, freed slave, loyalist settler, and later preacher in Nova Scotia and Sierra Leone; married to Violet.

JOHN MARRANT, freed slave, ordained Huntingdon Connexion minister, missionary.

BENJAMIN MARSTON, Marblehead businessman, seafarer, Shelburne deputy surveyor.

JOHN MURRAY, EARL OF DUNMORE, last royalist governor of Virginia, author of the 1775 Dunmore proclamation freeing slaves who left their masters to fight for the British.

LORD FREDERICK NORTH, British prime minister, 1770–82.

GEORGE PANTON, Shelburne Anglican minister, 1783–85.

JOHN PARR, governor of Nova Scotia, 1782–91.

THOMAS PETERS, freed slave, unofficial leader of black settlements in Annapolis and Digby, agent for Sierra Leone Company, Sierra Leone settler.

WILLIAM PETTY, LORD SHELBURNE, British prime minister (1782–83), responsible for negotiating peace treaty with the new United States of America, patron to John Parr.

EDMUND PROUDFOOT, SAMUEL PROUDFOOT, William Booth's brothers-in-law; Samuel operated a Grenada plantation; Edmund was a merchant in London.

JOSEPH PYNCHON, first president of the Port Roseway Associates, their agent in Nova Scotia before the founding of Port Roseway.

JAMES RIVINGTON, New York bookseller, printer, and infamous publisher.

JAMES ROBERTSON, ALEXANDER ROBERTSON, loyalist printers in New York and Shelburne.

JAMES SWORDS, THOMAS SWORDS, brothers who apprenticed to the Robertsons in the printing trade and followed them to Shelburne.

MICHAEL WALLACE, Halifax businessman and politician, involved in a
dispute with William Booth, appointed agent to assist John Clarkson in
arranging fleet for Sierra Leone.

WILLIAM WALTER, Shelburne Anglican minister, 1783–91.

BROOK WATSON, commissary general under Sir Guy Carleton during the
evacuation of New York, 1782–83.

MARGARET WATSON, widow of British soldier, loyalist refugee,
Shelburne innkeeper.

JOHN WENTWORTH, last loyalist governor of New Hampshire, John
Parr's rival for the governorship of Nova Scotia, surveyor of his
Majesty's woods.

GIDEON WHITE, *Mayflower* descendant, member of one of
Massachusetts' most powerful families, British army volunteer, Port
Roseway Associate, Shelburne merchant and politician, cousin to
Benjamin Marston and Edward Winslow.

MOSES WILKINSON, freed slave, Methodist minister in Nova Scotia and
Sierra Leone.

EDWARD WINSLOW, *Mayflower* descendant, member of one of
Massachusetts' most powerful families, muster master of British
forces in North America during the revolutionary war, Nova Scotia
agent for loyalist regiments after the evacuation, cousin to Benjamin
Marston and Gideon White.

THE UNITED STATES AND THE BRITISH COLONIES
IN NORTH AMERICA (1763–1803)

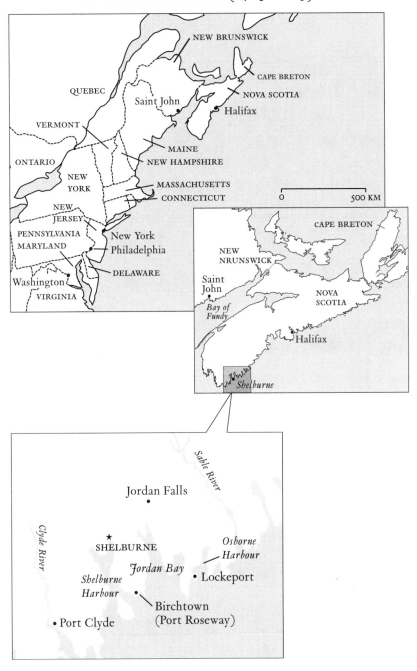

INTRODUCTION

I am not now, nor ever have been an historian. By training, I'm a journalist; by inclination, a storyteller.

I knew from the beginning of this project that trying to translate the usual fragmentary, sometimes contradictory, often dubious details of the lives of ordinary people, all of them long dead, into a narrative that captured not only the reality of their lives but also the larger truth of how and why a 225-year-old city rose and fell within the historic blink of an eye—and do all of that without playing fast and loose with the known facts—was going to be challenging, and probably frustrating.

And it was.

As a journalist, I'm accustomed to writing about recent events. When I do that, I have the luxury of interviewing flesh-and-blood human beings. Later, if I can't make sense of some sequence of events, or simply want to know more about an interesting incident that I'd missed or that they'd casually passed over the first time we talked, I simply pick up the telephone, call, and ask them.

Unfortunately, it's impossible to ask the dearly departed to clarify or elaborate when you discover something in their life-on-paper that puzzles or confuses. You're stuck with what you know and—just as importantly—what you don't.

I still don't know enough about the women of Shelburne, for example. When I began my research, I had hoped to discover a strong female character whose story could become part of this book. There undoubtedly were many of them in Shelburne. Unfortunately, they didn't have the time to write about their experiences because they were too busy living them, or if they did, those diaries and letters have largely long since been lost to history.

During the course of my research, I came tantalizingly close on a couple of occasions to finding the female character I was seeking. Margaret Cowper-Fletcher-Watson-Cutt, for example, could have made a fascinating central character. She certainly lived an extraordinary life. In the mid-1770s, she and her two young children followed her soldier-husband from London across the ocean to America, where she witnessed his death in a revolutionary battle. Then both of her sons died. A few years later, she married again, to a man who'd been her late husband's cellmate while they were prisoners of war. Margaret had two more children by him. In 1783, she and her second family became part of the historic exodus of refugees who sailed from New York to Shelburne. They'd barely begun to settle into their new lives when husband number two died, probably of a heart attack, leaving Margaret to fend for herself once again. Which she did by marrying a third time. That husband died too. Margaret, having had so little luck with husbands, eventually became an innkeeper in Shelburne. There is undoubtedly the makings of a novel in her Perils-of-Pauline life. But there aren't enough letters, diaries, and accounts to make a full-fledged non-fiction narrative out of all those fascinating facts. I know. I tried.

Just as I did with Mary Swords, who was the mother of two young Shelburne printers. For more than a decade after the war, Mary relentlessly pressed her seemingly reasonable claims for compensation for her wartime losses, which included a husband and another son, as well as valuable property. No one listened. Despite that, she continued to be the most resolute and steadfast of Loyalists. Until she wasn't. In 1795, she had a sudden and unexplained—and now inexplicable—change of heart and swore an oath of allegiance to the new United States of America.

Hannah Booth, the too-delicate wife of a British soldier stationed in Shelburne, also seemed at one point to be a candidate for principal-character status. But all I could find out about her came from her husband's diaries and letters, written from his perspective. There is no written record to explain what was going on in her mind when the fates—and her husband's superiors—dispatched them both to Shelburne.

These women do make cameo appearances, but I would have preferred to focus more on their personal narratives—if only I'd been able to find the details I needed.

That, of course, is the difficulty of writing non-fiction. And the reward, too.

The writer's joy comes in those occasional *aha* moments when he discovers something unexpected, or suddenly connects the dots between seemingly disconnected events or characters.

During the course of my research, I did discover some incredibly rich and tellingly detailed first-person accounts of eighteenth-century life in the diaries and letters of a number of people who had called Shelburne home: Benjamin Marston, an acerbic surveyor who chronicled the town's founding and first tumultuous year; William Booth, a British army captain who spent two melancholy years in Shelburne during its precipitous decline; and perhaps most intriguing, David George and Boston King, two former slaves who were central to the development of both Shelburne and Birchtown, the black loyalist community on Shelburne's fringes. Their "slave narratives" offer another, quite different window to the story of the rise and fall of a loyalist town, as well as to black life in North America in the 1700s.

Their personal stories—and others, too—are the threads that interweave to tell the larger story of Shelburne. In many ways, the history of any place is the sum of the flesh-and-blood stories of those who lived it. During the period I'm writing about, Shelburne went through tumultuous, turbulent times. People came and went, oblivious to my narrative needs and desires. Benjamin Marston, who is such a central character in Shelburne's founding and early days, for example, departs its stage forever after little more than a year, while William Booth, whose own diaries chronicle the town's eventual demise, doesn't begin his Shelburne sojourn until more than three years after the arrival of the first Loyalists.

Since I've chosen to tell the stories of these central characters as much as possible in narrative form, and usually from the point of view of the characters themselves, it's certainly fair to ask whether I'm making anything up, or at least imposing my own notions of what these people must have been thinking at any particular time.

The short answer is no.

Charlotte Gray, one of Canada's most respected writers of historical narrative non-fiction, put it this way in attempting to explain how she wrote *Sisters in the Wilderness*, her brilliant, best-selling account of the lives of two nineteenth-century English sisters in backwoods Ontario: "I don't invent. But I take known facts, and imagine. . . . From the relatively little documentation available, I tried to read between the lines of those of their letters that have survived. I used my judgment in what to include and what to omit; what to emphasize and what to ignore; how to distill an untidy, sprawling mass of facts into a tidy package."

Me too. Or at least that is my aim.

You can find at the beginning of the Endnotes an example of how I have developed my source material into a narrative. To maintain the narrative flow, I've consigned to those Endnotes most of the details of my sources. Through that section and the Bibliography, any reader should easily be able to discover the factual underpinning of what I've written. (Throughout the text, Roman numerals refer the reader to an endnote, while Arabic numerals refer to a footnote.)

Part of the fun of writing a book like this is in the occasionally rewarding "detective" work of trying to fill in the gaps in knowledge, or find the missing piece that will solve some puzzle or another. But there are still many gaps and puzzles, such as whatever happened to the mysterious Eliza, Benjamin Marston's love interest during his early days in Halifax? Freshly widowed but clearly smitten, Benjamin wrote love poems to her and once confided in his diary that "the pleasure of again seeing that dear girl has abundantly rewarded me for all the disagreeable feelings of a six-months' imprisonment." And then, nothing . . . Eliza suddenly disappears from the pages of his diary and, so far as we can tell, from his life, too. Did they have a falling out? Did she move away? Take up with another lover?

In a novel, it would be a simple enough matter to tie up that loose end with a plot twist; in the messier world of non-fiction, however, we're bound by what we know—and don't. That's what makes it non-fiction.

Stephen Kimber
Halifax, September 2007

"An ornament to the British empire"

Prologue.

F irst, you had to meet with Joseph Durfee at his home on Water Street so he, and perhaps a few of the others, could personally vet you.[i] Not everyone was eligible to join their exclusive club of "loyalists associated for the purposes of removing and settling at Port Roseway in Nova Scotia," as their articles of association described them. You needed to be a true Loyalist. And a proper British citizen. Which meant you couldn't be a Jew; British law didn't allow Jews to own land, and land was what this organization was all about. No one needed to inquire whether membership was open to the thousands of freed black slaves who'd also ended up in New York because of this American Revolution; it wasn't. British promises of freedom were fine during wartime, but the war was ending and many of the members of this group had slaves of their own. They certainly didn't want them getting the wrong ideas.

Once you had passed muster with Durfee and obtained your prized letter of recommendation—the other key needed to enter this exclusive club—you were eligible to attend a meeting. Tonight's was being held at New York city hall at the corner of Broad and Wall streets.

It was November 30, 1782, yet another millstone-milestone day in the tumultuous seven-year war between England and her estranged American colonies. In Paris that day, British negotiators at the peace talks had formally agreed to recognize American independence. Communication being what it was then, the news wouldn't officially reach New York for close to four months, but no one in tonight's jostling, anxious, milling crowd of several hundred needed official notice. They knew. Which is why there were now so many more applying to join them that they'd had to move tonight's gathering to city hall and even post a doorman to make sure only those with letters of recommendation got inside.

Previously, they'd gathered at Charles Roubalet's tavern, a smoky establishment on Cortland Street near the Paulus Hook ferry that had become a favoured loyalist gathering place during these last few years of war. The refugees would meet to forget their troubles. They'd watch entertainers like the famous magician Isaac Levy, whose handbills boasted that the "hand is quicker than the eye." Or they'd enjoy an evening of music— usually a three-hour musicale followed by dancing—at one of Roubalet's regular Tuesday night public concerts. Whatever the entertainment on offer, of course, the real purpose of the gatherings was to give the dispirited Loyalists the chance to drink a few pints; puff on what *Rivington's Gazette*, the popular loyalist newspaper, characterized as some "monstrous good smoking tobacco"; and complain, commiserate, and contemplate.

Although bands in many taverns, including Roubalet's, still played "God Save the King" on the hour, and some among the Loyalists still optimistically toasted their shared dream of "a happy reinstatement of the loyal refugees," most had finally become more realistic. The British had let them down, made a balls-up of the war strategy, ignored their advice and offers of help, and treated them . . . well, as if they were the enemy, too. And now they who had been so loyal had lost—or would soon lose—everything. Because they'd supported the wrong side, their homes, farms, land, businesses, careers, sometimes families, and, of course, country were gone.

Even those lucky enough to still have the resources to take care of themselves could no longer count on being able to buy what they needed in this teeming, overburdened city where what wasn't in short supply was overpriced. Many once proud, successful, independent men had been reduced to subsisting on government largesse. By the time Sir Guy Carleton had arrived in the spring of 1782 to preside over this foregone conclusion, in fact, more than six thousand civilian men, women, and children were on the dole in New York.

New York was the last loyalist stronghold in the thirteen revolted colonies. After New York, what?

With the British army obviously preparing to depart and many former New Yorkers—rebels, patriots, winners to their losers—showing up to reclaim their abandoned homes and demand payments of past rent from the loyalist squatters, it was obvious they could not remain in New York much longer. Which invited the question, what was to become of them?

The Loyalists at Roubalet's weren't the only ones trying to answer that question. Loyalist societies had been spawned in taverns and pubs all over New York, their meetings often advertised in the newspapers with messages that hinted obliquely at "secret and important business [to] which all should attend." Many of the gatherings were geographically based: Pennsylvania Loyalists, for example, gathered at Birkets Tavern near Maiden Lane, while those from Virginia met at the Queen's Head, and Massachusetts refugees congregated at Hicks' Tavern on Broadway. Some of these informal gatherings had evolved into associations, often the official successors to loyalist military organizations set up during the war. Others, including the group at Roubalet's, had sprung up more recently and spontaneously, their members drawn from all of the rebellious colonies.

The Port Roseway Associates had had its beginnings the year before when a group of twenty-six men—"chiefly of the number of those who, for their attachment to [the British] government and after numberless fatigues in support of the royal cause, have been obliged to quit their all and take refuge within the King's lines"—met to launch a search for an "ideal Loyalist refugee township" where they could settle together after the war.

Their leader was Joseph Durfee, a former Newport sea captain and merchant who'd parlayed his valuable work piloting British vessels for General Clinton during the successful siege of Charles Town in May 1780—how long ago that seemed now!—into his current job as the director of vessels in New York Harbor. Others in the group came from almost all of the about-to-become United States: New York, New Jersey, Massachusetts, Connecticut, New Hampshire, Pennsylvania, Virginia, South Carolina, and Georgia. And though they represented the spectrum of professions, crafts, and trades—there were seven merchants, four farmers, two carpenters, two tailors, a hat maker, a printer, a bookbinder, a doctor, a grocer, and a mariner among their number—they were, by and large, the good burghers of a suddenly bygone colonial America. That was deliberate. Their goal was to create a new and better New York—more exclusive, more sophisticated, more loyal than the one they were leaving behind.

Where should this new loyalist mecca be located?

There were plenty of options, of course, including relocating to England. But most of the Loyalists had been born in America; many, like Joseph Durfee and Gideon White, another original Associate, could trace their American roots to the beginning of European settlement. For most, England seemed far more foreign than the former colonies of which they could no longer call themselves citizens. Canada was another possibility, but it was far away and cold, and besides, most of the inhabitants there spoke French. There was still the West Indies, but it was occupied by alien races and plagued by yellow fever and tropical diseases.

Which, by process of elimination, led them to Nova Scotia, the closest British territory to New York. Though some of the

Loyalists could tell stories about the chilly—in more ways than one—unwelcoming city of Halifax (Gideon White had been among those who'd endured time there after the British evacuated Boston in 1776), there was no particular reason why Halifax itself needed to be their destination. In fact, they would prefer to settle in a new, unoccupied territory they could make their own.

In 1781, Durfee had written to Andrew Snape Hammond, the lieutenant-governor of Nova Scotia, and his secretary, Richard Bulkeley, seeking their advice on a suitable location for their new city. Hammond and Bulkeley had encouraged the Loyalists to consider Port Roseway, a barely inhabited patch of land on the southern shore of the province less than two hundred miles down the coast from Halifax. Not only was its deep, commodious harbour one of the most "capital" ports in America, Hammond enthused, but its location also offered an ideal stopover for European vessels on their way to the Bay of Fundy or American ports, or for American ships heading up the coast to Halifax. As well, Roseway Bay was surrounded by thousands of acres of wild timberland, which might offer the Loyalists the possibility of making their new community the base for a lucrative trade in lumber with England and the new United States. As if all that wasn't enough, Hammond claimed that conditions for fishing, farming, and the fur trade were the best in the entire province.

Hammond wasn't alone in his enthusiasm for Port Roseway. Though he'd never spent any time ashore, Gideon White told the others he remembered sailing past its fine harbour and could attest to its excellent fishing.

By the summer of 1782, they'd settled on the location and an appropriate name for their new group—the Port Roseway Associates—but they still had to deal with the nagging issue of who they wanted to accompany them to their loyalist nirvana.

Initially, their number was to include only the twenty-six original members and their families, but that quickly grew. Gideon White invited his brother-in-law, Pelham Winslow, who was married to his sister Joanna. Thomas Courtney, a tailor from

Boston, wanted to include his sons, Richard, James, and Thomas, Jr., also tailors. Alexander Robertson, the New York–based printer, recommended his brother James, with whom he'd established loyalist newspapers in British-occupied cities, including Philadelphia and Charles Town; and his friends George Chisholm and William MacKenzie; and, oh yes, the Swords boys, Thomas and James, who were apprentices at his newspaper.

When Durfee wrote again to Hammond in August 1782 to ask for a grant of land at or near Port Roseway, he was making the request on behalf of himself and about a hundred families.

By the time the provincial secretary, Bulkeley, replied, informing Durfee that the governor had directed "inquiries be made" to ensure Port Roseway would "answer the views and intentions of yourself and other loyal associates so the same may be reserved," the numbers of Port Roseway Associates had doubled again. And others—disbanded soldiers as well as Loyalists—were clamouring to be added to the list. So much for their dream of an exclusive club.

According to the minutes of tonight's New York city hall meeting, in fact, the Port Roseway Associates now numbered more than two hundred subscribers, plus their families. To determine how serious they really were, the Associates adopted a resolution that night permitting anyone to withdraw his name without penalty by December 17. After that, those refusing to follow through "should have their names transmitted to the Governor of Nova Scotia as persons forfeiting their word and their honour."

The group then elected two delegations. Durfee and four others would handle the New York end of the negotiations with Guy Carleton while Joseph Pynchon, a Connecticut farmer who had been in the process of being groomed for the governorship there before the war, and James Dole, a former Albany merchant, would sail to Halifax to meet with John Parr, the recently appointed governor, and other officials, and also to scout out their promised land. They were "totally invested with full and ample power . . .

to settle and determine all matters, grant, etc., of the settlement of Port Roseway," a city which, as they wrote to Parr, would be "not only happy for themselves but . . . an ornament to the British empire."

"Emanations of the leaden George"

Chapter I.

O f course, the story of Shelburne—née Port Roseway—doesn't really start in some smoky, overcrowded meeting room in New York city hall on a crisp fall night in 1782. It doesn't even begin on the town's actual birthday—May 4, 1783—on that fresh spring afternoon when the first fleet of vessels from New York dropped anchor in what was to become Shelburne harbour and thousands of exhausted, frightened, hopeful Loyalists spilled onto the decks to see their new home.

To understand how and why Shelburne came to be, you have to begin by going back two decades and following the many separate strings of decree and division, miscalculation and misunderstanding, incident and insult, shove and shout, push and punch, pistol shot and cannon fire, and calamity and catastrophe that inexorably tumbled and twisted and tangled themselves into the unbreakable, unshakeable, irresistible, unstoppable force of history that became the American Revolution—and that, inevitably, spawned the dream that would turn into the reality of Shelburne.

The ink was barely dry on the treaty that sealed the British victory in the French and Indian War in 1763 when London made the first in a series of seemingly reasonable, seemingly inconsequential decisions that would have unintended and often unfortunate consequences for its American colonists, especially those who remained—often in spite of themselves and certainly despite their own best interests—loyal to the Crown.

It is popular now to paint them as one-dimensional stick figures, as Loyalists or traitors, depending on which side of the forty-ninth parallel you sit. But it was always more complicated than that. And so were they. The Loyalists were a mixed bag: men, women, children, black, white, British, American, aristocrats and artisans, politicians and preachers, merchants and mariners, soldiers and soldiers of fortune, hustlers and hangers-on, slaves and slave owners, recently freed blacks and not-so-freed "servants." For the most part, they didn't set out to change their world; they wanted things to stay the way they were. The Loyalists didn't always, or even often, agree with the actions of the mother country. Many had their doubts. Some would change their minds about what they should do next, a few more than once. But they were products of their upbringing and of often random decisions, carried forward by larger currents they couldn't control or change.

In the beginning, Shelburne was really just an idea, a hope, a sweet dream on a dark night.

But we're getting ahead of ourselves. The story of the story that became Shelburne could begin in any number of other places with any number of people. With snobbish, snappish Benjamin Marston, for example, a successful merchant obliviously reading in his library in Marblehead while the mobs gather at his door, or with frustrated, frightened David, a black slave with no last name searching in vain for the face of God in Glory in the woods of his master's plantation in South Carolina. We could even begin farther afield. In London, perhaps, with sinecure-seeking John Parr still trying to buy himself his lieutenant colonel's rank, or with aging bachelor Brigadier Guy Carleton, who already had a title—captain general and governor-in-chief of the British colony at Quebec—but desperately wanted a bride he could take back to America.

But let's begin our story instead on the shores of Narragansett Bay in Rhode Island, where the man who would become Shelburne's first founding father is in the process of discovering that his home no longer feels like home.

Joseph Durfee stood alone on some rocks at the far end of the beach, staring but not quite seeing, comprehending but not really understanding.[i] Half a mile across the bay, on the shores of Goat Island, sat the burned, grounded hulk of what, only yesterday, had been His Majesty's Ship *Liberty*. Down the shore from where he stood, many of his fellow Newporters eagerly scavenged the vessel's charred timbers as they washed ashore, piling them one on top of the other and making huge bonfires that licked the midsummer sky.

The crowd's mood was festive, Durfee's anything but. As Shelburne historian Mary Archibald would later reconstruct this story from the records of the Newport Historical Society, Durfee's own correspondence, and his eventual claim for compensation for his losses, Durfee had gone down to the harbour that day from his home on School Street before dawn, and spent the entire day watching, mesmerized. Now, with the sun's light finally fading, along with the ship's embers and his own hopes for the future, Durfee turned and began his lonely walk home. He couldn't have helped but imagine what all this might mean for him, for his family, and even for Rhode Island, the colony his family had called home for four generations.

Before dawn this morning—July 17, 1769—a mob had clambered aboard the *Liberty*, forced her crew to flee, smashed her lifeboats, ripped down her mast, cut her cables, and set her loose to drift helplessly in Narragansett Bay. At some point, the sloop had grounded on the island and a few of the hooligans, their desire for vengeance not yet fully sated, had boarded her once again and set her ablaze.

The ostensible reason for all of this was that the *Liberty*[1]—a British revenue vessel under the command of one of the Royal Navy's many overbearing, overzealous captains, this one named William Reid—had the day before seized two ships, a brig and a sloop from Connecticut. Reid had accused their masters of not paying the required duties on their cargoes, and immediately proceeded to confiscate them in the name of his Majesty. It was not the first time since Reid had arrived in Newport in May 1769 to enforce the unenforceable Molasses Act that the *Liberty* had seized contraband. But it was—at least to the locals on shore who'd watched it unfold like a play in front of them—the most outrageous yet. When one of the captains tried to argue his case, Reid ordered the *Liberty* to open fire on the man's vessel and the captain was forced to flee in a small boat. In that one moment, years of simmering resentments, frustrations, and anger had finally boiled over into menacing, mindless violence.

Was it, Durfee wondered darkly, just a harbinger of things to come?

It was crazy. And frightening. Not that Durfee hadn't seen it coming. If it wasn't one British "Act," it was another. The Sugar Act, the Currency Act, the Stamp Act, the Quartering Act, the Declaratory Act, the Townshend Revenue Acts[2] . . . It seemed

---

1. The *Liberty*'s previous owner was John Hancock, Boston's leading shipowner and merchant. British customs officials seized it in Boston Harbor on June 10, 1768, after it arrived from Madeira with an untaxed cargo of wine and other commodities. The seizure, which followed a scuffle between Hancock's supporters and sailors from the Royal Navy, came on the heels of street demonstrations by the Sons of Liberty, during which customs agents had been physically set upon and their homes attacked. Perhaps as a kind of payback, the British sent the *Liberty* to Newport to make Rhode Islanders adhere to the laws too.

2. For those who like to know such things, the Sugar Act, passed by the British Parliament in 1764, was designed to help offset the costs of the French and Indian

the British government was determined to make its North American colonies foot their share—and maybe more—of the bill for its Seven Years War with France. Durfee was not entirely unsympathetic to this. The war, after all, had sent the French packing, neutralized Spanish influence in North America, and largely subdued the Indian threat, making it possible for colonials to imagine the grand possibilities that might follow from westward exploration and settlement.

But if the New World's future seemed prosperous, the Old World was beginning to founder. In spite of—or perhaps because of—its now sprawling empire, Britain's national debt had climbed to a previously unheard of £140 million.[3] What especially galled British politicians—and taxpayers—was that the Americans appeared eager to reap the benefits of empire without sharing its costs.

To add insolence to insult, the Americans had been dodging many of the too few duties they were obligated by law to pay. The Molasses Act was a case in point. The law, which had been in effect since 1733, required anyone importing molasses from the French Caribbean into the American colonies to pay a duty of sixpence per gallon. But the Board of Trade in London estimated that £700,000 worth of goods slipped, untaxed, into the

---

War and the ongoing expenses of the colonies. It increased duties on imported sugar and other commodities, doubling the duties on foreign goods reshipped from England to the colonies. The Currency Act (1764) prohibited the colonies from issuing their own paper money. The Stamp Act (1765) became the first direct tax on the colonies; the Quartering Act (1765) required colonists to provide food and shelter to British troops; the Declaratory Act (1766) gave the British Parliament total authority to legislate and impose whatever laws it wished on its American colonies; and the Townshend Revenue Acts (1767) added a range of new taxes on everything from tea to glass and set up a new colonial board of customs commissioners in Boston.

3. In a contemporary context, Britain's national debt would have been £14.5 billion.

American colonies each year through cracks—more often gaping holes—in the customs collection process. Customs agents were as much the problem as the solution. There were only two hundred of them for the whole of the North American seaboard from Nova Scotia to Barbados. Most were patronage appointees who found it easier—and more lucrative—to look the other way. So easy, in fact, that customs agents collected four times more in wages than they did in duties.

Durfee's fellow Rhode Islanders were among the worst scofflaws. Rhode Island was awash in molasses, most of it arriving untaxed from the French Caribbean, which was known for supplying molasses that produced a "fiery, high-quality" rum. In the mid-1700s, Rhode Island (population less than fifty thousand) boasted one rum distiller for every sixteen hundred citizens. Even Rhode Island's legislature conceded that rum had become "the main hinge upon which the trade of the colony turns."

Thanks to see-no-wrong customs inspectors and the colony's smuggler-friendly bays, coves, and inlets, molasses had escaped the outstretched hand of the taxman for far too long. That, at least, was the view of Britain's new prime minister, George Grenville, "a man of little mind, blinkered judgment, obstinacy and bad temper."[4] His only claims to his job were that he was the brother-in-law of a still-revered former prime minister, William Pitt the elder, and that he had been the most senior minister in

---

4. This quote comes from historian Don Cook in his book *The Long Fuse: How England Lost the American Colonies,* but the judgment seems widely shared. Thomas Babington Macauley called Grenville's "the worst administration . . . since the revolution" of 1668, arguing that his public acts were either "outrages on the liberty of the people [or] outrages on the dignity of the crown." A later historian, O.A. Sherrard, said Grenville was "intolerably conceited, and to make matters worse, added to his conceit an excessive measure of those faults that often go with it—obstinacy, rancour, resentment, an implacable temper, an inability to forget and forgive."

the cabinet of the unpopular former prime minister, the Earl of Bute. Bute, young King George III's mentor, confidant, and "dearest friend," had abruptly resigned as prime minister in 1763, having grown tired of being jeered at in theatres and stoned in public for his role in ousting Pitt.

Although the king detested his new first minister and airily dismissed him as a man with "the mind of a counting house clerk," George and Grenville were of one mind on one important subject. Both men believed the colonies should shoulder more of their own costs, including those of garrisoning the ten thousand British troops now stationed there. And Grenville had no compunction about imposing new direct taxes on the Americans in order to raise that revenue.

To begin, however, he simply ordered his American customs agents to start collecting that which was already owed—or lose their jobs. He also issued new regulations requiring shipowners and merchants not only to fill in all proper forms, "certificates, affidavits, warrants, bonds [and] clearance orders" but also to pay what they owed, even if that meant making them post bond on cargoes before their vessels left port. And he sent the British navy across the Atlantic to prove he meant business.

Predictably, none of this went over well with the colonists, including Joseph Durfee. Durfee, after all, was a sea captain, the co-owner of a fleet of vessels that plied what was known as the triangular trade. His ships carried fish and lumber from Rhode Island to the West Indies, trading them there for rum and molasses to sell in Britain. There, he'd fill up his ships' holds again, this time with the wares of British merchants he would peddle in Boston and other New England towns. Since Durfee often captained his own vessels, he knew how frustrated people in those communities had become with the prime minister's new rules. As for himself, he certainly didn't need—or want—to fill out more forms. Or pay more taxes.

But he was also a pragmatic businessman who feared the protests that had now turned violent would ultimately be bad for his business. And, unlike many of his fellow colonists, he was a man of conservative inclinations who respected the authority of king and Parliament, even if he didn't always agree with either.

He had been born in Portsmouth in 1734 but relocated to the bustling port city of Newport as an adult so he and his wife, Ann, could raise their five children—their youngest, Elizabeth, was now just a year old—and so Joseph, 35, could establish himself as a respected member of the local community. He had done just that.

After his father had died and his mother remarried, Joseph and his stepbrother Oliver had gone into the shipping business together, and their fleet had continued to grow and prosper. But Durfee had begun to feel increasingly out of step with his fellow citizens, including his stepbrother and business partner who—like his mother—was becoming more vocal in his opposition to the British authorities.

As the differences between the colonies and the mother country had intensified and the number of Acts had multiplied, Rhode Islanders had become among the most openly defiant of all North American colonies, spitting out a series of petitions, protests, and arguments. After Parliament passed the Stamp Act, Rhode Island's legislature declared it null and void. When the new stamp distributor arrived to set up shop, an angry mob greeted his vessel, and neither the distributor nor his stamps made it ashore. Having become the only colony to successfully refuse to allow stamp distributors to operate within its borders, Rhode Island officials then generously offered to send ten thousand men to Boston to help that city rid itself of the plague of the stamp men.

What would happen now, Durfee wondered again? Would the British send more naval ships and men to compel the rebellious Newporters to bow to the king's will? And if they did, how would the colonists react? How should *he* react? Should he and his family uproot themselves and start over again in a more congenial, less combative community? But where?

Durfee couldn't stomach the thought of returning to his Portsmouth birthplace, if only because his mother still lived there. The two of them, not to put too fine a point on it, didn't get along. Mary Durfee was a Whig, and Joseph was not. "England has not the right to impose taxes on us in a parliament in which we have no representation," she told him, mouthing the popular sentiment of the day. "The war is over. We don't need the British army to defend us." Perhaps, in the end, there was nowhere left to escape to. There'd already been demonstrations in Boston and riots in New York.

Joseph Durfee would tough it out in Newport, and hope for better times.

"Our Father, who art in heaven . . ."[ii] It still wasn't working. Cyrus had put the fear of God in David. Or maybe it wasn't fear. Perhaps it was possibility? Or hope? Cyrus was a man of David's colour, from Charles Town. He and David both now worked for Mr. George Galphin, the master of Silver Bluff, a plantation that ambled along the banks of the Savannah River near the border between South Carolina and Georgia. One day, while they were in the woods together, Cyrus had turned to David and said, "You keep living the way you do, you'll never see the face of God in Glory."

As he would explain many years later in a memoir, David was taken aback. What did Cyrus know about the Lord? Was he even saved himself? And what did he know about David that would allow him to say such a thing?

Enough, David realized. Though he didn't like to talk or even think about the specifics himself, he had to acknowledge he'd "lived a bad life and had no serious thoughts about my soul." But he was in his mid-twenties now, newly married with a child of his own. Perhaps it was past time he started thinking, and praying. So he'd said the Lord's Prayer over and over, hoping it would help. It hadn't.

He tried to snatch what inspiration he could from his memory of the few times he'd attended the English Church in

Nottoway, which was eight or nine miles' walk from the plantation in Essex County, Virginia, where he'd been born. But invariably it was the image of Mr. Chapel, the master of the plantation,
that flooded out all other memories of that childish time when he
"did not steal, did not fear hell, was without knowledge."

Mr. Chapel was cruel, "a very bad man to the negroes." And
especially to David's family: his father John, his mother Judith,
and his four brothers and sisters. David's parents had been captured and brought over from Africa as slaves. He and the other
children had been born into it. They knew nothing else. Perhaps
this was what hell was.

David had seen his older sister Patty whipped so badly her
back was "all corruption, as though it would rot." His mother
was the master's cook. When he was displeased with her he'd
"strip her directly and cut away" with his whip. His brother
Dick had tried to run away, was caught, escaped again. When
they finally recaptured him, the master had him hung up by his
hands to the branch of a cherry tree, his feet a foot-and-a-half
off the ground, naked except for his breeches. They tied his legs
together and then put a pole between them. The master's sons
sat at either end of the pole to weigh Dick down while the master gave him five hundred lashes, maybe more. Then they
washed his back with salt water and whipped it some more, and
then used a rag to rub the salt deeper into his wounds. Finally,
when they were finished, they sent him back out into the field
to pull suckers off the tobacco. It was supposed to be a lesson to
the rest of the slaves about what would happen to them if they
tried to run away.

David also knew what the whip felt like. He'd been whipped
often enough, sometimes until the blood ran down over the
waistband of his pants. But that didn't stop him from trying to
get away too. The night that he ran for his own life, his mother
was on what David believed was her deathbed after another especially vicious beating from the master. That had been three years
ago. David still didn't know whether she'd lived or died.

Since then, his own life had encompassed more than enough for a lifetime. Soon after he'd escaped from the master's plantation, he found work on the Pedee River. But a few weeks later, word reached his new master that Mr. Chapel was offering thirty guineas for David's return. "I will have no hand in it," the man told David. "I would advise you to make your way south toward Savannah River."

David did as the man suggested, found work at another plantation, was discovered once more and escaped again, this time into Indian country where he was captured by an Indian king called Blue Salt. Unfortunately, his former master's son refused to be deterred and discovered his whereabouts one more time. The son travelled eight hundred miles to find King Blue Salt and offer him rum, linen, and a gun in exchange for the runaway slave. Before they could finalize the deal, David took off again, ending up this time in the employ of a man named John Miller who ran a remote trading post on the Ogeechee River for a plantation owner named George Galphin.

Galphin's forty-thousand-acre Silver Bluff plantation on the Savannah River, twelve miles from Augusta, was "a very celebrated place," and Galphin himself a legendary character. An Irish immigrant who became a prominent Indian trader after arriving in Georgia in 1737, Galphin had still been married to a woman back in Ireland when he wed another in America in 1741. Though both of those marriages were childless, Galphin did manage to father nine children, three with the daughter of a Creek Indian warrior, and others with slave women on his plantation.[5] "Red men and black men alike saw in him a man of kindly soul," wrote one observer. During the Seven Years War, Galphin, who was fluent in several tribal languages, had earned the gratitude of the mother country for helping maintain peace between the British and the Cree. But during the early 1770s, he had aligned himself with those colonists agitating for independence.

---

5. In his will, Galphin, who died in 1780, provided for all of his offspring.

STEPHEN KIMBER

During his time at Galphin's trading post, David tended the horses, mended deerskins brought in by the Indians, and, once a year, travelled with Miller four hundred miles along five or six different rivers from the trading post to the plantation to deliver the hides. After three years of this, David finally worked up the courage to tell Mr. Galphin: "I wished to live with him at Silver Bluff. He told me I should, so he took me to wait upon him and treated me kindly."

But today, as he stood alone in the forest, David wondered whether he was really ready for yet another life? For the eternal life Cyrus had told him about? David had tried and tried, but nothing seemed to help. He could imagine "no possibility of relief," he would recall later. "I must go to hell. I saw myself a mass of sin. I could not read and had no scriptures. I did not think of Adam and Eve's sin, but I was sin. I felt my own plague, and I was so overcome that I could not wait upon my master. I told him I was ill."

Which is how he'd ended up alone in these woods, trying to find a mind map out of this pain and frustration. He tried one more time: "Our Father, who art in heaven . . ."

He'd made it.[iii] Hidden from view by the black night, his small open boat had slipped, unmolested and undetected, out of Marblehead Neck into the choppy North Atlantic and turned starboard on its voyage to Boston. Now what? Benjamin Marston III—successful merchant, prominent landowner, and upstanding citizen of Marblehead, not to forget (and no one would have allowed him to forget even if he'd wanted to, which he most assuredly did not) loyal subject of the Crown—had to admit he had no idea what he would do now, or what would happen next.

Marston, who would soon become one of the central—and certainly most controversial—figures in Shelburne's early history, was an inveterate letter writer and diarist whose always colourful, usually acerbic, and sometimes melancholic writings during and after the American Revolution provide us with not only a singular—and singularly interesting—view of the great events of that period, but also a window into the often conflicted mind of a Loyalist.

On this evening—November 24, 1775—in the waters off Marblehead, Marston tried to calm himself, convince his still-racing heart that the immediate danger had passed. Wispy trails of his breath danced in the moonlight; the chill November air bit through his too-light-for-this-night greatcoat. He'd had no time to gather his valuables, let alone to pack a valise or dress appropriately when that assortment of thugs and hoodlums who dared call themselves the Marblehead Committee had battered down his door and swarmed into his house looking for him.

He'd had to make a run for it. He wouldn't have been the first Tory tarred and feathered. The humiliating and horrific procedure was notorious. First, the gangs would heat the tar until it was thin, then strip their victim naked and either pour the hot sticky liquid over his body or paint it on with a brush, then sprinkle it with "as many feathers as will stick to it." If they were feeling especially brutish, they would, as per the instructions circulating in their ranks, "hold a lighted candle to the feathers and try to set it all on fire; if it will burn, so much the better."

If not tarring and feathering, they might have made him "ride the rail," another painful punishment meted out to those who wouldn't support their shenanigans. Two louts would force their victim to straddle a sharp board and then lift it up on their shoulders and run through the streets, bouncing it up and down so the poor devil would suffer the most excruciating pain while hanging on for dear life.

Better not to even think of that . . . He'd have to write to Sarah, of course, let his wife know he was safe and find out what damage they'd inflicted on the house. He could only hope they'd left his library alone. He'd also need to get hold of his business associates and customers, inform them of matters. He could depend on Hooper. Robert "King" Hooper, who was also

Benjamin's brother-in-law and business partner, was a royalist. But the others? Which side were they really on?

In America in 1775, there was little, it seemed, one could be certain of. Even the traditional definers of place and class seemed relics of an earlier, simpler time. Which, Benjamin Marston III would be the first to tell you, had also been a better time.

Ben had come of age in those better times. His father, Colonel Benjamin Marston II, a Harvard College graduate, had been one of the most successful businessmen in Salem. He was also a colonel of militia, a justice of the peace, and had at one time represented Salem in the General Court of Massachusetts Bay. When he died in 1754, he left the bulk of his estate,[6] including Marston Farm, a 170-acre property in Manchester, New Hampshire, complete with a number of black slaves, to his widow and 24-year-old son.

Benjamin II's widow, Ben's mother, was a Winslow. Her father was the Honourable Isaac Winslow of Marshfield; her grandfather and her great-grandfather, Josiah and Edward Winslow, had both been governors of the Plymouth colony. Edward, in fact, was one of the original *Mayflower* pilgrims.

Young Ben, who followed in his father's footsteps to Harvard, had graduated at 19 as a member of the Class of 1749, and spent his immediate post-college years gallivanting through Europe and some of Britain's lesser colonies, enjoying the company of society ladies and doing what young male colonials of his age and background did before returning home, properly seasoned, to marry and establish themselves in business or the law.

Like his father before him, young Ben had also married well, wedding Sarah Sweet "of the pretty Sweet girls" in 1755. Sarah's two sisters had each married successful businessmen—Robert "King" Hooper and Jeremiah Lee, who between them controlled

---

6. The rest of his estate was to be used to propagate the gospel among the Indians.

the fishing industry in Marblehead. That was no insignificant matter, considering that Marblehead was widely conceded to be the most important fishing community in the colonies. Through their companies, they bought virtually every fish landed in Marblehead, shipping the sea's gold to Balboa and Spain to trade for real gold and silver, which they then used to buy goods in Britain to sell in America.

Soon after Benjamin's marriage, Hooper, Lee, and their new brother-in-law had formed a partnership to operate a store on King Street, which Benjamin initially ran as a kind of junior partner but eventually owned. With Lee and Hooper, he also operated a number of vessels in the London trade, and would occasionally travel there himself.

Though never quite as well-to-do as his in-laws, Benjamin had not done badly. In addition to the family land he'd inherited, he had acquired various warehouses and investment properties in Marblehead. For Sarah and himself, he bought a "pleasant and commodious" house on the hill at the head of Watson Street, on which he'd spent £450 to buy and an equal amount to renovate. One of its features was an impressive library, partly inherited from his father and partly acquired on Benjamin's travels. It included an extensive collection of books in Latin and Greek that Benjamin, who fancied himself something of a writer and scholar, had annotated in the margins.

Benjamin's own sisters also helped widen his social, political, and economic circles. Elizabeth, Patience, and Lucia had all married members of the Watson clan, the Plymouth Watsons whose forebears and descendants already freckled the pages of American colonial history. Unfortunately, from Benjamin's perspective, they were now all Whigs, and some had even become in thrall to the pernicious likes of that Samuel Adams in Boston.

Benjamin, of course, had his own powerful and well-connected friends and acquaintances, too. People like John Wentworth and others he'd met during his Harvard years. Wentworth was now the governor of New Hampshire, or at least he had been until the mob had driven him and his wife, Frances, into exile in August. Would Benjamin be next? Was that what was happening now?

How could this be happening to him? In the fifteen years between 1759 and 1774, the good burghers of Marblehead had chosen Benjamin Marston as moderator of their town meetings fourteen times, "selectman and overseer of the poor" thirteen times, fire ward twelve times, and, in 1760, assessor.[7] There was not an important local committee he hadn't been asked to chair, or at least serve on.

It wasn't as if he didn't understand, even sympathize with some of the frustrations the locals had with the government in London. In 1767, they had asked him—and he'd happily agreed—to be a member of a committee to compose a letter of thanks to the "Glorious 92," the ninety-two assemblymen who'd defied the governor's demand to rescind their resolution seeking a common front of all the colonies against some of the duties Britain had imposed. That letter praised the ninety-two "for their steady resolution in maintaining the rights and privileges of the government and resisting the aggressions of the mother country." The next year, he'd been chosen again to sit on another committee, this one encouraging their representative to press for the repeal of English tax laws and "renewal of harmony with the mother country."

As recently as last year, Benjamin was being elected to local office, but he was no longer asked to serve on the most important committees. Perhaps that was because he had begun to speak even more forcefully in defence of the Crown. That, in truth, was Benjamin's downfall; he could never hold his tongue, and he was known to be "an uncompromising adherent to the lawful government of the British colonies in this country."

---

7. One of his duties as assessor was "to examine and straighten the lines of several estates." It would be the closest he had come to being a surveyor before he was appointed deputy surveyor of the new town of Shelburne in 1783.

By March 1774, when a mob burned the smallpox hospital in Marblehead, just about everyone had been aligned on one side or the other. He and his Winslow relatives—his uncles, General John and Edward, and his cousins, Pelham and Edward—were royalists. As was King Hooper, who had even invited British General Thomas Gage to use his mansion in Danvers during the recent troubles at the port in Boston.

On the other hand, Jeremiah Lee, Benjamin's other brother-in-law and business partner, had become a member of the Massachusetts Committee of Safety, a kind of rebel provisional government chaired by John Hancock.[8] Last May, during one of its sessions in Watertown, word had come that the British army was approaching, so the members scattered. Jeremiah hid out in a swamp. He hadn't been caught by the British but he had caught a cold, which eventually killed him. Lee had been eulogized far and wide, including in an obituary in the *South Carolina Gazette*, which described him as "one of the most eminent merchants on the continent" and owner of the "most elegant and extensively finished house in the British colonies." All of which Benjamin Marston could gratefully acknowledge, but then the paper added that Jeremiah had been "a distinguished and resolute asserter and defender of the liberties of his country." Which stuck in Benjamin's craw. As did the news that Jeremiah had left his country "a legacy of £2000 sterling."

Benjamin's real sin, the one for which the thugs at his door tonight had wished to punish him, was that he'd been among the thirty-three Marblehead merchants, lawyers, and businessmen who'd signed a valedictory letter to Governor Thomas Hutchinson

---

8. These so-called committees of safety sprung up in the 1760s as ways for the colonists to gather to discuss issues and direct their local militias. At a local level, they often consisted of every adult male in a small community. As the times became more radicalized, the committees often took on more ominous, almost vigilante roles, ensuring that locals didn't stray from the popular view.

when he returned to Britain last year. At one level, it had all been rather innocuous, even pro forma, full of "sincere and hearty thanks" and "sincere esteem and gratitude" for Hutchinson's efforts in representing the king in the colony. There'd been some specific appreciations too, ones that should not have displeased even the most strident among the radicals. After he returned to London, the letter suggested Hutchinson should "embrace every opportunity of moderating the resentment of the government against us, and use your best endeavours to have the unhappy dispute between Great Britain and this country brought to a just and equitable determination." But the letter had ended on what some considered a provocative note—the wish that Hutchinson find a reception back home "as shall fully compensate for all the insults and indignities which have been offered you [in Massachusetts]." And yet, that was true, Benjamin thought!

Benjamin and the others who'd signed it—two hundred in the colony—became known as the "addressers," and were "sometimes harshly treated by the most noisy and turbulent." Benjamin, who'd tried to continue operating his business as usual, was frequently accosted in the street by people who berated him for his support of the governor. And now, on the evening of Friday, November 24, 1775, the verbal abuse had finally crossed a line. The mob that swarmed through his house didn't want to discuss; they wanted to attack. Benjamin had had to flee for his life.

For now, that was behind him. But what lay ahead? Benjamin Marston III stared into the blackness that, beyond the horizon, would be Boston.

David George stared nervously out into the motley gathering.[iv] On this sultry summer night, there were perhaps two dozen slaves arrayed in the field around him. Waiting for him to begin. He could see his wife, Phyllis, and his brother Jessie. Like him— praise the Lord—they'd been saved.

It wasn't as hard as he'd once imagined. The trick was to stop believing there was something you could do or not do, say or not say, and you'd be saved. That wasn't it at all. You had to give yourself up to the Lord, knowing that while your sins had crucified Christ, God's mercy would take them away. David George had finally accepted that. And God had done his part. "I was sure the Lord took [my sins] away," he would explain, "because I had such pleasure and joy in my soul that no man could give me."

Soon after David had been saved, Brother George Liele had come to Silver Bluff to preach to the slaves. David had known Liele, who was a few years younger, when they were slave children together back in Essex County, Virginia. But Liele had become a much different man since he'd been saved. "Come unto me all ye that labour," he'd said, "and I will give you rest." Afterwards, David confided in his old friend that he was that weary and heavy-laden man, "and that the grace of God had given me rest."

But living saved wasn't always easy. Sometimes, David told Brother Liele, he found it hard to express openly what was in his heart. Once, during one of Liele's services in a cornfield, "I had a great desire to pray with the people myself but I was ashamed, and went to a swamp and poured my heart out to the Lord." When he told Liele what had happened, the preacher urged him to meet with his fellow slaves between services to pray some more. David did, and "it gave me great relief." He had since taken on a new last name, George, to honour his mentor.

After Liele had moved on, Joshua Palmer, a charismatic white pastor of a church some distance from Silver Bluff, had come to the plantation—with the blessing of the master—and baptized eight of the slaves, including David, Phyllis, and Jessie, and organized a church for them. On Saturday evenings, Palmer would journey to the plantation to preach to the slaves. David became increasingly confident, beginning to "exhort in the church, and learned to sing hymns," even though he could neither read nor write.

He eventually learned to do those things too, with the help of the master's children. "I used to go to the little children to teach me a-b-c," he would write many years later. "They would give me a lesson, which I tried to learn, and then I would go to them, as when I was asleep." He was so consumed by his desire to learn "so that what I have in my heart, I can see again in the Scriptures . . . I think I learned in my sleep."

By the time of the Dunmore Proclamation in 1775, David was an elder in the Silver Bluff church. At first, it didn't seem as if anything that John Murray, the earl of Dunmore, the royalist governor of Virginia, might have to proclaim could have any direct effect on David's life. But it did. As, eventually, it would have an historic impact on thousands of other black slaves, not to mention their masters and the future of America. In the summer of 1775, however, matters seemed more mundane. Lord Dunmore's relations with his increasingly rebellious Virginia Assembly had grown so acrimonious he was forced to flee to a British warship for his own safety. He needed supporters. So, on November 7, 1775, from the deck of the *William*, he issued a proclamation in the name of the king, declaring martial law and calling on "every person capable of bearing arms to resort to his majesty's standard." What made his cry for help significant, however, was that he then expanded the meaning of "every person," adding: "I do herby further declare all indented servants, negroes or others free," if they agreed to bear arms on Britain's behalf.

Though Dunmore's proclamation had everything to do with pragmatism and almost nothing to do with principle, it instantly changed the dynamics of the incipient rebellion. Within a week, three hundred slaves from the Carolinas to New York had abandoned their masters' plantations to join the governor's Ethiopian Regiment.

The problem was that those three hundred made up fully half of Dunmore's troops, who were no match for several thousand rebel soldiers. Although Dunmore's gambit failed, the fact that he had brought the slaves into the conflict forced everyone, especially the rebels, to consider the potential power their slaves represented. "If that man is not crushed before spring," declared General George Washington, a Virginia slave-owner who'd been appointed commander of the newly formed Continental Army five months earlier, "[Dunmore] will become the most formidable enemy America has; his strength will increase as a snowball by rolling." To prevent that from happening, assemblies in the other colonies quickly did whatever they could to keep their own slave populations in check, including forbidding white ministers from holding services for them "lest they should furnish . . . too much knowledge."[9]

Not wanting to see his own missionary work among the slaves at Silver Bluff go to waste, Joshua Palmer encouraged earnest, enthusiastic David George to take over as the group's pastor. At first, David tried to beg off, said he was unfit, not ready, but Brother Palmer let him know it was not really in his hands anymore. "Take care that you don't offend the Lord," he said. So what choice did David have? Someone had to allow the Lord to speak through him to His flock. And David realized that the Lord would be guiding and directing him. Surely, God wouldn't have asked this of him if He didn't believe David was ready.

So on this night, David George looked out at the black faces in front of him and began with the words Brother George

---

9. Slaves who refused to give up their religion were often punished severely. John Marrant, a black minister who would later preach in Shelburne, recalled teaching religion to about thirty slave children while working as a contract labourer at a plantation outside Charles Town. The mistress of the plantation got it into her head that religion would "ruin" her slaves, and wanted them punished. So the master and his employees and neighbours raided the slaves' prayer meeting, grabbed them as they left, and tied them with cords. The next morning, all of the men, women, and children were stripped naked, their feet tied to a stake and their arms to a branch of a tree and beaten until they promised they would "lay off praying. . . . [It] didn't stop them," Marrant said. "They continued to pray in the woods, out of sight of the mistress."

Liele had used: "Come unto me all ye that labour, and I will give you rest."

The first black-ministered church in the Americas was open for worship.

There really was nowhere left to escape this madness.[v] Joseph Durfee had been more right than he could have guessed seven years ago. Good Lord, had it really been almost seven years since that day on the beach in Newport when he'd imagined he could outlast this insanity? It sometimes seemed like yesterday, but more often—like today, as he repacked his belongings once again—it felt like forever.

Year by year, the news had become ever more distressing. In Boston in 1770, a dispute between an off-duty soldier looking for a little extra cash and a waterfront rope manufacturer he'd asked for employment—"You want work?" the rope maker is said to have replied. "Clean my shithouse"—escalated into fisticuffs, then a brawl between the factory workers and the soldier's comrades. One brawl led to another and another, then to a standoff, and finally, after three days of lawlessness, to British soldiers firing rifles into a crowd. When it was over, five civilians were dead and six others wounded; the event quickly became known as the Boston Massacre.

So far as Durfee could tell, the area around Boston seemed to be the epicentre of the rebellion. Three years after the so-called massacre, a mob, disguised as Indians, had boarded three ships in Boston Harbor and dumped their cargoes of tea overboard. They had staged this pre-Christmas "tea party," Durfee noted, even after the British government had responded to colonial concerns by promising to repeal all of the unpopular Townshend duties, save one last three-pence-per-pound tax on tea. Nothing the British did, it seemed, satisfied these malcontents.

There were many more malcontents now. Thousands had watched the mob on the wharf while it rigged blocks and tackle to hoist the heavy chests of tea up from the hold, then opened them with axes in plain view of the onlookers and spilled their contents over the side. Not one person had come forward to identify the lawbreakers to the authorities.

The British response to this affront had been to shut down the port of Boston completely, not only until the East India Company was paid for the tea it had lost but also until the British government got its due in taxes. On June 1, 1774, the day the port closing was to take effect, residents in all of the colonies up and down the coast, including in Durfee's Rhode Island, lowered flags to half mast, closed up shops and marched through the streets, burning effigies of British officials such as the prime minister, Lord North. North had introduced what the British called the Coercive Acts, which he claimed were designed to restore order and civility to the American colonies. The colonists called them the Intolerable Acts and vowed they would not abide them.

It was especially hard to be a Loyalist in rebellious Newport. It became even harder after April 1775, the battles of Lexington and Concord, and "the shot heard around the world." That shot had certainly echoed through Newport, where news of the battle between the British army and the colonial Minutemen led to even more rioting and looting.

Which was why in the summer of 1775—a year ago now—the Durfees decided they had had enough. Daniel Goddard, a friend and cabinetmaker in Dartmouth, Massachusetts, a small inland town away from the front lines of what was now an undeclared but nonetheless very real war, invited the Durfees to stay with him. Joseph shuttered their house in Newport, closed the business, harnessed the two horses, and moved the family and as many belongings as would fit in their cart to Dartmouth.

It didn't take them long, however, to realize their mistake. Goddard's parents, suspected loyalist sympathizers, were under attack from their neighbours. Joseph and Ann were harassed themselves, and their children baited and jeered at by other children because of their parents' unpopular views. At least back in Newport, Joseph Durfee reasoned, the family would have their own house, their own refuge from the madness, and he might be able to run his business. It was time to harness those horses again.

At last! After lingering for more than a week at the mouth of Boston Harbor—as if threatening to change their minds about leaving (or perhaps just being their usual indecisive selves about whether to head for New York to engage the enemy immediately or retreat to Halifax to regroup)—the Howe brothers, General William and Admiral Richard, had finally given the order.[vi] The British fleet of seventy-eight ships, filled to bursting with soldiers, camp followers, Loyalists, guns, horses, and supplies, set sail for the safety—if that's what it would be—of Halifax.

It was March 17, 1776—St. Patrick's Day—and Benjamin Marston was eager to get on with it. He'd spent four months in the overcrowded British garrison at Boston living among the soldiers—officers, luckily—and other displaced Loyalists like himself who couldn't go home again. The food, even for the officers, was poor, and scurvy and smallpox were rampant in the quarters. Those had been difficult days for Benjamin personally. His wife, Sarah, had died in Marblehead and he'd been unable to be there with her. And, of course, those were bad times for America, too. "All America is in the most deplorable condition," he wrote to a business associate in Gibraltar, predicting: "Next summer will give my deluded countrymen some idea what it is like to live in a country which is the seat of war. God send us once more peace and good government."

Despite his and his country's troubles, Benjamin remained resourceful, even optimistic. He'd used his time in exile profitably, collecting on debts owed to him in Boston. He'd amassed £250 and begun making plans for a trip to the West Indies to buy goods to sell to the British army and navy here.

But that, of course, was before the British army and navy had decided the previous week to evacuate Boston.

The British army had been driven back into Boston nearly a year ago after the battles at Lexington and Concord, and found itself trapped there after Bunker Hill, the costly June victory that stung like defeat. By July, General Washington had arrived to take charge of the ill-equipped but ever-increasing numbers of rebel soldiers of the newly formed Continental Army. They ringed the city, preventing supplies from reaching the British by land. To make matters worse for the British, most of what remained of the civilian population in the city that had so recently given its name to an iconic and inspirational "massacre" and a "tea party" was hostile to British presence.

The British initially had planned to evacuate in the fall and regroup in more loyal New York, but then hadn't. Then, their planned spring departure had to be postponed after the British transport vessels that were supposed to carry the troops were slow in arriving.

But then Dorchester Heights changed General Howe's mind, and hastened the departure.

It had all come to a sorry head less than two weeks before on the night of March 4, 1776, when American soldiers stealthily moved prefabricated fortifications into place on Dorchester Heights, which overlooked and commanded Boston and its harbour. Behind those hastily configured ramparts, the Americans placed cannons they'd captured from the British at Ticonderoga and hauled three hundred miles through the winter snows to Boston.

The next morning, when General William Howe, commander of the British forces, saw what the Americans had done, he was stunned by the audacity of their move and astounded at the difficulty of what they'd accomplished. He estimated it must have taken twelve thousand soldiers to put those fortifications in place so quickly.[10] It was also, he understood immediately, a bold and brilliant tactical strike. Not only could his own artillery not be elevated high

---

10. The number, in fact, was just twelve hundred.

enough to attack the new American position but the Americans were able to fire with impunity at his ships in the harbour.

Howe briefly considered attacking the American position, thought better of it, and issued the order to withdraw immediately all British forces from the city.

The new problem was that there was no evacuation plan.

Benjamin Marston wasn't surprised. And he wouldn't have been alone in wondering whether the real reason for the lack of planning might have been that the good general was a trifle distracted. Since he'd taken over from General Thomas Gage in October, Howe's only real conquest—at least according to the garrison gossips—was the wife of Joshua Loring, Howe's commissary of prisons. The blond and beautiful Mrs. Loring was now the general's mistress, constant companion, and chief preoccupation.

Others put an even more sinister spin on Howe's failure to outwit and outmanoeuvre the Americans. The Howes—William's older brother, Richard, was the British admiral in charge of the naval fleet at Boston—were both considered Whigs and American sympathizers. Before he'd heeded the call of King George III to return to uniform in 1775, William had served as a British Member of Parliament, where he'd not only opposed the Coercive Acts but also reassured his Nottingham constituents in 1774 that he would refuse to serve in the American conflict. So much for that promise.

Still, Benjamin found it hard to believe the general could be anything but loyal to the king's cause. For a start, there was his heroic performance at Bunker Hill. Despite the fact that the Americans had twice repulsed his forces, Howe refused to concede and led his troops back up the hill a third time, finally forcing the Americans to retreat. By the time the battle ended, he'd lost 40 percent of his soldiers, including every member of his personal staff, but he'd won.

If that wasn't convincing enough, there was the reality—the gossips again—of the Howes' "close" connections to the British royal family. Their grandmother had been King George I's mistress,[11] making them the illegitimate uncles of King George III. Surely, that would be reason enough to support his cause in battle.

Whatever the merits of such idle and probably ill-informed speculation, Benjamin understood that the more pressing matter was to get the British out of Boston, and quickly. It was going to be no easy task. There were rumours that food, already in short supply, would soon be gone. There were more than nine thousand soldiers, plus another two thousand camp followers—wives, children, mistresses, prostitutes, servants, and assorted others—and perhaps a thousand more Loyalists, all needing food and transport.

For the Loyalists, the first days after General Howe's evacuation announcement had been filled with fear and anxiety. Would there be enough room on the transport ships for them? Would they have to stay behind and face the wrath of the Americans?

In the end, there'd been room—barely—for everyone, plus some of the stores and a few of the horses. On their way out the door, they'd blown up the British army headquarters at Castle William to prevent the Americans from finding anything useful there. All that remained of British Boston was crammed into seventy-eight vessels on a journey to Halifax.

The Loyalists' initial relief that they had escaped was replaced almost immediately by trepidation at what might be in store for them in Halifax. They knew Halifax was small—they would, upon their arrival, double the population of the entire colony—and there would likely still be snow on the ground. There would be no housing for them, and no jobs.

Perhaps surprisingly, Benjamin Marston wasn't worried. He had already decided he would follow through with his plan to sail to the West Indies to acquire goods he could sell to the British forces. The only difference was that those forces would now be in Halifax rather than Boston.

---

11. The Howe brothers, it was suggested, resembled George I.

Perhaps he should track down Dr. John Prince, a fellow Loyalist from Marblehead who'd been among the signatories of the letter to Governor Hutchinson in 1774 and was now among the Loyalists heading to Halifax. He might be interested in investing in Benjamin's trading venture. Or maybe Benjamin should talk to Gideon White, a cousin from Plymouth, a loyalist cousin from the Winslow side. Gideon, a sea captain and merchant trader, had just happened to be in Boston last spring at the time of the Battle of Bunker Hill, and immediately volunteered to serve in the British army. He too was on one of the vessels bound for Halifax. Gideon might be interested in his scheme, Benjamin thought.

It would all turn out all right. This damned war couldn't last forever.

After the statue was toppled, everyone wanted to take credit. Colonel Oliver Brown of Wellsburg, West Virginia, for example, reported that he had led a raucous group of forty soldiers, sailors, and civilians down Broadway to Bowling Green on the evening of July 9, 1776, where he claimed it took them two tries to get a rope around its neck. But local rabble-rousers Isaac Sears and Peter Cortenjus would both later brag that the perpetrators were members of their patriotic Sons of Liberty group, and each would claim that *he* was their leader that day.

Regardless, there is no doubt about what triggered the attack—or its symbolic import. At 6 p.m. on July 9, copies of the freshly minted Declaration of Independence, which had been formally approved in Philadelphia five days earlier, finally arrived in New York and were officially read out to General Washington's troops in their various parade grounds. The news that the thirteen former British colonies had suddenly and unilaterally declared themselves the independent United States of America was greeted with loud cheers and an understandable desire to do something spectacular to memorialize the momentous occasion. It didn't take long to figure out what that something should be.

Ten years earlier, New York merchants—grateful that the British government had repealed the hated Stamp Act—had commissioned the construction of a gilded lead statue of King George III at Bowling Green, a parade ground and marketplace at the foot of Broadway near the harbour. But by the time the four-thousand-pound monument, which depicted the king on a horse and dressed as a Roman emperor, was finally erected in 1770, many New Yorkers were feeling decidedly less grateful to their king. In 1771, officials had to put up a wrought-iron fence to protect the statue from vandals. Two years later, they passed an anti-desecration law to discourage people from damaging it.

But no fence nor law could protect the statue on this night. The soldiers, sailors, and citizens surged onto Bowling Green, managed to throw ropes around the king's head and horse's neck, and pulled the whole thing to the ground. Someone cut off the king's nose; someone else managed to separate the crown of laurels from the top of his head. The mob then jammed what was left of their former sovereign's head onto a spike and propped it outside a tavern for all to enjoy.

Toppling the hated statue not only seemed as good a way as any for New Yorkers to mark their newfound independence but also served as a very practical contribution to the cause when the lead was recast into much needed musket balls for the army.[12] As one jaded loyalist soldier wrote in his diary, the colonists "hoped that the emanations of the leaden George will make as deep impressions in the bodies of his red-coated and Tory subjects . . . as the super-abundant emanations of the folly and pretended goodness of the real George have made upon their minds."

The war for America had seemed to stutter into existence over the course of more than a dozen years as the legalistic feint and parry of British act and colonial resistance slowly but inexorably gave way to harsher measures on both sides. Had

---

12. According to one account, 42,088 bullets were cast from the statue.

the tipping point been Lexington and Concord? Or had it come a few months later, in August 1775, when the British government ignored the Americans' Olive Branch Petition and issued its own Proclamation of Rebellion, declaring the American colonies in a state of "open and avowed rebellion," and calling on its subjects to "withstand and suppress" it. Or had it actually come on July 4, 1776, the day the Continental Congress approved the Declaration of Independence?

For Benjamin Marston, Joseph Durfee, David George, and thousands of their fellow loyalist colonists, trying to determine when disagreement had turned to rebellion no longer mattered. The fact was that the Americans had now—symbolically, at least—toppled their king. And none of their lives would ever be the same again.

"Oh God, it's all over"

Chapter 2.

Benjamin Marston hadn't expected he'd end up back here in this province—"state, I mean, I beg pardon"—so soon. And certainly not in these circumstances. Bad luck and worse timing. Not that any of that mattered. He was here now, in Plymouth, Massachusetts, a "guest" of the local Committee of Safety, and he would have to make the best of it.

It was November 24, 1776, exactly one year to the day since he'd made his hasty exit from Marblehead by cover of darkness. As he confided almost giddily in his journal, "I have seen more variety than in all my life before. I have lived in a town besieged, on board ships, both of war and others, have been at sea, in the West Indies, have been in the woods, have travelled by land and carried my baggage on my back, have been taken and am now in prison, not worth a groat . . ."[13]

His "prison" wasn't such a bad place. For which he could thank his patriot brothers-in-law. John and William Watson had posted his bail, and William had agreed to let Benjamin serve an indefinite term of confinement in his home. Their generosity

---

13. A groat is a silver coin worth fourpence.

may have had more to do with the entreaties of their wives, Benjamin's sisters, than any desire to help an unregenerate Tory, but Benjamin had to allow that it was "upon the whole . . . not a disagreeable way of life."

That said, given the state of affairs in this new state of the union, he would have preferred to be back in Halifax to try to put the wind back in the sails of his life. He'd made the most of the short time he'd spent there after arriving with Howe's fleet at the end of March.

Though he was 45 and had been a widower for only a few months, he'd already fallen in love with a younger woman from Windsor named Eliza. "The grave folk, should they see this," he confided to his sister Lucia, "would doubtless think me a very ridiculous fellow to be thus earnestly engaged in such (as they would call it) a frivolous pursuit, and you, my good sister, will perhaps smile at your brother to see him a second time so entirely engrossed by the tender passion. But all this would not cool my ardor, for I frankly confess that I do (and always did) look on a sensible, well-bred, accomplished person of your sex as the most valuable thing the world has in it."

On a more prosaic level, during his time in Halifax Benjamin had also teamed up with Dr. John Prince and British merchant George Ervin to acquire a schooner named the *Earl Percy*. On June 10, 1776, with a cargo of fish, he'd set sail for Dominica under the benign protection of the British fleet, which was ferrying General Howe's troops to New York for what had become, Benjamin had since learned, a very successful assault on the American forces there.

His own adventure had not gone nearly as well. The *Percy* had taken forty days to make Dominica, spoiling much of its fish. This had resulted in what Benjamin conceded was an "indifferent sale." To make matters worse, he'd been within a few hours of the safety of Halifax harbour on his return voyage when the *Percy* was set upon by the *Eagle*, an American privateer "of six carriage and eight swivel guns," and forced to return with it to Plymouth where its captain, Elijah Freeman Paine, claimed his prize and the local Committee of Safety claimed Benjamin.

The day after his arrival in Plymouth, nine members of the committee had interrogated him, and ordered him to jail. Benjamin was unimpressed. In his journal, he wrote disparaging comments about each of his inquisitors. Mr. Mayhew, for example, the host of the gathering, was "a simpering how-do-you-do-sorry-for-your-loss kind," while Silas Bartlett was "a good sort of a man made a fool of to serve the purpose of the occasion." Mr. Lothrop, who'd "been handsomely and kindly entertained at my house," Benjamin noted tartly, "can do dirty work."

Eventually, the committee agreed to turn him over to his brother-in-law, giving him the liberty of William's yard and garden and permitting him to go to meetings on Sunday. (Would they have been so accommodating if they'd been able to read his journal?)

Benjamin used the journal, in which he wrote most days, to give vent to his many and various frustrations, including his views on his "deluded countrymen" and their doomed infatuation with independence. "Salt is now about 10 shillings sterling per bushel; flour about six dollars per hundredweight; woolens and linens are scarcely to be had," he wrote one day. "Bread corn has got to a price which was hardly ever known of in times of greatest dearth. . . . And yet this miserably deceived people are made to believe they can support independency."

He added: "God have mercy upon them and open their eyes," thinking perhaps of Howe's recent routing of the Americans in New York. "Their army is now broken to pieces. Their general [Washington] is not to be found—so that General Howe has been obliged to send to the governor of Connecticut about an exchange of prisoners, of whom he has great numbers. [The Americans] have likewise lost a very great part of their cannon, tents and baggage. And yet the managers of the game in this province affect to talk in high style—still push the drafting of every fourth man to relieve the army, who are every day running home, sick, lowzy, ragged and full of all manner of nastiness. Nay, General Washington, who moves the puppets of this place, has the effrontery to give out that a French fleet and army will be over early in the spring. A fleet from France! There will be one from the moon as soon. Strange stupidity to expect assistance from that quarter, for can it be thought that any European power who has colonies in America would lend a helping hand to form an independent State here, so large as the British Colonies would make if all united?"[14]

For all his considerable consternation at the unhappy turn of events in what had once been his homeland, Benjamin was not, strangely, unhappy himself. He had lost his wife, his home, his business, and his homeland, it was true, but all of the adventures, intrigues, setbacks, and excitement he'd experienced in the past 365 days had invigorated him in ways that merely being a successful middle-aged, good-citizen businessman in Marblehead never could. "I conclude that health of body and peace of mind are more essential to human happiness than either riches or honours," he wrote on the anniversary of his night flight into exile. "I thank heaven I am amply possessed of the two first."

Now if he could only get back to Halifax, and the business of making a living for himself, and the pleasure of seeing Eliza again . . . Would she still be there for him?

In all likelihood, the moment only began to take on its mythic import three years later, in the fall of 1782, after Gideon White and his friends took to gathering regularly at Roubalet's Tavern in New York to consider their options.[i] Or perhaps its significance did not become clear, even to them, until later, perhaps deep into the following spring of 1783 after the first fleet of thirty vessels and three thousand people—Gideon not among

---

14. Ten years later, reading over what he had written, Marston added a note in the margin: "I find in this I was much out in my guess."

them—departed New York harbour so optimistically, so hopefully, and sailed off into the future. Or maybe it would not be until much, much later, when historians began rooting around in the fragments of their lives and decided that this particular incident was the start of it all.

The relevant fact everyone would ultimately note was that on a too-damp, too-cold spring day in 1779—or was it actually a crisp, sunny March day?—Gideon White sailed past the nearly deserted mouth of the harbour at Port Roseway and thought that it might, possibly, conceivably be a good place to establish a community someday. And said so to others.

He wasn't the first, of course. The Indians had called it Sawgumgeegum, or "bend of the water," to indicate that it was a place where the ocean bent deep into the land. They lived along the banks of the river that ran into the harbour, fishing, hunting, even cultivating the rocky soil where they could.

During the latter part of the seventeenth century, visiting French fishermen called it Port Razoir, apparently in honour of the prosaic razor clams that bred in a sandbar that jutted into the bay along the harbour's eastern shore.

But it wasn't until the mid-1700s, after the British had expelled the Acadians and the governor had issued several enticing proclamations, promising grants of up to a thousand acres for "peopling and cultivation [of] the lands vacated by the French," that anyone seriously attempted to settle much of the colony beyond Halifax. By then, the English had anglicized Port Razoir to the romantic-sounding Port Roseway.

An Irish-born Virginian named Alexander McNutt was among those who took up the governor's offer. Though he was granted a huge swath of the colony—2.5 million acres—in exchange for promises to bring in settlers, not much happened with most of it. In 1765, however, McNutt and his brother Benjamin obtained a grant of land around Port Roseway, where they planned to sow the seeds of a community they called New Jerusalem. There, they built a small settlement. Most of the dozen or so inhabitants were relatives or friends of the McNutts, and most had already decamped for more inviting locations by the beginnings of the American Revolution.

Benjamin and Alexander remained. They built their own homes on an island at the mouth of the harbour, which they aptly named after themselves. By the time of Gideon White's brief sail past, Alexander, who seemed to be in constant financial difficulties of one sort or another, had fallen on even harder times. Even though Alexander sympathized with the rebellious Americans, a party of "armed ruffians" from an American privateer had raided the island in 1778, ransacked his home, and taken away everything of worth.

This was, indirectly, one reason why, on this particular day, Gideon White was heading north, sailing past McNutts Island and the entrance to Port Roseway on his way to Ragged Island, twenty miles closer to Halifax. Gideon, the master of the *Apollo*, had become part of a loyalist patrol, which was attempting, without much success, to protect from American invaders the few scattered coastal settlements from Yarmouth to Halifax and the fishermen who plied the waters around them.

It certainly wouldn't have been Gideon's first voyage past the entrance to Roseway. Soon after evacuating to Halifax from Boston in 1776 with General Howe's troops, Gideon had teamed up with his brother Cornelius and their friend John Prince (who happened to be partners in another venture with Gideon's cousin Benjamin Marston) to ferry goods between Nova Scotia and the British West Indies. White's role was to handle the Nova Scotia end of the business, the milk run between Halifax and Yarmouth.

He didn't have much better luck than his cousin Benjamin. In September 1776, Gideon was captured by American privateers, served a few months' house arrest at his father's home in Plymouth, refused to sign an oath of fealty to the new government, and was designated "inimical to the United States" and unceremoniously shipped back to Nova Scotia. Where he became, at the age of 25, a man without a home.

Though he was far from ready to give up fighting the rebels, Gideon White couldn't have helped but see in Port Roseway's fine and sheltered harbour, a potential safe harbour for himself after the turbulence of the last few years. In the last year alone, his brother Cornelius had been lost at sea, his father had died in Plymouth, and he himself had been among those legally banished from Massachusetts as an "enemy of the state." If he returned, the law declared, he would "suffer the pains of death without benefit of clergy."

That would have been an ignominious fate for a man whose great-great-grandfather Peregrine had been born aboard the *Mayflower*. After Peregrine's father died, his mother remarried Edward Winslow, later to be governor of Massachusetts, and began a prestigious colonial family line that would eventually encompass the Whites, Winslows, and Marstons, among others.

Port Roseway may have beckoned but, in 1779, Gideon wasn't yet ready to answer its call. There was still a homeland and a heritage to recapture.

Benjamin Marston stood slack-jawed on the wharf in Santa Cruz, appalled at the parade of human misery before him: "men and women, boys and girls all together, each as naked as God made them, saving a piece of coarse linen just to cover what nature most commonly dictates to human creatures to hide."[ii] They were being driven like cattle from the deck of the Danish ship that had brought them here, past the docks and into a huge pen where they could be put on display and sold to the highest bidder. Each had a wooden identity tag around his or her neck. Benjamin had never seen a slave auction before and, watching now—wanting not to, but mesmerized by the awfulness of it all—he hoped he would never have to see such a thing again.

It had been a long, strange voyage. And not just this most recent trip on the *Ajax*.

It was March 20, 1779, almost two years to the day since he had been unceremoniously put aboard a cartel vessel in Boston Harbor with other captured Loyalists and shipped to Halifax as part of a prisoner exchange after serving his house arrest in Marblehead.

During his time in captivity, Benjamin had hired a lawyer to try to recover his vessel but, even before they'd gotten their case to court, a judge had ordered the *Percy* sold, along with its cargo of rum and cocoa. In earlier, better times, Benjamin might have been able to challenge this travesty, but no longer. As he wrote dejectedly to Paine, the privateer captain who'd claimed what had been rightly Benjamin's: "I have now no other object in view but to obtain my liberty and return to Nova Scotia as soon as I can."

The best thing about being in Halifax once again had almost certainly been the opportunity to reunite with Eliza. "The pleasure of again seeing that dear girl has abundantly rewarded me for all the disagreeable feelings of a six-months' imprisonment," he wrote in his journal. But such psychic rewards did little to allay his more worldly wants. Circumstances had reduced him to living in a dingy, one-guinea-a-week room in Mrs. Lyde's boarding house, which may explain why he was soon writing Eliza another farewell poem:

> *Eliza dearest maid farewell*
> *From you I now must part*
> *Leave you in Halifax to dwell*
> *And ply the seaman's art.*

A few months later, however, he was a captive again. He had been sailing south from St. John's to St. Kitts in the schooner *Polly* with a load of fish when a Yankee privateer named *General Gates* gave chase. Six hours later, the wind died down and the crew of the *General Gates*, "by means of oars, overhauled the schooner" and took it to Boston.

At first, Benjamin was lucky enough to end up a "prisoner" at the home of a friend, Samuel White, but word soon got back to Marblehead. Thanks to "the littleness of mind of some person at Marblehead who wrote to [Boston's Committee of Safety] to inform them that I was such an inveterate enemy to the country that it would be dangerous for me to be at large," he was forced to spend ten days aboard a prison ship in the harbour. "I have learned that a man may enjoy himself in prison," he noted obliquely in his journal. A few days later, he and 170 other prisoners were exchanged, and he once again found himself back in Halifax where he took up "lodgings at my old quarters at Miss Lyde's. So ends my second captivity."

Not all of his trips ended so badly, of course, though it was a rare voyage that didn't include at least some adventure. On this most recent run aboard the *Ajax*, it had come in the form of a gale. The *Ajax* had left Halifax on December 7, 1778, for Surinam on the northern coast of South America. Thanks to the storm, which denuded the *Ajax* of its foremast, main topmast, bowsprit, boats, anchor, and three deck guns—not to mention washing one man overboard—Benjamin had had to spend five weeks at sea before finally limping into port at St. Eustatius for repair.

The lengthy wait for a replacement mast was frustrating. "Could I with a wish waft hither one of the many thousands of useless trees, which are now standing in the woods of Nova Scotia," Benjamin wrote plaintively. Still, he found St. Eustatius ("Statia" to the locals) a fascinating place to be. And why not? This little Dutch island in the middle of the northeastern Caribbean was a major supplier of arms and ammunition to the American rebels, and one of the main links between Europe and the new American nation. Even Benjamin Franklin, who had decamped from London to Paris after the hostilities broke out, had his mail to America routed through the island to ensure that it arrived safely at its destination.

But St. Eustatius, for all its American connections, was also a cosmopolitan crossroads for adventurers of all allegiances, and Benjamin had an opportunity to exchange yarns with more than a few sailors like himself who'd been captured by privateers and spent time as "guests" of those new United States of America.

One man who'd also spent time in Marblehead told Benjamin about the town's new way of determining who was and was not a Tory. They'd call a town meeting, the man said, and someone would read out a list of all male inhabitants of the community. And then the group would vote. "Is A. a Tory?" the chair would ask. "If he is, signify it by holding up of hands." Using this "scientific" method, Benjamin's former neighbours had identified thirty of their number as Tories. Benjamin could only shake his head in wonder at the lunacy of it all. "This is being tried by one's peers," he noted, "with a vengeance."

Finally, on March 20, new mast in place and repairs completed, the *Ajax* had set sail for Santa Cruz,[15] ninety miles to the west. It was as interesting in its own way as Statia. "This island," he wrote, ever the social anthropologist, "belongs to the King of Denmark, but nine-tenths of the inhabitants are British and Dutch subjects. Strangers coming into this island are inspected by the officers of government like other goods. . . . Natural Danes coming hither find themselves in a strange country, though in the dominions of their prince. All religions are tolerated here and, besides the Danish Church, there are the Church of England, a Presbyterian congregation, a Dutch Church, the Roman Catholics, a Quaker meeting house and a Moravian preacher. The last is intended principally, if not totally, for the slaves, over whom he has great influence, and whom he keeps in very good order."

Benjamin was no stranger to slaves. His family had had a few of its own at Marston's Farm, and he encountered them in the finer homes of Halifax, too. But it was another thing entirely to watch human beings be sold in a marketplace. "Great God. What must be the feelings of a sensible human being," he wrote that day in his journal, "to be torn from all that is reckoned valuable and dear, and to be condemned to the most servile drudgery and infamous uses without the least hope of relief?"

---

15. Now known as St. Croix.

For the first time, he tried to imagine what it would be like to be on the other side of slavery's lash. "If the Misses B and L and S and G, with the young gentlemen of those families, should be torn from their country and carried into perpetual servitude, we should see and feel the atrociousness, the dreadfulness of the wrong. But as it is only Miss Yawyaw and Miss Pawpee and the young gentlemen Messrs. Quashee and Quomino, whose skins are black, whose hair stout and curled, whose noses flat and lips thick, why we think there can be no great harm in it." With grim irony he concluded: "I fancy there is some mistake in the very trite maxim that all men are by nature equal. If so, why such an inequality in their conditions. 'Tis a phenomenon, which Omniscience only can account for—to Him I leave it." Benjamin had concerns enough of his own. It was time for the *Ajax* to head north, run the gauntlet of marauding privateers, and Benjamin hoped, against the odds, that he'd make the trip safely this time.

Boston King knew all about that which Benjamin Marston could only imagine. He had been born a slave but was now free—or as free as it was possible for a black man to be in America in these turbulent times. Like David George, the slave preacher whose physical and psychic path he would cross more than once in the next thirty years, Boston King would ultimately leave behind a fascinating, full, and vivid account of his own life and times.[iii] He was, initially at least, an almost accidental adherent to the king's cause, as were thousands of other black Loyalists. In his memoir, which was first published in an English Methodist magazine in 1798, King writes about one pivotal moment—probably sometime in 1780—when his loyalty was put to the test.

For the previous two days, he would write, he had smacked up against one new and still more troubling revelation after another. And now *this*. Fifty horses! All of them stolen from the British army, probably a few at a time, and then hidden on this island by the traitorous militia officer who'd laid claim to Boston too! Boston knew he had to escape and get word to his British captain, but he also knew he would have to wait for his opportunity. Otherwise . . . well, best not to think of that. There'd been enough of *that* in his life already.

So much had happened since yesterday morning when he had left the British camp to catch a few fish to fry for Captain Grey's breakfast. By the time he returned an hour or so later, his regiment had gone. One of the few remaining soldiers told Boston that an express messenger had come bearing urgent orders: "Decamp in fifteen minutes," he'd said. And they had.

"You need not be uneasy," Captain Lewes assured Boston upon noticing his distress. "You'll see your regiment before seven o'clock tonight." Boston had no reason to doubt the man, who was in charge of the small band of Rocky Mount Militia the regular army had left behind to disband the camp. Two hours later, he and Lewes and the others set off together, ostensibly in search of the rest of the regiment.

But as they were marching, Lewes surprised Boston with an out-of-nowhere question. "How will you like me to be your master," he'd said, more a statement of fact than a question.

"But I'm Captain Grey's servant," Boston answered, hoping he sounded less indignant than he felt.

"Yes." Lewes was dismissive. "But I expect they're all taken prisoner by now." How could he know such a thing? Boston wondered. He didn't have much time to ponder that question before Captain Lewes said something even more startling—and offensive. "I have been long enough in the English service," he confided, "and I'm determined to leave them."

Leave them? *Desert* was what he meant. Captain Lewes was going to turn his back on the British king, the same king who had given Boston King, a poor black slave from South Carolina, his freedom and his name. Boston King was indignant. And he let Captain Lewes know it.

But Lewes was not about to be criticized by an uppity coloured boy barely out of slavery. "If you do not behave well," he informed Boston sharply, "I will put you in irons and give you a dozen stripes every morning!"

Boston had had enough experience with this sort of white man to believe that Lewes would do as he said. Boston had been a slave almost all of his twenty years. A few months ago, he'd run off to escape just such a whipping and "[threw] myself into the hands of the English." He was not about to go back to being a slave after he'd tasted freedom.

Boston's father had been stolen from Africa and sold into slavery. His master was Richard Waring, the owner of a spectacularly beautiful five-hundred-acre plantation on the banks of the Ashley River at the east end of Dorchester, one of the largest villages in all of South Carolina. Boston's father had quickly become a favourite of the master, serving as his driver. Boston's mother, who knew all about the medicinal powers of herbs from the Indians and had a way with a needle and thread, was also much in demand among the ladies of the plantation.

The happy result was that young Boston enjoyed many privileges other slaves on the plantation did not. Not that he was ever free. By the time he was six, in fact, Boston was working in Mr. Waring's house as one of his personal servants.

Three years later, Waring assigned him to join a group of slave boys minding the cattle. They taught him to curse, Boston would recall years later, but God soon scared that badness out of him. One day after lunch when he was 12, he fell asleep and dreamed that the world was on fire. In the dream, God himself descended from his white throne to separate those who, from among the millions of souls on earth, would go to heaven and those who were "rejected, and fell into the greatest confusion and despair." When he woke up, Boston vowed to give up both bad company and swearing. Which he did. But it wasn't always easy. There was much to curse in his life.

When he was 16, his owner apprenticed him to a carpenter in Charles Town named Waters who frequently beat him, once so severely he was laid up for three weeks before he could go back to work. When Waring heard how badly Boston was being treated, he came to town and threatened to take the young man away from Waters and allow him to finish his apprenticeship elsewhere. Things got better after that, and Boston became accomplished at his trade.

But when word came in the winter of 1780 that the British under Sir Henry Clinton were preparing to attack Charles Town, Waters decided to evacuate to safer territory thirty-eight miles beyond the city. He took Boston with him. The new quarters were just twelve miles from the plantation where Boston's parents were still slaves, so one day Boston got permission from Mr. Waters to borrow a horse and visit them. While there, Boston impetuously agreed to lend the horse to one of Waring's other servants, who claimed he needed it for "a little journey." But the man arrived back several days late. Boston knew he would be the one to suffer the "severest punishment" for the servant's tardiness since Waters "knew not how to show mercy." So he decided to do what tens of thousands of other slaves like him were already doing: he fled to the British side. Not out of some profound principle, but to escape a beating.

In the four years since Lord Dunmore had offered freedom to American slaves who took up arms against their masters, the British had broadened their campaign to convince Southern blacks to join them. In 1779, General Clinton, by then commander-in-chief of "all His Majesty's Colonies laying on the Atlantic Ocean" had issued what became known as the Philipsburg Proclamation, promising "every negro who shall desert the rebel standard, full security to follow within these lines any occupation which he shall think proper." This meant that slaves didn't actually have to join the British military to gain their freedom, and better, might even be able to bring their families with them.

Promising freedom to everyone, of course, was less the result of royal altruism—and certainly not a reflection of the reality that the British, whose forces had since been augmented by Hessian mercenaries, no longer needed black troops to serve as

58

cannon fodder—and more about gaining a tactical advantage. Allowing runaway slaves to bring their families with them meant that runaways wouldn't have to worry about their masters taking revenge on their families back on the plantations. Perhaps more important, planting the insidious notion that their slaves might leave them could distract Southern soldiers from their fight with the British. They'd be torn, the British hoped, between their soldiering duties and figuring out how to prevent their own slaves from leaving; or—better—worrying too about what their suddenly empowered slaves might do to their plantations or the families the slave-owner-soldiers had left behind.

Boston, for his part, had made his escape alone and hoped that Mr. Waring, who by the standards of Southern plantation owners had been a good master, would not punish his parents for his desertion. The British, Boston explained later, "received me readily, and I began to feel the happiness of liberty, of which I knew nothing before, although I was also much grieved at first to be obliged to leave my friends and reside among strangers."

His situation, however, became considerably worse before it got better. Almost immediately after he'd joined the British, Boston fell ill with smallpox, which had been epidemic in America from the first days of the siege of Boston in 1775. While most British-born soldiers had survived less virulent strains of the disease as children and therefore were immune to it, their American cousins, white and black—but especially black—had no immunity. In the cramped, often unsanitary conditions of the military encampments, the disease—whose first symptoms could easily be mistaken for flu—spread quickly from person to person. Thirty to 40 percent of those who contracted smallpox died as a result.

As soon as the pustules began spreading over Boston's skin—visual confirmation that an all-too-common flu was really a potentially lethal case of smallpox—the British slapped him into quarantine with other blacks afflicted with the disease. He spent a miserable month there, isolated and ignored, often losing entire days laying on the hard ground without anything to eat or drink. His saviour came in the earthly form of a York Volunteer he'd known in his former life: "He brought me such things as I stood in need of and, by the blessing of the Lord, I began to recover."

By then, however, the British had abandoned the camp, leaving their ill black comrades to their fate. Luckily, the Americans, realizing that Boston and the others had smallpox, wisely left them alone too.[16] Boston was eventually able to make it back to Lord Cornwallis's new British headquarters at Camden, where he discovered that the soldier who'd nursed him through his bout of smallpox had been wounded. Boston tended him for six weeks—"rejoicing that it was in my power to return him the kindness he had [shown me]"—before finally rejoining his regiment as Captain Grey's servant.

He was Grey's *servant*, not his slave. It was an important distinction for Boston in this new and different world of freedom, but one he knew was lost on the traitorous Captain Lewes. So Boston bided his time, waiting for his chance to escape. It would come soon enough.

The morning after they'd left the British camp, Lewes had ordered Boston and a small boy to wade across to a nearby island and fetch him some horses. Boston soon discovered that the

---

16. Sick blacks were occasionally used as weapons of war. Later in the conflict, in fact, the British apparently deliberately set out to infect American troops with the virus. In 1781, as Elizabeth Fenn notes in "Biological Warfare in Eighteenth-Century North America: Beyond Jeffery Amherst" published in *The Journal of American History*, one general, who had seven hundred blacks with smallpox among his forces, wrote to a fellow general: "I shall distribute them about the rebel plantations." Those who were not deliberately sent back among the enemy were often "freed" by the army to wreak even more havoc. Simon Shama, in *Rough Crossings*, quotes one Hessian officer: "We drove back to the enemy all our black friends whom we had taken along to despoil the countryside. We had used them to good advantage and set them free and now, with fear and trembling, they had to face the reward of their cruel masters."

horses had been stolen from the British. When he and the boy brought them back to the captain, Lewes immediately mounted one and went off on his own. Which is when Boston slipped away, too. In the other direction. He had to find his regiment, inform Captain Grey that Lewes not only had deserted but also was the one who'd taken the king's horses. He hoped the British would believe the story that he, Boston King, a freed black man, a loyal subject of the king, had to tell them.

Finally, Joseph Durfee had something to show for his efforts on behalf of the cause.[iv] And he didn't just mean General Henry Clinton's fifty-guinea thanks from a grateful nation either—although that too was more than welcome, especially given his own straitened circumstances these days. His personal contribution had been critical. Not to put too fine a point on it, Joseph Durfee—in the process of skilfully guiding the British armada across the treacherous Charles Town Bar, through heavy enemy shelling, and into the harbour from where its forces had been able to complete their stunningly successful siege of Charles Town— had helped Britain win the war, or at least, he hoped, finally turn the tide of battle.

Despite his very best efforts, the tide had been running against the British—and Durfee, too—for far too long.

After he and his family had returned to British-controlled Newport from their self-imposed exile in Dartmouth, Massachusetts, in 1776, Durfee joined the Loyal Newport Association as a captain and placed both his sloop *Friendship* and his schooners *Peggy* and *Dolphin* under British command. Unfortunately, all three vessels were soon lost to privateers.

Later, the British asked Durfee to undertake a census to determine what sort of assistance they might hope for from the locals in the event of an American attack. The answer, it turned out, was very little. And not just from Newport's large rebel-sympathizing contingent. The often oafishly ham-handed British occupation had bred dangerous resentments, even among the most kingly of royalist sympathizers. British soldiers seemed to view all Americans—rebels and Loyalists alike—with contempt. They'd indiscriminately plunder the colonists' fields of fruits and root vegetables and then, to mock those they'd stolen from, would hand over the ill-gotten booty to their wives, who would then attempt to sell it back to the locals. The situation got so bad that, early in the fall of 1779, the British commanders in Newport finally had to issue a proclamation declaring that if those peddling produce couldn't prove ownership, the goods would be seized and the miscreants expelled from the garrison.

Not that it mattered much. Within a month, the British forces had pulled out of Newport anyway. Their generals had decided it made more sense to concentrate their forces in New York. The Durfees, having no choice any longer, followed them there, taking up residence at 125 Water Street. Back home, they quickly learned, the rebels had confiscated their properties.

Perhaps that was why Durfee hadn't hesitated when Clinton, who knew that the former sea captain and trader had an intimate knowledge of the many navigationally tricky rivers, bays, and shoals that dotted America's southern coast, asked him to accompany his forces as they prepared their assault on Charles Town. For Durfee, it marked the final step of his transformation from moderate Loyalist to fighter for his king.

The fleet—ninety troop ships and fourteen warships carrying eighty-five hundred soldiers and five thousand sailors—set off on Christmas Day 1779. After a horrific month-long journey through almost continuous storms—the first storm, which hit on December 27, lasted three days; the next came after a single day of clear weather and continued for six days—many of the ships had been blown so far off course they ended up near Florida and had to sail north again. Clinton set up his command headquarters on Tybee Island, near Savannah, which British forces had captured the year before.

Durfee, as befitting his own importance to the mission, had sailed from New York aboard the *Romulus* with Clinton and his most senior officers. Seeing the British high command at such close range must have been fascinating, though not entirely encouraging.

Clinton and his second-in-command, Lieutenant-General Charles Cornwallis, didn't like each other much to begin with, and relations only got worse as the days passed. Clinton had been talking about resigning his command for close to two years, which would have made the impatient, often impetuous Cornwallis his logical successor. But the cautious Clinton never actually followed through, frustrating Cornwallis so much that he finally "abruptly withdrew to his tent and improved upon Achilles by trying to turn the officers against their commander in chief."

Clinton's relations with Vice Admiral Marriott Arbuthnot, the man in charge of the naval contingent, were not much better. Arbuthnot, nearing 70 and in failing health, would be described by later historians as "vacillating, irascible and timid." Worse, his "strategic sense was usually meagre and his tactical ideas . . . were in the worst tradition of the period." Clinton had pleaded unsuccessfully with his superiors to replace him. Which may explain why Clinton not only often kept his own counsel but also served as his own naval strategist.

Clinton had learned the lesson of his 1776 defeat in the first Battle of Charles Town, when he had accepted what turned out to be the disastrous advice of Admiral Sir Peter Drake to launch a direct assault on Charles Town harbour. So this time, Clinton decided instead to land his forces thirty miles south at Edisto Inlet. The army would then march overland across the Johns and James islands to the Charles Town peninsula while British ships sailed north along the many rivers that snaked inland south of the city, delivering supplies as needed to the men on the ground.

In early April, after the British had taken control of most of the land around Charles Town, the fleet, with Joseph Durfee piloting the frigate *Richmond*, had been dispatched to take control of the city's strategically vital harbour.

It had not been easy. To enter the harbour, the ships not only had to get past the American guns guarding the northern entrance from Fort Moultrie on Sullivan's Island but also navigate the ship-sucking Charles Town Bar, a series of sandbanks lurking just below the surface of the water southeast of the island. Although there were half a dozen channels through the sandbar, the large British warships could only navigate through two of them.

Even though his vessel faced "heavy and incessant fire" from the American batteries at Moultrie, Joseph Durfee skilfully led the fleet through the deepest channels and into an area known as Five Fathom Hole, a huge anchorage between Charles Town Bar and Morris Island from which the British could command the harbour with impunity.

Within the month, the American commander, Major General Benjamin Lincoln, surrendered, and he and all of his remaining troops—about forty-five hundred in total—became British prisoners of war. That left the Americans with no army at all in the southern colonies. Better, it also meant that the British had secured a much needed cache of arms, artillery, and munitions from the rebels, which they could now use to put down what remained of the American resistance in the region, and finally begin the trek north to end this so-called revolution once and for all.

In early June, Clinton, with Joseph Durfee aboard, set sail to New York to shore up that city's defences in anticipation of the arrival of a French fleet rumoured to be on its way across the Atlantic. Clinton, with more than a little trepidation, left his rival Cornwallis in charge of consolidating the gains they'd made in Charles Town. Securing the city, he said, should be Cornwallis's primary objective, and any new offensive "must be subordinate" to it. "I leave Lord Cornwallis here in sufficient force to keep [the city] against the world," Clinton wrote to his superiors.

No one could know what was to happen next. All Joseph Durfee knew was that he had done his job, that General Clinton was grateful for his efforts, and that he had been asked to return to New York with the general to assume control of traffic in chaotic, uncontrolled New York Harbor. In a few months, a year at most, he would be back in Newport.

New York in the summer of 1781, as Benjamin Marston quickly discovered, was a crazy quilt of mass confusion, constant kerfuffle, and complex contradictions.[v] Benjamin had landed in the city in early April in search of the *Ranger*, which—as had become all too common—he'd lost to privateers. Worse, he'd been thrown back into jail, a real one this time, in Philadelphia, where he spent a winter month with little fuel and fewer rations. Luckily, he was befriended by local Quakers who sent the prisoners "fresh meat and vegetables, fruit, milk, eggs and goodies," and by an Irishman named Collins who eventually helped win his freedom.

By the time Marston had followed up on rumours that the *Ranger* had been recaptured by a British ship and taken to New York, the vessel had already been sold to a man on Long Island. Benjamin's new plan was to wait in the city in hope that the vessel would return so he could reclaim her unless, in the meantime, "I should be able to lay out my money to better advantage in some other."

Within the month, he found that "some other." It was a small, 110-ton brig called the *Britannia*, which had been built in New England and employed for the past seven years in the whaling business. While he waited for the vessel to be refitted for trading—and suffered through the continuing annoyance of having roving press gangs scoop up the tradesmen he hired to work on the refit and force them into service in the royal navy— Benjamin had plenty of time to visit with old friends like the Winslows and, of course, to wander through—and wonder at— the strangeness of life in occupied New York.

From its harbour approaches, the city did not look much altered by its changed circumstances. It was full of ships, though even more of them now that it was the British navy's main home away from home in the Americas. Beyond the sails and masts, Ben could glimpse the traditional multicoloured horizon of wood and red-brick buildings, rising four, five, and even six storeys into the sky. Most New York buildings were still in Dutch architectural style, with steep-gabled facades and rooftop balconies. Above them, the skyline was dominated by the spires of many churches.

But as he made his way beyond the docks and into the city, Benjamin quickly recognized that this was not the New York he'd known before the revolution. It was very much a British military city now. Though General Howe had allowed the governor, mayor, and chief justice to keep their titles, they exercised authority in name only. Howe appointed a military commandant, who reported directly to him, to oversee the city, and the commandant, in turn, delegated administrative responsibilities to his soldier subordinates, and so on down the line.

This, not surprisingly, had upset many influential local Loyalists who believed they deserved better treatment. In November 1776, barely a month into military rule, 547 of them had signed a petition pleading for a return to civil government. "We wish," they wrote in an almost wounded tone, "that our conduct in maintaining inviolate our loyalty to our sovereign against the strong tide of oppression and tyranny . . . may be marked by some line of distinction, which cannot well be drawn from the mode of representation that has been adopted for the inhabitants in general." Howe ignored their requests.

Soldiers, of course, were everywhere. Fifteen thousand of them had marched into New York as General Washington retreated in 1776. Though their numbers waxed and waned with the British military campaigns in other colonies, there always seemed to be more of them than civilians. The luckiest were garrisoned in churches and large public buildings like King's College, which the army had claimed for itself. Most, however, were not that lucky. They, along with their dependants and camp-followers, had turned the neighbourhoods ravaged by the great fire of 1776—which had wiped out a quarter of the city— into what everyone referred to as Canvass Town. It was a forest of tents, ramshackle huts, and lean-tos, many erected against the charred ruins of what had once been fine homes.

The landscape was desolate. If the trees that the early Dutch settlers had planted so carefully a hundred years before hadn't been reduced to stumps in the great fire, they had long since been chopped down for firewood. In the five years since the beginning of the occupation, in fact, the winters had been so cold the British had also needed to dismantle derelict vessels to use as fuel. Last winter, New York Harbor had frozen[17] and some of the sentries assigned to guard the city from the Americans had frozen to death at their posts.

Living conditions in Canvass Town—as in much of the city—were abysmal. Nicholas Cresswell, an Englishman living in New York at the time, suggested that "if any author had an inclination to write a treatise on stinks and ill smells, he never could meet with more subject matter than in New York. . . . Ditches and fortified places are full of stagnate water, damaged sour crout and filth of every kind. Noisome vapours arise from the mud left in the docks and slips at low water, and unwholesome smells are occasioned by such a number of people being crowded together in so small a compass almost like herrings in a barrel, most of them very dirty and not a small number sick of some disease, the itch, pox, fever or flux . . ."

Given that men dramatically outnumbered women in the occupied city, the fact that prostitution and venereal disease were rampant in Canvass Town wasn't surprising. For some desperate women, especially those who'd lost their husbands to war, prostitution may have seemed their only viable option. Which could, as one notice in the city's largest newspaper dramatically illustrated, lead to unfortunate consequences. Joshua Hamilton had taken out the notice in *Rivington's Gazette* in 1780 to disown his wife, Elizabeth, publicly. It seems Hamilton had gone south with

---

17. The only time that's ever happened.

British troops in late 1779 and been captured. He was eventually exchanged and returned to New York, only to discover that his wife—possibly assuming that he was never coming back—had become what he claimed was a common prostitute for both soldiers and sailors.[18]

Housing was in short supply all over the city, thanks not only to the presence of the soldiers but also to the ever-growing ranks of frightened Loyalists who made their way to the sanctuary of New York in order to escape the dangers of life as Loyalists in the rebel-held colonies. Rents in private homes had doubled, and then doubled again. And you usually had to know someone who knew someone to even get the chance to pay too much money for a roof over your head. The roof was often all you got.

Necessities were in short supply or expensive, usually both. In part, that was because, between being battered by storms and attacked by American privateers, many of the ships that were supposed to be carrying vital supplies for the residents never made it to New York. That's not to say no supplies arrived. New York was also the home port for hundreds of loyalist privateers who would bring their captured American ships to the city and overcharge often desperate residents for the cargoes they carried.

Corruption was rampant. Those who depended on government rations (soldiers' families qualified for half rations, though that was frequently reduced to quarter rations when there were shortages) were often shortchanged by unscrupulous contractors, who preferred to sell what they could skim on the thriving black market.

---

18. Hamilton could not have been much happier when he discovered a few months later that Elizabeth had married John Puff, a Hessian soldier from Brigadier General De Lancey's brigade. (The brigade's chaplain, William Walter—who would later be a central figure in Shelburne's religious conflicts—performed the ceremony.) Though not usually about matters of the heart, tensions between the British soldiers and the Hessian mercenaries ran so high they had to be garrisoned separately.

And yet, during his spring 1781 visit to the city, Benjamin also glimpsed another, very different New York—the refined society of the senior soldiers and their ladies, or their mistresses, or sometimes both at the same time—that coexisted uneasily with life on the streets. These women all wore the latest in London fashion and shared the latest in London gossip. The men enjoyed each other's company and that of well-to-do Loyalists during afternoons spent gambling and gamboling at popular horse tracks like Ascot Heath, five miles east of the Long Island ferry landing. At night they'd join their ladies at delightful dinner parties and fancy dress balls, or head off to the theatre.

While this social whirl itself did not upset Benjamin Marston—after all, his cousin Edward Winslow, now the master of the loyalist troops, and Edward's sisters were members in good standing of local society and would certainly have invited Benjamin to join them at some soirees—the stupidity and, worse, hypocrisy of the military brass drove him to distraction. Members of some of the militias "cannot obtain even an allowance of rations," he wrote, while at the same time "a very elegant music house is built at Fort George in New York, and subscriptions are taken at Rivington's [newspaper] office at a guinea a piece to lay out a walk at the upper fort for the use of the military gentlemen."

Benjamin had already endured an encounter with one of these powerful—and arbitrary—military gentlemen, the rebel-turned-Loyalist Benedict Arnold. While Arnold was out of the city in June, someone had stolen a cargo of his tobacco. So he promptly ordered all tobacco cargoes in New York to be confiscated until their owners were able "to make out the justness of their title by proving that their tobacco could not be any of the plundered tobacco." It was, complained Marston, "just the reverse of . . . the good old law of the land."

Even after demonstrating to Arnold's satisfaction that the tobacco in his hold really was his, Marston had been obliged for other reasons to remain in New York for more than a month—and counting.

The Admiral had decreed—perhaps rightly, given Benjamin's own history—that all merchant vessels must now sail under convoy. The latest rumour was that the next fleet bound for Halifax, under the protection of the British warships *Garland* and *Warwick*, would set sail at the end of July. That gave Benjamin a few more weeks to observe—and criticize—the military rulers who inhabited that other New York.

It centred around the mansions along the west side of Broadway above Fort George. The army had confiscated these homes to accommodate its generals. General Howe had his headquarters at the foot of Broadway which, like other homes reserved for the military brass, was marked on the front with the letters *G.R.*, for George Rex.

When they weren't entertaining each other in their mansions, the military command was out celebrating royal birthdays or other festive occasions. The hosts of such events usually went out of their way to impress. The proprietor of Loosely's Tavern, for example, set up a pyramid of lamps from the base to the top of his flagstaff, including one lamp representing "George Rex with a crown imperial, illumined and finished with a globe of fire." Inside, the guests admired a painting of their majesties with a single crown above their heads supported "by angels elegantly illuminated by different colored lights." On either side of their majesties, the tableau featured images of a British sailor trampling on the rebels' thirteen-striped flag and a "very apropos" devil at the elbow of the American Congress. Above the painting, there was, as *Rivington's Gazette* delicately understated, a decorated canopy "which shone like their majesties' virtues, conspicuous to the world." All of which, along with much good food and many and various toasts, led the assembled guests to lift up their voices in hosannas of praise to their monarch.

Inspired by this auspicious morn
When George the Great, the Good, was born!

Young officers gathered at the City Tavern north on Broadway twice a month for a Garrison Assembly, a dance that was mostly an opportunity for the officers to woo the city's few remaining young society ladies. Or they sat listening to an orchestra on a specially built platform opposite the burned-out Trinity Church (this had become such a popular pastime that the church walk had to be widened, necessitating the removal of some tombstones and graves in the church cemetery). Or, of course, they attended the theatre.

Within three months of their arrival in 1776, the British had renovated an old building on John Street, an unsightly red structure set back sixty feet from the street. They reopened it as Theater Royal, ostensibly for "the charitable purpose of relieving the widows and orphans" of those who had died in war. Though the theatre was usually sold out—each afternoon, the well-to-do would dispatch servants to stand in line for tickets—the cost of doing business in occupied New York was high, so there was rarely much left over for charitable purposes.[19]

General Howe himself commissioned a play, a satire called *The Battle of Brooklyn*, in which Howe's rebel rival, George Washington, was portrayed as a "whore-mastering barbarian" whose mistress—a mistress of the playwright's imagination, it is worth noting—charged him £30 a night. Given the rumours Benjamin had heard about the extramarital affairs of British military brass, he was certain that the play had inspired more than a few local wits. There was much to inspire wits in occupied New York.

The most delicious gossip had to do with Sir Henry Clinton, who'd replaced Howe as commander-in-chief in 1780. He was widely regarded as a vain, bad-tempered, indecisive fellow. Ben Franklin had probably summed him up best when he said that

---

19. Given the chaos of the city at that time, no one was collecting taxes, so the only funds for relief for the poor—not to mention maintenance of streets and other public works—came from such charitable donations.

Clinton, who had become paranoid about the possibility of losing New York to the rebels, was "incapable of forming any plan himself, and too weak or too proud and conceited to follow that of another." The general, it was said, much preferred watching "Clinton's Thespians" perform at the Theater Royal or spending time at Beekman House, his country estate in Turtle Bay, where he partied with cronies like his aide-de-camp, Major John Andre, and prominent local loyalist leader Oliver De Lancey. They would drink, sing, and impersonate those they didn't like until they were too drunk to stand.

There was also, of course, much wagging of tongues over the widower Clinton's relationship with his housekeeper, Mary Baddeley, who was apparently pregnant with his child but also still married to one of Clinton's sergeants. Clinton had paid the man off and transferred him out of the city, but still . . . [20] Nothing new in that, of course. Benjamin recalled that General Howe's mistress, Elizabeth Loring, had accompanied Howe from Boston to Halifax and then New York while her husband continued to serve, without public complaint, as Howe's well-paid commissary of prisoners. Many of the gossips believed that Mrs. Loring's presence had been the cause of Howe's eventual resignation as commander-in-chief. "As Cleopatra of old lost Mark Anthony to the world," wrote Thomas Jones, a loyalist judge, "so did this illustrious courtesan [Mrs. Loring] lose William Howe, the honour, the laurels and the glory" of nipping the American Revolution in the bud.

Not that many New Yorkers doubted, even now, that the British would ultimately triumph. In part, this confidence was

20. Although Clinton and Baddeley's sergeant-husband apparently reached a mutually agreeable financial understanding over Mary's favours, the sergeant eventually died of fever in the "hardship post" to which Clinton had dispatched him, leaving Clinton feeling guilty. After he returned to London, he ended up supporting both families and even divided his time between them.

the result of incessant propaganda, especially in James Rivington's newspaper. He not only made it a policy to minimize American military victories while exaggerating—often wildly— British successes, but also filled the paper's pages with false stories designed to encourage his loyalist readers. At various points, *Rivington's Gazette* reported that George Washington had been wounded, been captured, was dead. None of it was true. Benjamin Franklin fared no better—in Rivington's newspaper, the alive-and-well Franklin had been mortally wounded in Bordeaux. To shore up loyalist morale, Rivington even invented the news that eighteen thousand Cossack troops were on their way from Russia to help the British put down the rebellion.

Perhaps he'd been reading too much Rivington, but Benjamin Marston still shared the expectation of most Loyalists he knew in New York that the summer of 1781 would prove the last of the "Kingdom of Congress." On the other hand, he cautioned himself, "I have had my sanguine expectations too— supposing that integrity and capacity had a hand in the conduct of our military operations—but experience has shown that one or the other has heretofore been wanting. I hope better things of the present times."

The news that swept through the city in late October 1781 was all the more profoundly disappointing to New York's Loyalists for being so stunningly and completely unexpected.[vi]

During the early fall of that year, the city's loyalist press had been brimming with upbeat reports of royal victories and rebel routs, as usual. And most of them seemed to be grounded in the inevitable, relentless reality that a British victory in its war with the colonies was only a matter of time.

The southern strategy was working. The British army had taken Savannah and Charles Town, and everyone was expecting more good news from the rest of the South soon. The rebels, meanwhile, were still reeling from the desertion of Arnold, one of their top generals, the year before. And there were more and more frequent reports of mutinies in the ranks of the American army in New York and New Jersey. With good reason. Washington, or so the loyalist viewpoint had it, had proved himself to be an absolute disaster as commander-in-chief. Even the new currency the Continental Congress had issued—derisively referred to in the loyalist press as King Cong—had turned out to be worthless.

Despite the uncomfortable, unspoken reality that this rebellion had taken far longer to put down than anyone had expected, New Yorkers could—and did—take comfort in the fact that their king obviously remained steadfast in his commitment to their cause.

On September 24, 1781, in fact, George III's 16-year-old son, the youthful but dissolute Prince William Henry, had arrived in New York for a spirit-buoying visit among the colonials. Giddy locals welcomed him with a twenty-one-gun salute and a dizzying round of dinners, parties, and concerts. The taverns, noted *Rivington's Gazette*, "rang with loyal toasts and song until early morning." Some speculated that the prince planned to bide his time in New York until Cornwallis reported that the rebels had been sent packing from Virginia, at which time his father would name him that rescued royal colony's next governor.

On October 19, less than a month after William Henry's arrival, a much-delayed British supply fleet arrived in the city, filled to bursting with enough foodstuffs to feed thirty thousand people for another six months. Which increased everyone's confidence. It now seemed certain that the unpleasantness of the revolution would soon be history and they could return home to reclaim their houses and farms and businesses and lives, and put this unhappy business behind them.

It was not to be.

On the very day those British supply ships arrived in New York, the disaster the Loyalists were hoping to prevent was occurring 350 miles to the south.

While a British band played "The World Turned Upside Down," Charles Cornwallis's seven thousand soldiers—a quarter of all British forces in America—marched desultorily out of their base at Yorktown, Virginia, down a mile-long path through two rows of armed opponents—American soldiers to the right and the French to the left—and into an open field where they "sullenly" obeyed their officers' orders to "ground arms."

The unthinkable had happened. Cornwallis had surrendered.[21] The war, for all intents and purposes, was over. The Americans had won!

This stunning turnabout was far less surprising than it must have seemed to most New Yorkers at the time. The British defeat at Yorktown was, in large part, the end result of the still-simmering feud between Henry Clinton and his supposed subordinate, Charles Cornwallis. After the British victory at Charles Town, Cornwallis—who had the support of Lord Germain, the British secretary of state for the colonies—ignored Clinton's orders to consolidate British gains in the Carolinas, and decided to push north to Virginia instead. Later, when Clinton ordered Cornwallis to send some of his troops to New York, Cornwallis instead set up a new base at Yorktown, a tobacco port on the York River near Chesapeake Bay, and insisted he had no soldiers to spare.

Soon after, a French fleet from the West Indies arrived in Chesapeake Bay, chased off the British navy, and took control of the bay's entrance, thus cutting off Cornwallis's forces from reinforcement or escape by sea. At about the same time, Washington, having abandoned his original scheme of attacking too-well-defended New York, swept south with sixty-five hundred American and French troops and joined up with ten thousand soldiers already on the ground there. They soon surrounded and trapped Cornwallis's army.

---

21. Cornwallis himself didn't participate in the official surrender. Pleading "indisposition," he remained at his headquarters and forced his deputy, General O'Hara, to lead his soldiers to surrender instead.

It took five days for news of Cornwallis's defeat to reach New York, and another month for it to arrive in London. The reaction was the same in both places.

"Oh God," summed up Lord North, the British prime minister, "it's all over." Many in Britain who already despaired at the cost of this war used the defeat at Yorktown to step up their efforts to end it, even if that meant abandoning the American colonies to the rebels.

No one, least of all the thousands of Loyalists left in New York, doubted that the British had lost their stomach for this fight. The real question now was what would become of them. Many had learned what had happened in Yorktown—and how British soldiers had responded to their defeat—from the few Loyalists who'd managed to escape aboard the overcrowded British sloop *Bonetta*, which had fled just before the surrender. The *Bonetta* was "sagging with British officers" as it sailed away from "hundreds of loyalists [who] frantically rowed after." Only fourteen were allowed to board the vessel; the rest were overtaken by the pursuing Americans and returned to Yorktown and their fate. The fact that Washington was refusing to consider those captured at Yorktown as ordinary prisoners of war—meaning that they could be tried as traitors, even executed—did little to assuage the Loyalists' fears, or those of the three thousand black slaves who began hearing rumours that, British promises of freedom notwithstanding, they were to be returned to their masters.

Perhaps not surprisingly, advertisements began appearing in the loyalist press informing readers that so-and-so, who "intends to leave for Britain in the first fleet," was eager to settle his affairs and sell off his possessions.

Thousands of others, however, were left in fearful limbo. They didn't have the means to start new lives in Britain. And even if they did, they had been living in America for so long that the notion of the mother country was little more than an abstraction. But if they couldn't go to Britain nor could they stay where they were. Many of the rebel colonies already had laws on their books against the Loyalists. In New Jersey, for example, "anyone teaching, speaking or writing acknowledged loyalty to the king or [who] suggested he might rule New Jersey [should] suffer death without benefit of clergy," while in Pennsylvania, merely having accepted a commission in the enemy army was sufficient to merit "death and forfeiture of property" as punishment. Would the rebels really enforce those laws?

Everyone had heard stories of vengeful patriots. One Loyalist who'd ventured outside of New York to visit friends in rural Dutchess County, for example, had been turned back by a patriot justice of the peace who told him that "such Tories as he was should not be permitted to go through the country nor to come back among them." On his way back to New York, he was stripped of his clothes twice, robbed, and barely avoided a whipping. He was one of the lucky ones. One old man died soon after a beating by a mob of thirty men led by the local sequestration commissioner,[22] who derisively ordered the man's son to "drive his corpse to Nova Scotia."

Nova Scotia? Where was that?

As he dragged his skinny, ragged, aching body up out of the overcrowded shallop in which he'd passed the last ten days and tried to establish his footing on the terra firma of a Halifax dock, Benjamin Marston knew he must look more like a rescued, real-life Robinson Crusoe than the cocky young Harvard graduate and successful middle-aged businessman he had once been. Truth to tell, he felt more like Crusoe, too. Like Defoe's creation, he'd certainly had more than his share of "strange, surprising adventures . . . having been cast on shore by shipwreck," and had even kept his own account of "how he was at

---

22. A sequestration commissioner was the official in charge of confiscating loyalist property during the revolution.

last as strangely delivered" from almost certain death by local Indians. Benjamin clutched the journal—blotted, stained, the ink now pale on the recently frozen pages—in which he'd recorded everything that had happened to him. It was the only possession he'd managed to save after the grounding of the *Britannia*. How long ago had that happened? He'd have to check his diary. Perhaps it only seemed like forever.

It was April 10, 1782, nearly ten months since Benjamin had sailed out of New York, and he knew nothing of the calamity of Yorktown, or the roiling it had created among his loyalist friends, or the world-changing events now transpiring in far-off London. He knew only that he was still alive, if considerably the worse for wear, and that he was going to have to rethink his future—now that he still had one.

It had all seemed so different on July 29, 1781, when Benjamin and the crew of the *Britannia* sailed out of New York for Halifax in a merchant fleet under the protection of two British warships. His ship's hold was filled with a cargo of salt and tobacco, which he partly sold in Halifax before departing with another fleet bound for the Bay of Fundy, where he hoped to sell the remainder and take on more goods he could peddle back in Halifax.

It was hard to remember now, but the voyage had seemed so routine at the time that Benjamin had devoted one of his journal entries to catching a halibut. It "came running up after a cod I had hooked, and while he was gaping about to see what [I] was doing to the cod, I clapped the boat hook into him. Many a one has shared the poor halibut's fate," Benjamin had added with a smile, "while staring about what he had no business with."

By mid-September, the *Britannia* had docked in Annapolis, where Benjamin made a deal with Colonel Christopher Prince to sell what was left of his original cargo and take on a load of "bricks, boards, oats, vegetables, apples, cider and sundries" to deliver to Halifax. It wasn't as simple a chore as expected, so Benjamin was forced to spend more time than he wanted in Annapolis which, he noted in his journal, was "once a place of

consequence . . . now a heap of ruins." The inhabitants were anything but neighbourly, living in "an unsocial monastic way.
Seldom you see them in the streets, nor do they pay any of the
attentions to strangers, which is common to be shown by
mankind in general in places where strangers but seldom come."

They weren't especially efficient either, if his experiences were
anything to go by. He had had to wait while his shipment of bricks
was brought down the river in gondolas, and then he almost got
into a "wrangle" with a prominent local businessman who tried to
foist a load of bad apples on him. In the end, Benjamin had to cull
fully one half of the apples. "When people fall into mistakes, but
yet think themselves in the right," Benjamin noted in his diary,
"they are to be borne with. But for a man to lie—and to know he
lies—and yet want you to believe them, beats all my patience."

Between those difficulties and the Valley's always changing,
never agreeable weather, the *Britannia* had remained tied up in
Annapolis for two months, giving Benjamin plenty of time to
miss "sweet Halifax." Eliza was no longer in the picture—he'd
stopped referring to her in his diaries—and he craved compan-
ionship. One day in his journal he lamented: "Oh! That I had the
wings of an eagle, or an owl, or any flying thing, that I might fly
right into some friendly circle this evening, and there discover
someone whose feelings are in concord with my own."

It was early December before he managed to load the last of
the apple cider, escape the grip of the Annapolis Basin, "and then
for Halifax, so it please Heaven."

It did not please heaven. Or earth. Or Benjamin Marston.
Within days of setting sail, the vessel found itself in hell, beset by
one violent, vicious nor'easter after another. They lost the long-
boat overboard. The *Britannia* began to leak so badly that the crew
was forced to dump its cargoes of apples and grain overboard—so
much for the profits Benjamin had been calculating in his mind!—
in a desperate attempt to keep the brig afloat. By the time the
storms finally subsided and calm was restored, Benjamin discovered they'd overshot Halifax by close to 150 miles! Worse, the

Britannia was now well and truly stuck in ice near Cape Canso, a barren summer fishing village at the northern tip of Nova Scotia.

There being no hope of rescue, Marston, his crew, and Tiger, the ship's dog, abandoned the vessel on December 19 with an ambitious scheme to walk through the woods all the way back to Halifax.

Within the week, they'd run out of food, had had to kill their "poor faithful" dog for sustenance, and seemed not much closer to their destination. Worse, Benjamin—the oldest of the group—had become so lame he couldn't continue. Realizing he would only slow them down, he offered his colleagues his share of Tiger and ordered them to continue on without him. They left reluctantly. Benjamin, who now had only a bit of dried moose meat to stave off hunger, waited for darkness and wondered if he would live long enough to see in the new year of 1782.

He did. On the third day, the *Britannia*'s mate returned with two Indians his shipmates had discovered living in the nearby woods. The Indians had "received them with great kindness, and treated them with the utmost care and hospitality." They helped bring Benjamin to their camp in Country Harbour where he stayed "with my Indian landlord Michel," built a hut of his own, and slowly began to rebuild his health. That accomplished, Benjamin trekked overland thirty miles to Chedabucto, where he stayed with a white family until he could arrange passage in an "uncomfortable" shallop, "where there was not room to walk, stand, or sit."

Ten days later, he was finally home in "sweet Halifax." But now what? His cargo was gone. As was the brig and most of his worldly possessions. Except, of course, his diary. He still had that. Perhaps he should count his blessings. After all, he was still alive. But maybe it really was time to think of a different future. One that did not include a life at sea!

In London in the late fall of 1781, the British were also thinking about the future, and about the vexing question of what the country should do now to bring this wasting, wasteful war with America to some sort of conclusion.[vii] The problem was that there was little agreement on how to answer that question.

On the one hand, King George III and his principal secretary for the colonies, the hawkish, micromanaging Lord George Sackville Germain,[23] continued to insist that Britain should never, could never, and would never accept American independence. Americans, Germain declared, must be prevented from "stealing a constitution they had no right to," though even he had to admit after Yorktown that "the mode of [fighting] may require alteration."

On the other hand, more and more ordinary parliamentarians —already lukewarm in their support of this costly and apparently unending overseas adventure—were pressing the government to walk away, especially after Yorktown, no matter the consequences.

In the middle, as usual, was the country's ever-vacillating prime minister, Lord Frederick North, a jowly, slope-headed, perpetually wary-looking man of 49 years who'd been England's reluctant prime minister for much of the decade during which simmering colonial tensions had escalated into all-out American revolution. A lifelong politician with a flair for matters of public finance, North might have been a successful prime minister in simpler times but seemed overwhelmed and uncertain as events in America kept escaping his grasp.

---

23. One later historian described Lord Germain's role in the American Revolution this way: "When in 1775 the king and Lord North wanted to coerce the Americans, they entrusted the task to a man who had been court-martialed, declared unfit to serve the king in any military capacity and ejected from the privy council." A more sympathetic biographer put it more kindly: "He was brought into office as a man of outstanding ability at a time when the ministry was notably lacking in such men; and as a determined advocate of a definite policy of coercion, when the principal ministers felt the need of a leader and could not take such a policy upon themselves."

North's refusal to remove the hated tax on tea, for example, had triggered the Boston tea party, which led him to introduce even more punitive measures. When those didn't work, he attempted to switch direction, offering to eliminate the tea tax if the colonies would pay the salaries of the colonial civil authorities. The rebels, having already moved past such easy reconciliation, answered with musket fire at Lexington and Concord. Realizing he'd miscalculated his way into an all-out war, North offered his resignation to the king who—for the first though not the last time—refused to accept it, perhaps more because he despised North's likely potential successors than because he believed North was the man for the job. When the French joined the fight on the side of the Americans after Saratoga, North again tried to quit, and was once more rebuffed. After that, he resumed his peacemaking efforts, establishing a commission that offered the rebellious colonists virtually everything they wanted except independence. They rejected that too. And so North became a supporter of Clinton's southern military strategy as the best way to win the war. When Cornwallis surrendered at Yorktown, a shaken North submitted his resignation one more time, but the king—unsurprisingly—ordered him to face Parliament one more time. There, an emboldened and growing opposition was prepared to do what the king would not.

Though he was unwilling to let North quit, the king—like everyone else—realized that General Henry Clinton would have to be replaced as commander-in-chief of the British military in North America. Rightly or wrongly, he was blamed for the failed Southern strategy and the Yorktown debacle. Cornwallis, who ordinarily might have succeeded Clinton, was not only personally implicated in the failure at Yorktown but also unavailable. He was a prisoner of war.

Still, the king believed that choosing Clinton's replacement should be a simple matter. "The country," he noted in a letter to Germain on December 15, "will have more confidence in a new man, and I believe, without partiality, that the man who,

in general, by the army, would be looked upon as the best officer is Sir Guy Carleton."

Which was where it got complicated.

The king was correct that Carleton would be a popular
choice. Britons remembered how he'd saved Quebec and driven
the Americans out of Canada at the beginning of the North
American conflict. Better, Carleton's hands were unsullied by
General Johnny Burgoyne's defeat at Saratoga, even though
Carleton himself had conceived the general plan for that campaign before Germain had arbitrarily parachuted Burgoyne in.

Germain and Carleton still didn't like each other. While
Germain took a hard line against all American rebels, Carleton
believed that the revolution was the work of "a few wretched and
designing men who first deceived, then led the credulous multi-
tude to the brink of ruin." He preferred to treat the enemy well,
even those Americans he'd captured at Quebec, in order to let
them know that "the way of mercy is not yet shut against them."
There were less high-minded differences between the men, too.
During Carleton's stint as governor of Quebec, Germain had
appointed one of his own friends as Quebec's chief justice over
Carleton's objections. That still rankled both parties.

Relations had not improved in the three years since Carleton
had returned to Britain. When the king rewarded Carleton for his
defence of Quebec by appointing him Governor of Charlemont, a
largely ceremonial position that nonetheless provided him with
£1000 a year, Germain threatened to resign. He objected again
when the king made Carleton a Knight Companion of the Order
of the Bath, a chivalrous order the king used to honour his top
generals.

"Whatever disagreements have been between you and
[Carleton]," the king noted gently in a letter to Germain, "I have
no doubt if, on consideration, you should think him a proper person, that both you and he will, by some common friend, so
explain yourselves that . . . will make the public service be cheerfully carried on."

Germain rather pointedly ignored the king's advice, putting forth instead General James Robinson, "a desk officer and a man in his dotage," to replace Clinton. That prompted the king to write to North on Christmas Eve, once again touting Carleton and suggesting a clever, political way out of the impasse. "Lord George," he noted archly, "is certainly not unwilling to retire if he gets his object, which is a peerage."

By the end of February 1782, the deed was done. Germain took a seat in the upper house as Viscount Sackville, and the king announced Carleton's appointment.

The question, of course, was what exactly he had appointed Carleton to do. The king certainly wanted to fight on. But on March 4, 1782, Parliament passed a motion unequivocally declaring that "this House will consider as enemies to his Majesty and this country all those who shall endeavour to frustrate his Majesty's paternal care for the ease and happiness of his people, by advising, or by any means attempting to further prosecution of offensive war on the continent of North America, for the purpose of reducing the revolted colonies to obedience by force."

Within the month, Lord North, facing a non-confidence vote he was likely to lose, formally resigned as prime minister—and this time the king was unable to talk him out of it. King George briefly considered abdicating himself, but didn't. The new prime minister, Lord Rockingham, immediately set about the business of making peace with the Americans.

Despite their other differences with the king, Rockingham[24] and his new secretary of the colonies, Welbore Ellis, pronounced themselves delighted that Guy Carleton had accepted the job of commander-in-chief of the thirty-four thousand British soldiers still in North America. But the larger question remained: what did they expect him to do once he got there?

---

24. Rockingham, a long-time opponent of the war, had proposed to repeal the Stamp Act.

On the one hand, according to his orders, the job seemed routine, a military mopping-up operation. He was to evacuate the troops from the remaining American colonies, including Charles Town and Savannah, sending some to garrisons in the West Indies and the remaining regiments to Halifax. Although this was ostensibly "the immediate object to which all other considerations must give way," there was more. In a letter dated March 26, 1782, the day before Rockingham officially assumed office, Ellis assigned Carleton and Admiral Robert Digby the far larger and more significant—and less clear-cut—task of "restoring peace and granting pardon to the revolted provinces in America."

In New York and the few remaining loyalist settlements along the eastern seaboard, the question now became what Carleton's arrival would mean for the thousands of American Loyalists, white and black, trapped between vengeful former owners and neighbours, who remembered what they'd done all too well, and a mother country that didn't seem to want to think of them at all.

"THE CONSEQUENCE . . .
TIME ONLY WILL REVEAL"

Chapter 3.

Guy Carleton's world had unravelled quickly since that glorious day in May 1782—impossible to believe it was only four months ago—when he'd returned in personal triumph to America, sailing into New York Harbor with the spring fleet to take up his job as commander-in-chief of His Majesty's Armed Forces in North America, not to forget "restorer of peace and grantor of pardon" to the revolted colonies.[i]

His arrival had been celebrated with welcoming cannon fire from his troops at Fort George, as well as "a party of horse and foot, the gentlemen of the army, most of the respectable inhabitants of the city and a numerous concourse of people, who all testified their joy in his happy arrival."

Carleton had barely settled into his new accommodations,[25] however, before George Washington began making mischief. Though the fighting between regular British forces and

---

25. Carleton's headquarters were at 1 Broadway, the same mansion his predecessors had occupied, as had General Washington himself during the brief American occupation at the beginning of the war. It was a stunning piece of real estate with a

America's Continental Army had officially ended, troublemakers on both sides were still venting their hostility toward one another. During the winter, a captured loyalist militia captain had been killed trying to escape. At least that's what his patriot captors had claimed. But some Loyalists, led by a hothead named Richard Lippincott, claimed the captain had died as the result of torture, and decided to extract revenge by killing an American prisoner, Captain Joshua Huddy, in return. They left him hanging from a tree with a note attached to his chest saying that they had "made use of Captain Huddy as the first object to present to your view," and threatening to retaliate for the "cruel murder" of any more of their brethren "man for man while there is a refugee standing."

Soon after that incident, Washington had written to Carleton's predecessor, General Clinton, demanding he turn Lippincott over to the Americans so they could try him for murder. Clinton refused, though he did convene his own board of inquiry into the matter, which accomplished nothing.

Three days before Carleton was to arrive in New York to take Clinton's place, however, Washington upped the ante, ordering one of his commanders to choose a soldier, by lot, from the British captains captured at Yorktown. Captain Charles Asgill's was the unlucky name drawn. Washington then welcomed Carleton to America by repeating his demand that the British turn Lippincott over to him for trial (and, most likely, hanging)—but this time coupled with the threat that he would hang Asgill, the 19-year-old son of a prominent baronet

---

back garden that swept down to the water's edge. On a clear day, you could see across the river to the New Jersey shore. Carleton's next-door neighbour in New York was his old nemesis from his days in Quebec, Benedict Arnold, now, of course, a British general. The two had met again in London the winter before Carleton's return to North America when Arnold made his first appearance at court "ushered into the Royal presence on the arm of Sir Guy Carleton."

who'd once served as a lord mayor of London, if Carleton failed to comply.

At first, Carleton tried to appease Washington by launching his own court-martial proceedings against Lippincott. That failed when the court martial acquitted him. He then offered to return to the Americans two soldiers who'd been captured by a loyalist band and appealed to what he hoped was Washington's better judgment. In a civil war, Carleton noted in a patronizing tone, there could be no such crime as treason. Otherwise, each side would be forever inventing new rules to justify murdering neighbours who'd chosen the wrong side in the conflict. As for Washington's threat to use young Asgill as a pawn in the dispute, Carleton wrote, "it has not been usual, I think, since the barbarious ages to use any menaces, however obscure, towards prisoners, and still less to practise towards them any barbarity."

In case such an appeal to reason failed, Carleton also wrote to Asgill's parents in Britain, suggesting that they make a direct plea to the French king to convince the government there to ask its American allies to spare the young soldier. While he waited for a reply from the Continental Congress,[26] Carleton had more than enough to keep him occupied.

Corruption in his own ranks, for starters. Carleton knew better than most not only how bad the situation had become—the army was often spending twice what it should to purchase basic supplies, due to bribes, graft, kickbacks, and other assorted payoffs—but also how to go about fixing it. During his most recent sojourn in London, Carleton had served as the head of a high-powered, ten-member civilian commission auditing Britain's public accounts. He'd come away from the experience with a reputation of incorruptibility that King George described as "universally acknowledged," not to mention a few ideas on how to discourage bad behaviour. Though he didn't accuse anyone of

---

26. In November 1782, the American Congress ordered Asgill released.

corruption directly, he shook up his procurement office, firing its civilian employees and moving its military officers to other jobs. Then he appointed his own commissary of accounts and, above him, a civilian oversight board that Carleton himself chaired. Within the year, Carleton was able to claim he'd saved the home government more than £2 million.

Figuring out what to do about corruption, however, was easy compared to trying to satisfy the swelling ranks of the city's unhappy Loyalists. They'd been streaming into New York since the war began, of course, but the flow had increased dramatically after Yorktown. Still more had arrived this summer after the British withdrew from Savannah and Charles Town.[27] There were families who'd been driven from their homes, their properties confiscated; citizen-soldiers who'd served with the British forces and now, rightly, feared for their lives; and blacks who had joined the fight on the British promise of freedom and worried they were about to be returned to their masters. Most wanted to relocate to someplace safer, someplace British, and soon.

Carleton was sympathetic. In his few short months in New York, he'd become well known and, unlike his recent predecessors, well liked—not only among his soldiers but also among many otherwise disaffected Loyalists. In part, that was because, according to one admirer, "he sees everything with his own eyes and hears everybody." He met many of the Loyalists during his daily morning horseback rides around town. "Before a quarter part of the army have opened their eyelids, he has perhaps rode 10 or 12 miles. He comes almost every day to the parade, which is a signal that immediately after he will have a levee, where everyone may tell their story, or request a private hour . . . and those who have had conversation with him go away very much satisfied with his patience and condescension. In short,"

27. After retaking control of the city, the Americans renamed it Charleston to have it sound less British.

suggested the writer, "his conduct has procured him the respect of the army and the love of the loyalists."

In response to their pleadings, Carleton wrote to his new bosses in London to ask for their support in finding new homes for those who wanted to leave. His new bosses! Who could have guessed that Lord Rockingham would be dead within months of taking over as prime minister? Or that Rockingham's successor, Lord Shelburne, and Shelburne's new secretary of state, Thomas Townshend, would not only support what amounted to peace at any price but also cut Carleton out of the promised negotiation loop. Since the chief American negotiators—Ben Franklin, John Jay, and John Adams—were already in Europe, the Americans demanded that peace talks take place in Paris. Shelburne, who could personally oversee the talks from across the channel, agreed. The prime minister then wrote to Carleton not only to tell him about plans for the negotiations but also to inform him that Britain had decided to grant the colonies independence, immediately and unconditionally.

Where did that leave the man who was supposed to be the "restorer of peace and grantor of pardon"? Was he now just the "inspector of embarkations"? That wasn't what Carleton had signed on to do, so he wrote back to Shelburne and Townshend, asking them to relieve him of this onerous and unworthy post.

While he waited for a reply, there was still the refugee issue to contend with. Some of them had expressed an interest in relocating to Nova Scotia, the last remaining British colony on the east coast. Carleton did his best to accommodate them, writing a letter to Andrew Snape Hammond, Nova Scotia's lieutenant-governor. In it, he noted that there were about six hundred Loyalists who planned to emigrate to Nova Scotia. Would the governor grant them a few acres each to help them start new lives?

For his own part, since the army clearly would not need to use its stockpile of provisions to supply warring troops, Carleton offered to authorize the king's stores to provide each refugee with enough provisions to last a year, as well as supplies of clothing, medicine, farm tools, a musket, powder, and ammunition. Carleton hadn't yet received permission from London to do this, but, given the sacrifices the Loyalists had made for their king, it seemed the least the king—and Carleton—could do for them. Besides, how many of them could there be?

John Parr was feeling more than a little smug.[ii] And who could blame him? Governor of Nova Scotia! He must have let the sweet sound of that phrase roll around in his mind as he contemplated how to describe these first few blissful days in his new domain in a letter he was writing to his friend General Grey back in Britain. "I have found everything here to exceed my expectation," he wrote. And he had.

The offer of the governorship had come suddenly and unexpectedly, more the happy result—if he was to be honest—of Lord Rockingham's timely demise and his own past support of Lord Shelburne, the replacement as prime minister, than from any particular ability or experience he could bring to his new position. Not that the job seemed likely to prove onerous. The Nova Scotia governorship had actually been half vacant ever since its last official occupant, Francis Legge, decamped to England six years earlier.

Parr knew there were others who'd wanted this plum he had plucked from the patronage vine. Andrew Snape Hammond had been serving as lieutenant-governor for the past year, and logically expected to be promoted to the top job. Though Hammond had been at the dock to officially greet Parr when he, Lady Parr, and their youngest daughter arrived two weeks before, Hammond had made "his chagrin and anger" abundantly clear to Parr. He'd already tendered his resignation to London. John Wentworth, Benjamin Marston's college friend, who had also been lobbying for the job for at least a year, was among the disappointed, too.

By the time Shelburne's offer came, Parr, a career soldier, had already found himself a comfortable sinecure as a major in the Tower of London, a job that offered a good salary but was "a position of negative importance." Not that Parr had regarded it as such, at least until the lure of a colonial governorship had made its perks pale in comparison.

The Dublin-born son of an impoverished Irish officer, Parr was 19 when he joined the British army as an ensign in the 20th foot regiment in 1745. Over the next twenty-five years, he served— often at great personal cost—in all of the major European battles of the day, from Culloden to Minden. He was wounded so badly at Minden, he'd spent nearly six months in hospital recovering from his wounds. By 1771, he managed to purchase a lieutenant colonel's rank and command of his regiment. But five years later, when the regiment got orders to ship out to Quebec, Parr, by now 51 years old, resigned. (In truth, he'd never set foot on North American soil until he arrived in Halifax in October 1782.) He took the job in the Tower instead, and expected, contentedly, to finish out his career there. Until, of course, Shelburne had made him an offer he did not want to refuse.

Parr—a short, fat, balding man with a "brisk, strutting gait," a quick temper, and a taste for liquor, not to mention, as later historians would describe him, "a stickler for formalities [who had] the tetchy stubbornness of an independent but narrow mind long accustomed to military discipline"—considered Nova Scotia's governorship more a reward for services rendered than a task needing to be accomplished.

Which may explain why, in his letter to Grey, Parr dwelled mainly on the many and sundry perquisites of his new position: "a most excellent house and garden; a small farm close to the town; another of 70 or 80 acres at the distance of two miles, where I propose passing two or three months in summer . . . a beautiful prospect, with good fishing, plenty of provisions of all sorts, except flour, with a very good French cook to dress them, a cellar well stocked with port, claret, Madeira, rum, brandy, Bowood strong beer, etc.; and a neat income . . . of £2,200 per year, an income far beyond my expectations, plenty of coals and wood against the severity of the winter, a house well furnished, and warm clothes . . ."

There were, of course, duties to perform, some ceremonial and therefore welcome, some more pressing and less welcome. Not that Parr had not resolved, as he explained it to Grey, "to be happy and to make every one so who comes within my line." In this vein, as one of his first duties as governor, Parr had written a reply to a letter that Guy Carleton had sent to Andrew Hammond in September, requesting the government's assistance to resettle some loyalist refugees after the recent unpleasantness in the former colonies.

"I am to assure you, sir," Parr wrote effusively, "that no assistance which can possibly be derived from this government shall be wanting to those who have made so great a sacrifice to their loyalty, and they shall receive every accommodation that I can afford them . . ." Having promised that, however, Parr was quick to add a number of caveats. "At the same time sir, I must inform you . . ." The simple truth, as he'd discovered during his short time in the capital, was that there was already a housing shortage in Halifax. There was no lumber prepared for building, and many of the soldiers garrisoned there were living in huts in the woods themselves. The situation in other parts of the colony, he'd been told, was worse, and winter was quickly coming on.

Carleton had written that he knew of at least six hundred refugees who wanted to move to Nova Scotia from New York during the fall, though he could only arrange transport for about three hundred of them. While promising to do his best for them, Parr also did his best to encourage Carleton to discourage the refugees, at least for now. "Many inconveniences and great stress these people must suffer if any of them come into this province this winter," he wrote.

John Parr was not anxious for inconvenience or stress. As he put it in his letter to General Grey, "Your friend Parr is as happy and comfortably seated as you could wish an old friend to be."

It would not last.

"My time," said Benjamin Marston in a fit of melancholy, "lies very heavy on my hands. . . . For employment, I walk. When

tired with that, [I] read and, when tired of that, [I] write."
Which is what he was doing now, writing it all down in his journal on this Friday, the first day of November 1782.[iii]

The year had begun as badly as any he could recall. He'd celebrated the dawning of it in the wilds of Nova Scotia, having lost
everything he owned to the vagaries of nature, and had even been
forced to ask himself whether he would survive to tell the tale.
Now, it seemed, 1782 was likely to end almost as badly.

There was "nothing to do." He had few friends left to spend
time with. Eliza was gone, and no one had taken her place. He
had an acquaintance who occasionally invited him to join in a
game of backgammon, which was "a very charitable action without [him] knowing," he wrote with barely concealed self-pity.

Benjamin had taken a room in William Sutherland's inn,
which was filled with rowdy officers from a number of independent military companies who had been waiting since the summer
for a ship to take them to England. It could not happen too soon
for Benjamin: "Such another set of riotous vagabonds there never
were." With luck, the louts would take Andrew Hammond with
them when they finally sailed.

Or perhaps this would not be good luck for Benjamin. One of
the few amusing moments he'd enjoyed this past year had come
while watching the lieutenant-governor's wife engage in an
unseemly argument over precedence with the wife of General
Campbell, the commander of British forces in Nova Scotia. The
dispute had scandalized Halifax society, and was ended only after
Campbell was shipped off to Penobscot and replaced by General
Patterson and, of course, after Governor Parr arrived last month
and Hammond tendered his resignation.

Benjamin himself had no job from which to resign. "No business offers, nor do I know where to look for any," he wrote plaintively. "Go? I can't stir from this place; I have not the means of
transporting myself a single day's journey."

After he'd recovered from his winter ordeal, Benjamin thought
he'd found work again on a vessel owned by his former associates,

John Prince and Benjamin Holmes, but they ended up selling the boat instead. Holmes had then hired him to go to Liverpool to meet some people with whom he had business, but these people showed up in Halifax before Benjamin could make the journey there. He'd even applied to British officials in New York for an administrative job—similar to the one his cousin Edward Winslow had enjoyed with loyalist troops in New York—as muster master for the king's forces in Nova Scotia. He didn't get the courtesy of a reply.

He did hear from a relative in Marblehead, however, who wrote to tell him that all of his confiscated real estate had been sold, but that the expenses incurred in selling them on his behalf had wiped out most of the income he should have received. Which was unfortunate. The only coins in his pockets were a moidore, one of those Portuguese gold coins worth two-and-a-half dollars, and a lone guinea no merchant would accept because a large slice of it had been cut off. There were days when he didn't even have enough to buy food.

Partly to keep himself occupied, Marston had volunteered this past summer to help defend Halifax from a rumoured American invasion. He'd been sent to George's Island near the entrance to the harbour to help prepare its defences. But it turned out there were no supplies, and the weapons there were so old they'd be useless in beating back an invading force. Would he even care if the Americans overran the place? What difference would it make in his life?

"Heaven knows what is to become of me," he continued writing. But then his dark mood seemed to lift. "I have one thing to thank Heaven for," he added with a final, hopeful flourish. "My hopes do not fail me. . . . My friends or enemies—if I have any—shall never have it to say that I am indolent and won't take business when 'tis offered."

Perhaps 1783 would bring better times.

John Parr had glimpsed his future, and he didn't like what he'd seen.[iv] He had spent the day at the Halifax docks playing governor-greeter to some of the first of the refugees from the American war. There were 501 bedraggled souls altogether— Loyalists, disbanded soldiers, and fifty-six negroes[28]—who had survived twenty-two days in the blustery North Atlantic after the British evacuated Charles Town. They were in a "wretched situation," having arrived, as Parr would put it in a letter to London later that day, "almost naked from the burning sands of South Carolina to the frozen coast of Nova Scotia." Parr knew they weren't the first arrivals—three hundred had reached Annapolis a few weeks earlier—and they certainly wouldn't be the last he'd have to deal with.

Despite a continuing upbeat exchange of correspondence with Carleton—Carleton predicting that the new settlers "will bring a great accession of strength and wealth to the province" and Parr replying that "nothing in my power shall be wanting to them"—Parr was, by now, all too well aware of just how woefully prepared Nova Scotia was to accommodate significant numbers of refugees. It was even worse than he'd first been told.

Strange as it might seem in such a sparsely populated colony, there was very little land available to the newcomers. The problem dated back to the years immediately following the final conquest of the French, when London was so desperate to populate the colony it offered sweet deals to speculators, who made grand promises to bring in new settlers but rarely delivered. In one seventeen-day period in 1765, for example, speculators had gobbled up three million acres, most of which—nearly twenty years later—was still pristine and unsullied by Europeans. Because many of these original grants required that the land be settled within a specified time frame, however, Parr had been able to

---

28. Including David George and his family. George had nearly died from smallpox. He and his family had relocated to Charles Town where David befriended a British major who "advised me to go to Halifax in Nova Scotia" and offered him free passage. He was seasick for most of the voyage.

begin the arduous legal task of recovering some of it for the Loyalists. But that would not be accomplished easily, or quickly.

In the meantime, he'd roughly sketched out the boundaries of one new community—400,000 acres of land, running from the eastern boundary of Barrington township along the shore to Port Mouton Harbour and then, well . . . far back into the wilderness—and begun assembling 400,000 boards, about 1300 for each of the 300 families he'd been told to expect to take up residence in Port Roseway in the spring. The lumber would have to be kept under wraps until then.

But there were complications. Some of the Carolina refugees had already told him they were interested in joining forces with the group that wanted to settle Port Roseway. Would the Port Roseway Associates willingly open up their membership to such a ragtag lot? Parr would have to put that question to their representatives, who were coming to Halifax soon to meet with him. But even if they were amenable, was Port Roseway the right place to send them? There was plenty of other land in Nova Scotia in at least as much need of settlers, and John Parr had a few ideas of his own on how best to develop his new dominion.

Those were problems he would deal with on another day, however. It was quickly coming on to Christmas and much remained to be done to make sure these newcomers could survive their first Nova Scotia winter in any condition to settle anywhere come spring.

Joseph Pynchon had glimpsed the future too, but *he* liked what he saw. He had written to his fellow Associates in New York to tell them that some people he'd spoken with in Nova Scotia were already admitting the possibility that their soon-to-be shining city of Port Roseway would someday replace Halifax as the capital of the colony. "Halifax," he informed them, "can't but be sensible that Port Roseway, if properly tended to . . . will have much advantage. . . . What the consequence will be time only will reveal."

Pynchon and James Dole had come to Halifax as a kind of advance scouting party for the rest of the Port Roseway Associates. They met with Alexander McNutt, an earlier grantee who'd established a small settlement on an island at the entrance to Roseway Bay. He told them there was plenty of prime forest, which would provide excellent timber for building, and that the soil was conducive to growing crops, especially fruits.

They also met with Charles Morris, the colony's surveyor general, who reassured them they'd chosen "the best situation in the province for trade, fishing and farming." Morris also said they should "expect indifferent land in every part of the province," but Pynchon, like most enthusiasts, heard much more loudly what he wanted to hear. While he was keen to report that government officials had informed him that Port Roseway offered "the best landfall in the province to all European vessels," better even than any port in New England, he was dismissive of those "many persons at Halifax" who had warned him that the new settlement was bound to fail. Some had suggested they look for land on the shores of the Bay of Fundy or the banks of the St. John River instead. Such naysayers, Pynchon believed, were just jealous.

Pynchon's reports to New York were also filled with practical advice for the would-be settlers: "Each family should bring all the stoves they can procure for it may be possible that all the chimneys cannot be built by winter." They should also plan to bring their own supplies of nails and building tools since they were hard to find in Halifax.

Pynchon met with Parr too, of course. He told the governor there were now 224 subscribers on the rolls of the Port Roseway Associates, and he enumerated their demands. Perhaps not surprisingly, given what they'd been through during the revolution, the Associates wanted as much control of their own destiny as possible, including the right to choose all of the officers needed to establish their settlement. They also wanted the "privilege of fowling and fishing reserved for them alone"; a guarantee that they would be "exempt forever" from having their new land seized by the Crown; and assurances that, by settling Port Roseway, they were in no way abandoning their legal "claims and demands" for compensation for their "former losses and sufferings."

As he reported to his fellow Associates in New York, Joseph Pynchon had come away from his meeting with Parr unsure of what to make of the man who seemed "tenacious of his own prerogatives" while at the same time "willing to accommodate everyone in his own way."

But for all of that, Pynchon couldn't contain his own optimism. Or resist reporting that "many respectable characters in this place [are] very friendly and wishing to join [us]." Colonel Hambelton, a leader among those who'd arrived from Carolina in late fall, was already making plans to sail to New York to make a pitch to be permitted to join the Associates. Given that the Associates were expecting a total grant of about 400,000 acres, Pynchon added, "we can't but on our part recommend them to partake with us in the share of lands."

Not everyone among the Associates in New York would feel the same way.

The rumour had spread through New York's black community faster than the pox had swept through their number in the southern states. And with almost as devastating results. Boston King hadn't been able to eat or sleep for days afterwards, and he wasn't alone.

Although the British and American negotiators had settled on the preliminary terms of peace and signed their treaty in late November 1782, news of its terms didn't reach New York until March.

Among the two thousand or so black refugees who'd fled to New York during the revolution, the immediate consternation was not about the broad strokes of agreement—"His Britannic Majesty acknowledges the said United States . . . to be free, sovereign and independent states . . . [and] relinquishes all claims to the government, propriety and territorial rights of the same and every part thereof"—but one specific section of one article of the treaty. In Article 7, the two sides had agreed that the British should leave the United States "with all convenient speed, and without causing any destruction, or carrying away any negroes or other property of the American inhabitants."

Without carrying away any negroes? What did that mean for former slaves like Boston King who had defected to the British side on the promise of freedom nearly three years ago and had served their king loyally and well ever since?

In the years since he'd escaped the traitorous Captain Grey and informed the British about that man's theft of British horses (for which, he would note in his memoir, he'd received British "approbation of my courage and conduct in this dangerous business . . . three shillings and many fine promises, which were all that I ever received"), he'd gone first to British-controlled Charles Town where he got work aboard a man-of-war that took him to New York. There, he spent time in service to two white masters, neither of whom paid him enough to survive, so he ended up finding work on a pilot boat instead. But it was taken by Americans, who made him a slave once more, this time in Brunswick, New Jersey.

The northern masters didn't usually treat their slaves as cruelly as their Southern counterparts. "The slaves about Baltimore, Philadelphia, and New York," Boston would report later, "have as good victuals as many of the English, for they have meat once a day, and milk for breakfast and supper. And, what is better than all, many of the masters send their slaves to school at night, that they may learn to read the Scriptures. This is a privilege indeed." But for all that, he still considered himself a former slave who had tasted the sweet fruit of freedom, so "all these enjoyments could not satisfy me without liberty!"

The problem had been how to get it back. Boston knew what happened, even in the north, to slaves who ran away. A slave he'd known in New York was caught trying to escape from his master in Brunswick. "They tied him to the tail of a horse and, in this manner brought him back to Brunswick. When I saw him, his feet were fastened in the stocks and, at night, both his hands." It was not only "a terrifying sight" but also a stark reminder of what would happen to Boston if he was caught "in the act of attempting to regain my liberty."

He vacillated between his desperate hunger for freedom and his resignation that, "if it was the will of God that I should be a slave, I was ready to resign myself to His will." Luckily, such was not God's will.

When he wasn't working, Boston would sometimes spend time near the Amboy River where the ferry crossed. Though he could see that some people waded across the mile-wide stretch at low tide, he also noted that the Americans had placed guards on the banks to keep prisoners and slaves from using it as an escape route. One Sunday, while he was at prayer, Boston heard the Lord telling him it was time to make his escape. By the time he got to the river's edge, it was one in the morning. At that hour, it seemed, the guards "were either asleep or in the tavern." So Boston waded into the water but soon heard guards "disputing among themselves: One said, 'I am sure I saw a man cross the river.' Another replied, 'There is no such thing.' It seems they were afraid to fire at me, or make an alarm, lest they should be punished for their negligence." He made it to the other side. "When I had got a little distance from the shore, I fell down upon my knees, and thanked God for this deliverance."

He travelled through the rest of the night, hid that day, and then continued, walking in the woods near the road until he reached the river separating New Jersey from Staten Island. There, he stole a large boat—almost a whaler—slipped across the river, and turned himself over to the British. "The commanding officer, when informed of my case, gave me a passport, and [I] proceeded to New York."

In New York, he was reunited with Violet, a woman he'd met and married during his first stay in the city. She was 35; he was 23. Like Boston, Violet had escaped from her master, Colonel

Young of Wilmington, and made her way to New York, which was already overflowing with negroes,[29] all hoping to collect on the British promise of freedom.

But did the British promise still mean anything, or were the blacks simply "property" to be returned to their rightful owners now that they were no longer useful to the British? Boston had heard the rumours. And seen the evidence. The first of the slave-owners, from Norfolk and Princess Ann counties in Virginia, were already wandering the city with a list of three hundred runaway slaves they wanted back.

What would the British do? What could Boston do? He wondered if this was God's punishment for his sins. His resolution to lead a better life following his escape to New York had "soon vanished away like the morning dew. The love of this world extinguished my good desires."

In the first days after "the horrors and devastation of war happily terminated and peace was restored," Boston had dared to imagine his new life as a free man. But now? Article 7? Property? Had it all been for nothing?

It was yet another item to pile on his already heaped plate, but at least this matter was near to Guy Carleton's military heart: the fate of the men of the provincial regiments.

During the course of the war, thousands of colonists—perhaps as many as fifty thousand in total—had signed on to fight for the British in dozens of local regiments, often raised and led by prominent citizens. What was to become of those citizen soldiers? Having fought—and killed—Americans in virtually every important battle of the revolution, they couldn't return to

---

29. Even before the revolution, there were many free blacks living in New York, working as labourers, carriage drivers, chimney sweeps, and dock workers. According to the 1771 census, in fact, blacks accounted for 14 percent of New York's population of fifty thousand.

their former homes and lives. And what of the many who'd been wounded while fighting for their king? Or the families of those who'd been killed in battle?

While Carleton had been inundated with demands and pleadings from clamorous civilian Loyalists—who wanted land, provisions, compensation, and often, not to forget, the eternal gratitude of a grateful mother country for their sufferings—he'd heard little from the officers of the provincial regiments. Their members were in at least as much danger—more, actually—from vengeful Americans. Which is why Carleton himself had prodded the heads of the loyalist regiments to apply to London for assistance.

On March 14, 1783, just a few days before the details of the preliminary peace treaty reached New York, the commanding officers of thirteen provincial regiments presented their petition to Carleton. Written in good part by Muster Master Edward Winslow, Benjamin's cousin, it pointed out that the provincial regiments had "persevered with unabated zeal through all of the vicissitudes of a calamitous and unfortunate war. Their hearts still glowed with loyalty, their detestation to the republican system unconquerable. [But] the personal animosities that arose from civil dissension," they added, "have been so heightened by the blood that has been shed in the context that the parties can never be reconciled."

"Relying on the gracious promise of their sovereign to support and protect them," the petition read, they now wanted the British government to give them grants of land in its remaining American territories—300 acres for a private soldier, 350 for a corporal, 400 for a sergeant, and so on—assistance in settling their new land so that "they and their children may enjoy the benefits of the British government," as well as continued half pay for themselves after the their regiments were disbanded and provisions for the wounded and the widows and orphans of those who'd died in battle.

Carleton was happy to forward the petition to Townshend,

along with his own letter of support. It was one more item he could check off on his to-do list—for now.

The New York members of the Port Roseway Associates were not amused.ᵛ They didn't like the tone of some of the reports they'd been receiving from Joseph Pynchon, their man in Halifax. They liked even less the sound of the new tune being sung by their erstwhile protector, Sir Guy Carleton.

The Associates had wasted little time that winter in replying to Pynchon's letter, in which he'd noted, favourably and optimistically, that others were interested in joining their number. At their latest meeting, they informed him by return mail, they'd unanimously passed a resolution declaring "that all lands, bounties and every other emolument granted by government, or the governor of Nova Scotia . . . shall be equitably distributed among such Associators as have signed at New York." Pynchon was to have no more dealings with would-be Associates. He, they made it clear, was "to suffer no person to associate with us—but such as you are clearly of [the] opinion are in our situation, and real suffering loyalists."

The Port Roseway Associates weren't the first to ask the question: who is a real Loyalist? The Board of Associated Loyalists, a group ostensibly established to look out for the interests of all Loyalists, had passed a resolution effectively dividing them into two groups: ultra Tories, who'd supported the king from the very beginning and suffered the consequences, and faux Loyalists, who included virtually anyone who'd ever supported the Americans, even if they'd later seen the royal light. These "cowards [and] despicable wretches," the board concluded, had probably only switched sides to qualify for free land and provisions. Like the members of that board, the Port Roseway Associates wanted to prevent such parvenus from becoming their new neighbours.

If they felt besieged on the one side by those wanting part of what was rightfully theirs, the Associates believed they were being buffeted from the other by the king's representative in

New York, Guy Carleton. Joseph Durfee reported that the general, who'd initially promised every family five hundred acres—three hundred for single men—now "absolutely refuses any other assistance than providing us with vessels and conveyances to take us [to Nova Scotia] and provisions for six months."[30]

The only concession Carleton seemed prepared to make was that the transport vessels that were to ferry them to their new home would remain at Port Roseway until they'd had time to build shelters from the weather. Though Carleton also reassured Durfee that the king would not allow loyal subjects to starve, he seemed to be tiring of their demands and their complaints. "The commander in chief," Durfee reported at the March 24 meeting of the Associates, "has asked me to say any who are dissatisfied had better NOT GO if they can better themselves."

Oh, yes, and by the way, Carleton had told Durfee, he wanted the Associates ready to set sail for their new home and lives by April 1, 1783.

Thirty tons per family? Eighty horses? A two-storey house! What were they thinking? Perhaps it was for the best that Guy Carleton didn't have time to consider the absurdity of what a few of the Loyalists were now asking of him. Or, indeed, perhaps to think too carefully about the absurdity of the impossible job he had taken on.

It almost seemed as if the entire population of New York—all fifty thousand of them—wanted to leave the city, and they wanted to go *now*. George Washington, of course, also wanted them gone yesterday, and said so often. And Carleton's bosses in London couldn't understand why it was taking him so long to ship their more than thirty thousand American-based troops back home. They were needed in Europe.

---

30. Men and boys over 13 were to qualify for full military rations—minus the usual rum—while women would get half rations and children one quarter.

Carleton had tried to explain. If he sent all of the troops back to Britain before the civilians had finished evacuating, who'd be left to protect the Loyalists? Besides, there weren't enough military transport ships to accommodate both the soldiers and the far-more-than-anyone-had-expected number of Loyalists seeking passage at the same time. So Carleton and Admiral Digby had to begin hiring private schooners, sloops, and brigs—even some owned by the hated Americans—to manage the exodus. By April, there would be more than 180 vessels involved, and many would make more than one trip to meet the demand for passage.

Demand for vessels in New York had become so intense by the spring of 1783, in fact, that Carleton had been unable to spare a single transport to sail to Philadelphia and Baltimore to pick up the sixty-four hundred British prisoners of war from the Yorktown debacle that the Americans had finally decided to release. Instead, they were forced to march to New York through hostile American territory. Their arrival, of course, could only create more chaos and confusion.

To complicate matters, Carleton also had to respond to those increasingly outrageous requests made by some of the Loyalists. Brook Watson, Carleton's commissary general, had reported incredulously that the Port Roseway Loyalists were asking to be permitted to bring with them on the departing ships up to thirty tons of goods per family.

No, he told them.

And eighty horses!

"Where," Watson wanted to know, "will you get the forage for them when you arrive?" *No*.

The most stunning request had come from a Loyalist, Alexander Dobbins, who worked in the commissary general's office and asked permission to load his entire, dismantled two-storey brick house aboard the ship that would take him to Nova Scotia. *Permission denied!*

As eager as Carleton was to get it over with, the situation on the ground had become so chaotic he had almost no choice but to accede to the request of the Port Roseway Associates and delay their scheduled departure from April 1 to April 15.

Not that there was much hope of that happening either.

Officially, it seemed, there was nothing left for the members of the Port Roseway Associates to do.

On March 25, they had completed a final inventory. There were now 306 male heads of families, 229 women, 557 children, and 420 servants—a total of 1512 people—on the list to sail to Port Roseway.

At Carleton's suggestion, they had divided themselves into companies of forty members each. Each company elected "proper persons" to serve as their captains. The captains would also function as magistrates and settle all disputes until the civil authorities assumed control in Nova Scotia.

All that was left was a motion to adjourn. "As no material business was left for the body to transact at New York," noted the Associates' minute book for April 8, 1783, "a motion was made that the meetings of this association do adjourn until the body arrived at Port Roseway."

Unofficially, of course, all was chaos. And no wonder. The Loyalists were in the process of turning their entire lives upside down, some for the second or third time since the revolution had begun. There were possessions to pack, goods to sell, borrowed items to return or retrieve, and, of course, too many friends to say goodbye to, perhaps for forever.

Emotions careened from bitterness (when the announcement of the official cessation of arms was read to a crowd in front of city hall at noon on April 8, "groans and hisses prevailed, attended by bitter reproaches and curses upon their king") to despair ("some have put a period to their miserable existences by drowning, shooting and hanging themselves," wrote one resident) to anger ("the town now swarms with Americans, whose insolence is scarce to be borne," complained another) to anxious anticipation of what the future would bring.

Joseph Durfee had spent most of his days since the final meeting of the Associates jostling with thousands of others along New York's overwhelmed waterfront, loading and reloading the dozens of small boats that ferried the physical evidence of the Loyalists' lives and hopes from the docks to huge transport ships anchored in the harbour.

And still the carts kept coming through the muddy streets, filled to overflowing with chests and trunks stuffed with clothing and personal effects; hogsheads and casks packed with china and more delicate pieces; carpets, linens, whatever could be jammed into whatever containers they could find. Many packed the tools of trades they'd plied before the revolution—there were carpenters, and jewellers, and tailors—in hopes they'd be able to start up again in their new city. Some brought crates full of fowl and geese, not to mention their farm menageries of hogs, sheep, even cattle to help sustain them after they'd landed. At least the "choice garden seed" many had purchased from Margaret Hembrow's establishment at No. 2 Pump Street didn't take up much room. How soon would they be able to plant gardens?

There wasn't room for everything, so the streets were also filled with the clamour of auctions—you could buy a horse, or a Chippendale chair, not to mention books, paintings, even entire estates for far less than they were worth. New York had become a buyers' market, and many of the bargain hunters were former New Yorkers who'd returned to the city in gleeful anticipation of the imminent departure of the Loyalists. Not surprisingly, emotions ran high; the British posted sentries at every corner to prevent looting and violence.

Amid all the commercial and human chaos, hundreds of slave-owners trolled the city's streets, anxious to grab back those blacks they believed rightfully belonged to them before they could escape from their clutches forever.

The British, supposedly, had come up with a scheme to protect blacks to whom they'd given their freedom. Any freed black who'd been living within the British lines for at least a year was to be allowed to leave on the transports. All they had to do was obtain an official Certificate of Freedom from Samuel Birch, the British general Carleton had placed in charge of keeping order in the orderless city. While Birch had quickly earned a reputation as a friend of the blacks, especially of the black loyalist veterans, for whom he'd arranged housing and meals, and although the certificates he signed were supposed to guarantee that the black Loyalists would be protected from their former masters, many had heard stories of fellow black Loyalists who'd been unceremoniously carted away by their old masters and of others who'd been denied permission to sail on the transports pending a hearing of some board of inquiry into their claim.

Blacks weren't the only ones whose fates seemed to be in the hands of others. Among the dozens of ads in newspapers selling this or seeking that, or looking for such-and-such a missing relative, were occasional poignant notices like the one in *Rivington's Gazette* from a Lieutenant Thomas Coffield, who announced plaintively that his wife, Martha, had been kidnapped, "conveyed from him and concealed by her mother of Queen's County to prevent her from leaving NY City with her husband to Nova Scotia." Martha Coffield would not be the only one not sailing off to Nova Scotia as planned.

Gideon White, one of the original Associates whose optimistic recollections of Port Roseway harbour had inspired his fellow Loyalists to choose it as the location of their new city, had spent most of the winter ill and confined to his room on Brewer Street. He offered his resignation so someone else could take his place, but his fellow Associates were quick to turn him down, saying they could "by no means think of accepting your resignation or choosing any other person in your stead."

Though he had indeed been ill, White's decision not to go to Nova Scotia immediately may also have had something to do with a letter he'd received around the same time from Lord Charles Montague, the former governor of South Carolina and commander of the Duke of Cumberlands, a private regiment that had fought for the British during the revolution. White had met Montague while he was serving as a captain of the city guard during the British occupation of Charles Town. Now, Montague wrote that he was hoping to establish a new battalion to continue the fight on his own, and he invited White to join him in Jamaica where they would establish their base.

Perhaps the war wasn't really over after all.

Finally, it was time. On April 26, 1783, more than two weeks after Carleton had triumphantly written to Townshend in London to inform him that four thousand to five thousand[31] Loyalists would depart "tomorrow" for Port Roseway and the St. John River—and, of course, to plead for many more ships to be sent in order "to accomplish the entire evacuation of New York in the course of the summer"—the first transports, accompanied by two British warships, finally slipped away from their moorings, raised their sails, and set off into a future none of them could yet foresee.

George Washington was aghast.[vi] "Already embarked!" he said in a voice that managed to represent his usual, careful, controlled self and still convey, with no uncertainty, his surprise, consternation, and frustration at what he was hearing. The first face-to-face meeting in months between Washington and his British counterpart, Guy Carleton, to sort out some of the trickier sticking points of the transition from British to American rule in New York had not begun well. And it wasn't just that Washington had a toothache, or that Carleton was laid low by a nasty cold.

---

31. The final count when the first of the spring fleet actually set sail on April 26 was closer to seven thousand, about three thousand of whom were bound for Port Roseway.

To this meeting—on the morning of May 6, 1783, at the de
Wint estate in Tappan, twelve miles north of New York on the
Hudson River—Carleton had brought along New York's loyalist
lieutenant-governor, Andrew Elliot, and his chief justice,
William Smith, who'd become one of Carleton's confidants. On
the American side, Washington was joined by New York's new
American governor, George Clinton, his attorney general, Egbert
Benson, and secretary of state, Morin Scott.

The American agenda was clear enough: they wanted British
troops out of New York *now*, and they wanted to put their impri-
matur on as much of their new territory as soon as possible, even
before the final British withdrawal. They also wanted the British
to agree to a timetable for their leave-taking. And, of course,
they demanded guarantees that the departing Loyalists wouldn't
vandalize what was now American property, or—perhaps even
more important—attempt to take any of it with them. They
were especially concerned about a particular class of property:
their slaves or, as Carleton would have it, their *former* slaves.

Washington had begun by reminding Carleton of the terms
of Article 7 of the peace treaty, which forbade the British from
"carrying away any negroes." Carleton responded, equally
unemotional, that the treaty's exact words were less important
than Britain's word of honour to the freed slaves. And besides, he
added, those Washington called slaves could no longer be considered the "property" of anyone because they'd already been freed
by British proclamation.

It's difficult now to read Carleton's motivation. Part of it was
certainly genuine.[32] But there may have been other factors at
work. Standing up to Washington—and, indirectly, to the
framers of the treaty—finally gave Carleton (who was officially
putting in time while he waited for his replacement to arrive

32. Carleton's valet, Pomp, was a freed slave, though Carleton hoped to take Pomp
with him when he returned to Britain.

from Britain) an opportunity to be something more than what he himself had dismissively referred to as an "inspector of embarkations." And, of course, this was an ideal opportunity to tweak Washington—some of whose own slaves had made their way to New York and freedom—for what Carleton still regarded as the American commander's ongoing efforts to embarrass him. Carleton had not forgotten the Asgill affair. So perhaps this was an opportunity too tempting to let slip.

"No interpretation," Carleton imperiously informed Washington, "could be put on the articles [of the treaty] inconsistent with prior engagements binding the national honour which must be kept with all colours." Besides, he added as if to twist the knife, some of the freed slaves had already departed New York on ships sailing to Nova Scotia—a small number the previous October, and a much larger group a little more than a week ago.

Washington couldn't believe what he was hearing. Already gone! Making off with their slaves was in clear violation of the treaty!

Not to worry, Carleton replied in a tone that made—and was probably intended to make—Washington and the other Americans even angrier. Carleton explained that he'd set up an official register, and only those who qualified would be granted a Certificate of Freedom declaring that "the said negro has hereby his Excellency Sir Guy Carleton's permission to go to Nova Scotia or wherever else he may think proper." If an American slave-owner disputed that designation, Carleton added, he could file a claim for compensation.

That failed to mollify Washington or the other Americans, and the discussion quickly degenerated into a shouting match until Washington, ever the good host, finally announced that it was time for dinner and "offered wine and bitters." In fact, he offered considerably more. Washington had hired the famous New York tavern owner, Sam Fraunces—ironically, a free black from the West Indies who was well liked by both sides—to cater the formal meal, which included huge quantities of all varieties of delicious food from oysters to puddings, and plenty of liquor to wash it down.[33]

But even a convivial dinner couldn't soften the hostility on both sides. A few days later, in reply to an angry follow-up letter from Washington, Carleton reiterated his arguments, then added pointedly: "I must confess that the mere supposition that the King's minister could deliberately stipulate in a treaty an engagement to be guilty of a notorious breach of the public faith towards the people of any complexion seems to denote a less friendly disposition than I could wish, and I think less friendly than we might expect."

Despite his own frustrations and continuing pressure from his fellow slave-owners, Washington eventually realized that, in the face of Carleton's implacability, there was little he could do to recover American slaves. He agreed, instead, to appoint representatives to the committees Carleton had promised to establish to consider appeals from aggrieved slave-owners.

Still living on the mean streets of New York, Boston King would never get the chance to read Guy Carleton's unequivocal words to Washington. But he certainly knew about General Birch and his Certificates of Freedom, which, as he would say years later, finally "dispelled our fears and filled us with joy and gratitude."

Soon, there would be more vessels arriving in New York harbour to take even more refugees—black and white—to their new land of hope and freedom. Boston and Violet King intended to be on one of those ships.

---

33. The final bill for entertaining Carleton's party that day would be £500.

"THIS CURSED REPUBLICAN TOWN MEETING SPIRIT"

Chapter 4.

Wandering along the storied streets of Shelburne's downtown district today, it isn't much of a stretch—a squint here, a twist of the head there—to imagine how the city must have looked to a visitor during its one brief, shining moment in history in the mid-1780s. The grid of broad waterfront streets and narrow lanes spilling back from the harbour's edge is much the same as it was nearly 225 years ago. If many of those streets now peter into seldom-walked footpaths and overgrown bush—a ghostly reminder that current-day Shelburne, population just over two thousand, is a shadow of what was once one of the largest and busiest cities in North America—the town's historic district retains the look and feel of those early days. Eight of the twelve waterside buildings along Dock Street, in fact, were built before 1785. To enhance the illusion of wandering into history—and, perhaps more importantly, to accommodate the desires of American filmmakers[34]—Shelburne buried all of its downtown utility cables in the early 1990s.

---

34. In the only two period films shot in the town 1992's *The Way of Duty: Mary Silliman's War* and the forgettable 1995 remake of *The Scarlet Letter* starring Demi

What is much harder to imagine, however, is the sense of shock and despair that must have swept through the legions of exhausted men and women on the afternoon of May 4, 1783, as they stumbled into the late afternoon sun from the holds of overcrowded ships that had been their shelter and their prison for more than a week—and beheld their future. Nine days after leaving New York to its fate, they had arrived at their destination only to discover there was no destination. There were no neatly divided town lots on which to build their new houses, not even the crudest beginnings of a town-site hacked out of the forest. No streets had been laid out for them, no roads leading out of this city that didn't exist to . . . well, some-where, anywhere. There was just forest—looming pines, hemlock, oak floored by thick scrub brush and heaved rock and then, beyond that, more forest as far as the eye could see.

For the men and women arriving in the harbour that day, it must have seemed like the worst possible ending to a long, unhappy journey. But for the eternally optimistic Benjamin Marston, who watched the ships drop anchor in the harbour that day from his own perch on shore, their arrival represented a new beginning—yet another new and hopeful beginning for him.

The transformation had been so sudden, so swift, it seemed almost unfathomable. Until a few weeks ago, Benjamin had been so distressed by his unpleasant present and even poorer prospects for the future that he'd almost given up writing in his journal. The only entry of note since the beginning of 1783, in fact, had been written in mid-February, and it simply recorded that the season had been so unseasonably cold that Halifax's normally ice-free harbour was "entirely choked" with ice for four days.

But then, on Monday, April 21, 1783, Benjamin's future

Moore—Shelburne plays a stand-in for American communities. To add insult to injury, in *Mary Silliman's War*, the setting is Fairfield, Connecticut, circa 1779, and the plot involves Mary's patriot husband being kidnapped by Tory Loyalists who turn him over to the British.

altered dramatically and unexpectedly. His cryptic journal entry—"This day Charles Morris, Esq., engaged me to go to Port Roseway to assist in laying out a new township there"—hardly did justice to the momentousness of the change that was to overtake his circumstance.

Consider that by now, just thirteen days after he'd received that job offer from the province's chief surveyor, Benjamin was standing on the eastern shore of Port Roseway harbour staring out at a wind-blown field of white sail. The ships, thirty vessels in all, were full to bursting—if what he'd heard from their agent was true—with three thousand anxious, eager, frightened men, women, and children for whom he, Benjamin Marston, was about to carve a new jewel of a city from the wilderness.

He was no longer the failed sea captain and merchant who couldn't even afford to leave Halifax. He was now Benjamin Marston, deputy surveyor! And his future . . . well, he'd already begun to imagine that.

Benjamin had his cousin Edward Winslow to thank. Winslow had arrived in Nova Scotia early in April. He'd carried with him a letter of introduction to Governor Parr from Guy Carleton, who'd appointed Winslow to take charge of finding settlements in Nova Scotia for the thousands of disbanded soldiers expected to follow. Apparently, the letter so impressed the governor that, as Winslow boasted, "there's not a man from this quarter that presumes to solicit from headquarters without my recommendation."

It was only natural then that Winslow should also use his influence to try to find a position for his unlucky cousin. Despite the fact that Benjamin had no experience or training as a surveyor, Winslow made the application on his behalf anyway. And Morris, who was at that time in desperate need of surveyors to deal with the hordes of new settlers about to descend on him, was more than happy to oblige Winslow's request.[35]

---

35. Marston, in fact, was just one of twenty-three deputy surveyors hired that spring.

Events had moved remarkably quickly after that. The same day Benjamin got his new position, Governor Parr approved Port Roseway's official town plan. The day after that, the *Royal Gazette* published the first notices of escheats, declaring the Crown's intention to take back millions of acres of lands it had previously granted to speculators who'd neither settled them nor kept up their quit-rent payments, and to parcel them out to the Loyalists instead.

Less than a week later, on April 28, two days after the fleet in New York had raised its anchors for the journey north, Benjamin himself set sail south from Halifax on the shorter journey to Port Roseway. He was accompanied by Charles Morris's son, William, who was to be in charge of the survey; Charles Mason, one of the three assistant surveyors appointed to work under Benjamin; and Joseph Pynchon, the Port Roseway Associates' agent who'd been organizing plans for the new settlement from Halifax. They spent one night in Liverpool where they had dinner with the captain of the King's Orange Rangers, a loyalist regiment from New Jersey that had been stationed there to protect the coast from American privateers, and—perhaps indicative of the rush in which they'd left Halifax—picked up some survey instruments they'd need for their task ahead.

The vessel arrived in Port Roseway harbour on Friday, May 2, anchoring in a sheltered cove at the head of the harbour's eastern arm. Benjamin set up his tent on a small island across from the timbered shore where they intended to begin laying out the new community. Over the next two days, while waiting for the fleet to arrive, they explored the land the Port Roseway Associates had chosen, sight unseen. The harbour, of course, was as advertised: deep, eight miles long, three-and-a-half to four-and-a-half miles wide, dividing at the inner end like an opened lobster claw into two sheltered coves. They quickly settled on the land along the far eastern arm of the inner harbour as the most logical spot for the town. The soil seemed better than Benjamin had been led to expect. The stands of white pine, hemlock, birch, and red oak as far as the body could wander would provide plentiful lumber for building, and, if their initial experiences were any indication, there would be no shortage of fish and game for the settlers. They'd already come face to face with one bear who'd lumbered off when it saw them, and the water was so full of fish that their ship's pilot had used his musket to shoot a salmon he'd then hauled aboard.

That night, his mood upbeat, Benjamin had written a letter to his sister Lucia in the United States. He'd discovered the ideal place, he told her, to finally "gather together the threads" of his life again and perhaps even rebuild his fortune. Though his immediate duties of laying out the city would keep him busy for a while, Benjamin told her, he was already looking forward to using his off-hours to begin some sort of business here.

That would have to wait, of course. His first task, on this fair, fresh afternoon would be to accompany his new boss, Morris, and the others out to the ships to welcome the arrivals to their new city. *His* new city.

You couldn't blame them.[i] When the Loyalists finally managed to escape the ships that had been their overcrowded prisons for what seemed like forever, many of the women simply sat down on the rocks on the shores of Port Roseway harbour and wept.

In part, of course, it was probably just relief. Many had boarded their vessels in New York harbour back in mid-April, expecting to sail immediately to Nova Scotia, only to find themselves trapped aboard ship for weeks while the captains waited for everyone else to board, and then for final okays from the military command, and finally for the weather to co-operate.

One woman, who'd spent two weeks waiting for her ship to sail, had written of "great confusion" in the cabins. "We cope with it pretty well through the day," she noted, "but as it grows toward night, one child cries in one place and one in another while we're getting them in bed." She added: "I think sometimes I shall be crazy."

When the ships finally set sail, many of the refugees probably wished they'd never left harbour. One brig carrying black loyalist refugees sank during a storm soon after reaching open water. The seas were too rough for any attempt to rescue them. Then another vessel, the *Martha*, with 174 disbanded soldiers from the Maryland Loyalists and Delancey's second brigade, sank off Cape Sable with a loss of ninety-nine men.[36] The refugees' spirits could not have been buoyed either when, after a week at sea, they caught their first glimpse of their new land—Cape Sable Island at the southern tip of Nova Scotia—and discovered it was still covered in snow.

Snow! In May! What had they done?

Whatever the Loyalists were hoping for, clearly this was not it. The expectation of many of the Associates had been that, upon their arrival, they would be handed title to a prime, surveyed lot in town where they could begin building their new home, and another title to a plot of rich farmland beyond the township boundaries where they could almost immediately begin planting the crops they would harvest in the autumn. They were disappointed on all counts.

If it had been a matter of satisfying only the initially anticipated few hundred Associates, Benjamin Marston and his fellow surveyors might have been able to complete the necessary survey work quickly. But now there were thousands of people, all clamouring for the same things. Which was a mixed blessing.

Though few would admit it, the Port Roseway Associates' initial determination to limit their number to the "better" sort of people now seemed sheer folly. Some among the refugees were accustomed to hard, physical labour, but the reality was that most—being of that better sort—were not natural pioneers.

Forty-eight-year-old Charles Oliver Bruff, for example, who'd landed in Port Roseway with his wife, Mary, five children, and

---

36. The rest were rescued by fishermen and eventually brought to Port Roseway.

eight servants, was a silversmith and jeweller by trade. His shop in New York—"at the sign of the Teapot and Tankard, in Maiden Lane, near the Fly Market"—had been a popular destination for society ladies and their gentlemen for decades. Bruff had been proud to offer an exhaustive range of products and services. According to one of his advertisements, he boasted that he "makes and mends all kinds of diamond or enameled work in the jewelry way; also all manner of stone buckles, solitaires, hair jewels, lockets, enameled sleeve buttons, mourning rings of all sorts, trinkets for ladies, rings and lockets, plain or enameled; gold necklaces and stones of all sorts. Likewise makes and mends all sorts of silversmith's work; also ladies' fans neatly mended. He gives the highest price for old gold, silver and jewels; buys rough coral, handsome pebbles and black cornelian, fit for seal stones. He has fitted a lapidary mill up where he cuts all sorts of stones, engraves all sorts of coins, crests, cyphers, heads and fancies, in the neatest manner and greatest expedition, with the heads of Lord Chatham, Shakespeare, Milton, Newton, Pope, Homer, Socrates, Hannibal, Marc Anthony, Caesar, Plato, Jupiter, Apollo, Neptune, Mars, Cleopatra, Diana, Flora, Venus, Marcelania, Masons arms, with all emblems of Liberty; Cupid fancies, hearts and doves neatly engraved for ladies' trinkets; likewise silver and steel seals. He also plaits hair in the neatest manner . . ." The more interesting question now, of course, was not whether Bruff could weave milady's hair into wondrous "visages . . . sprigs, birds, figures, cyphers, crests and cupid fancies," but whether he could chop down trees, build a house for himself and his family, hunt, fish, grow his own food, and do all the many and various other things necessary to survive in the wilderness.

James Courtney, one of three brothers—all tailors who'd catered to the carriage trade in pre-revolutionary Boston—who had arrived in Port Roseway, was initially struck by the "dark woods and dismal rocks [that] covered the ground." During his first foray ashore, he wandered through the forest, "traveling five or six hours, [and] returned quite dismayed," even though, as he also noted, he'd managed "in the course of my ramble [to] knock down two brace of partridges and one hare." That only highlighted what he saw as a critical issue confronting the newcomers: "I thought hunger looked every wretch in the face that could not hunt or shoot for his subsistence," he wrote, concluding dismally: "My stay here shall be very short."[37]

For others, however—even after having come face to face with the daunting reality of the obstacles ahead of them—Port Roseway still seemed heaven-sent. "As soon as we had set up a kind of tent," Reverend Jonathan Beecher wrote in his journal, "we knelt down, my wife and I and my two boys, and kissed the dear ground and thanked God that the flag of England floated there, and resolved that we would work with the rest to become again prosperous and happy."

The first few days had not gone according to anyone's plan, and Benjamin was already beginning to doubt his initial sanguine view of his future life in this new loyalist mecca.

For starters, it turned out that neither Benjamin nor his boss, William Morris, realized that Pynchon—the Associates' agent with whom they'd been dealing—had no authority to make any binding decisions, and that it would be the elected captains from the various Associates' companies who would ultimately choose the location of their new community. But there

---

37. Courtney soon changed his mind, writing that he had decided to "stay and think to do exceedingly well." But neither of his brothers, nor his father, remained long in the town. The story of Thomas, Sr.'s, stone house on the Shelburne waterfront, however, lasted for many years after his departure. The unique structure served as a convenient surveyor's mark—"to old Courtney's stone house, 3,000 feet"—and then, after its derelict walls finally collapsed, it became a gruesome legend. Inside a cellar closet, scavengers found the skeleton of a woman standing upright against a wall. No one ever determined who she was or how she ended up there. As for Thomas Courtney, Sr., he was long gone.

were twenty captains, an unwieldy number, and most of them—at least in Benjamin's view—were self-centred fellows "whom mere accident has placed in their present situation." Morris, "with some difficulty," had finally convinced them to select a few of their number to serve as a committee on behalf of all of the captains.

Eventually, that smaller contingent agreed on a site—the same one earlier identified by Morris and Benjamin—and the next day the two surveyors began their work. But not so fast! Other Loyalists, who'd finally begun to come ashore to explore, took one look at the land the committee had chosen and complained that the terrain was too uneven, too thick with trees and rocks, to make a suitable town.

So they selected yet another committee, this one consisting of three men from each of the twenty companies. Benjamin was appalled: "That is to commit to a mere mob of 60 what a few judicious men found very difficult to transact with a lesser mob of 20," he wrote in his journal. "This cursed republican town meeting spirit has been the ruin of us already and, unless checked by stricter form of government, will overset the prospect which now presents itself of retrieving our affairs."

Morris himself was no more impressed with them. He complained that the Loyalists showed "not the smallest appearance of that unanimity and disinterestedness and sentiment, which one would expect to find from people who say they have sacrificed their private fortunes and domestic happiness in support of government, and which is of the utmost consequence in fulfillment of a new country."

Finally, after much discussion and debate, this second committee decided on the same site already selected by the first committee—the site that was, in truth, the selfsame piece of real estate that Morris and Marston had recommended in the beginning.

The Town Plan, which had been drawn up—site unseen—by Governor Parr and approved by Guy Carleton, envisioned a well-designed settlement that would hug the shoreline and be built around a large public square. The land along the water's edge was to be reserved for warehouses and public buildings, and two parcels of land had been set aside for the inevitable need for burial grounds.[38] There would be five uncommonly broad, fifty-foot-wide streets running north and south parallel to the water, each criss-crossed by east–west thoroughfares dividing the town into forty-nine residential blocks. Each residential block was to be further subdivided into sixteen individual house lots—60 feet by 120 feet each—meaning that there'd be room in the initial plan for close to eight hundred homes. Still, some of the Loyalists complained; they argued that more of the public land should have been reserved for housing.

Despite their complaints and recalcitrance, Benjamin was pleased to see that the settlers had begun cutting down trees along Centre Street (though surely it should boast a better name than that) on May 9, less than a week after the ships had dropped anchor. Even though land-clearing was clearly "a new employment for many of them," as Benjamin noted in his journal that night, they did it "very cheerfully." By the end of the second day, despite the incessant fog and drizzle, they'd marked out the line for Water Street, surveyed another two blocks on either side of Centre Street and begun to clear away the underbrush.

Perhaps Benjamin, as he was occasionally wont to do, had been hasty—and harsh—in judging his new neighbours.

The settlers weren't the only ones with plenty to keep them occupied.[ii] On the small island directly across from what was to be the main settlement—where Benjamin had already pitched his tent—Lieutenant William Lawson was busy directing his men in clearing land for a military post and commissary. According to

---

38. According to a note in Marston's journal, the first death in Port Roseway, a Mr. Mason, occurred on May 12, less than a week after the fleet arrived.

the instructions the young army engineer had been given before leaving New York, he was to find a suitable location that would "afford a protection to shipping and be capable of defence towards the sea as well as by land, having in contemplation a town, wharfs, barracks and other public buildings necessary to a great and permanent establishment." To assist him, the army's chief engineer had assigned an assistant engineer, a foreman, eleven carpenters, a mason and a smith from the 33rd regiment, along with a sergeant, corporal, and sixteen members of the Black Pioneers to do the heavy lifting.

The military contingent was, necessarily, a more efficient lot than the Loyalists. Setting up a commissary, after all, was the most urgent priority for all concerned. Three framed storehouses were erected quickly to house food and other supplies.

Luckily, the end of the war meant there was a huge unused military stockpile of salted provisions and hardtack—which some less-than-grateful recipients would soon refer disparagingly to as "his majesty's rotten pork and weevily biscuit"—not to mention blankets, tents, clothing, weapons, and tools available to help the settlers establish their new lives.

The man in charge of the commissary, Edward Brinley, had more than enough to keep him engaged from morning until well past dark every day. He had to add each person to his official roll. According to a final head count done by the Associates' secretary, John Miller, just before the fleet left New York, there were now 1686 Loyalists in Port Roseway—577 men, 452 women, 354 children over age 10 and 303 under—not to forget their 415 servants, plus another 936 freed slaves. Every one of them needed food, clothing, and shelter immediately. Brinley not only was responsible for distributing the provisions amid the chaos around him, but also had to keep a careful count for his bosses of who got what.

Each man was to receive an axe, a spade, two pairs of shoes, one pair of mittens, four yards of woollen cloth, and seven yards of linen cloth. Women were each to get one pair of shoes, one pair of stockings, one pair of mittens, three yards of wool, and six yards of linen. For each child under 10, the family was eligible for an additional one-and-a-half yards of woollen cloth and three of linen.

As the settlers set up their tents—also provided by the commissary—Brinley gave each family a musket and ammunition.

During the first year, the settlers were entitled to full military rations (less for the women and children), with the amount dropping to two-thirds in the second year and one-third in the third year as the settlers became better able to fend for themselves.

That, of course, assumed that they would be.

One of Port Roseway's first official visitors was a taxman. Stephen Binney, a deputy tax collector and impost officer, arrived from Halifax less than two weeks after the refugees had landed. Although he did his best "to pick a little money out of the people's pockets under pretence of entering their vessels," Benjamin was delighted to report that most of the settlers had managed to get "windward of him."

Benjamin didn't escape so easily. He was forced to share his tent with Binney, but that only gave him fodder to mock him in his journal, reporting at one point Binney's day-long search for a barber. Though he eventually found someone to cut his hair, "the fellow," Benjamin noted with barely suppressed glee, "was clumsy and cut him pretty much. [Binney] was all the rest of the day examining his wounds. He won't live long with us. Our fare is too hard, our apparatus too indelicate and coarse." Binney thought otherwise. After a few days among the locals, he confided to Benjamin that he believed with a good house he could be "very well content to stay here a little while and endure hardships."

Luckily, there were no houses—good or otherwise—for Binney, and soon he was on his way back to Halifax. Never to be seen again.

Benjamin wrote down each number on a piece of paper and then carefully twisted it into a roll so the number couldn't be seen. As he prepared the tickets for today's first public draw for building lots, he couldn't help but shake his head in disbelief at the latest tortured twist in the saga of this sorry lot of would-be settlers. They'd done it again! They'd set up yet another cursed committee, this one a gang of sixteen who were supposed to "take it upon themselves" to determine who among them were "proper subjects of the king's grant."

Incredible! And this was, of course, just the first step in the long process each Loyalist would have to go through to take ownership of his new land. Once the local surveyors had measured the land for each grantee, the surveyor general for the province would issue a certificate which, along with the governor's initial warrant requesting the survey, would be sent on to the provincial secretary who would then draw up a draft grant and have it signed by the attorney general. Even after all that was accomplished, the grantee would still be required to take an oath of allegiance promising to "maintain and defend to the utmost of my power the authority of the king in his parliament as the supreme legislator of this province."

It was difficult to imagine Governor Parr, who was already complaining that he and his officials were overwhelmed by the Loyalists who'd arrived thus far, managing to cope with what promised to be ever increasing numbers of supplicants over the course of the next six months. Of course, it might never come to that. Not if the future settlement of the colony was dependent on this lot.

Benjamin's boss, Morris, was already beside himself with frustration; Loyalists who'd promised to show up at first light to assist in laying out the town would wander over to the site at eleven o'clock in the morning, if they showed up at all. "If they catch me waiting on them again like a lackey, they'll have good luck indeed," Morris had complained after a third straight day of tardiness. Finally, he asked Lieutenant Lawson and his crew to help with the survey. At least that way he could be sure it would get done. He also called in carpenters from Halifax to help with construction.

The problem was that the carpenters, along with a number of recently landed Loyalists from Marblehead, were eager to be part of the new settlement. The Associates resisted, claiming that only those of their number who'd signed on in New York were eligible to share in the land largesse. In fact, their latest republican committee had just informed Benjamin that only 441 individuals were to be allowed to draw for the lots. That was peculiar; there had been 136 more men than that on the official list of those leaving New York, not counting the black Loyalists—not that anyone was counting them.

The associates were a "curious set," Benjamin wrote in his diary. "They are upon the whole a collection of characters very unfit for the business that have undertaken. Barbers, tailors, shoemakers and all kinds of mechanics, bred and used to [living] in great towns." Benjamin, of course, sometimes found it easy to forget that, less than a decade earlier, this could have described himself. Not that that would have changed his opinion. "They are . . . very unfit for undertakings which require hardiness, resolution, industry and patience. Nothing so easy as to bear hardships in a good house by a good fireside with good clothes, provisions, etc., etc."

They were not all like that, of course. "While those engaged in settling them are justly exasperated at the insolence and impertinence of one sort of people," he wrote, "they can't help they must feel for the distress of the sensible feeling part, who have come from easy situations to encounter all the hardships of a new plantation and who wish to submit cheerfully to the dispensation of providence."

But what would providence provide?

Benjamin Marston's head had become "so full of triangles, squares, parallelograms, trapezias and rhomboids" and all the rest of the tools of his surveyor's trade "that the corners do sometimes almost put my eyes out." For his own mental and physical well-being, it was perhaps a good thing he'd been unable to work much these last few days—in part because of the welcome rain still pelting down on his tent today, but more, because everyone else was still recovering from their celebration of the king's birthday a few days earlier.

Benjamin was appalled. Barely a month after landing in Port Roseway, the settlers had decided to celebrate the king's birthday by declaring June 4 a holiday from labour. A holiday! Given the circumstances, Benjamin believed "any dissipation, any neglect of business, ought not to be in the least countenanced." Not that the Loyalists would have listened to him.

Bathed in the otherworldly glow of dozens of bonfires set among the tents, trees, stumps, rocks, and piles of still-uncleared brush, the Loyalists had staged a fancy dress ball, complete with music, dancing, and, of course, copious quantities of alcohol. It had lasted through the night and well into the next morning. Benjamin had refused to attend, preferring to spend his time in the "lonesome, solitary tabernacle" of his tent. He hadn't been allowed to avoid the revelry completely, however. Just after dark, the settlers had fired off their muskets in what Benjamin regarded as a "nonsensical" *feu de joie*. More than nonsensical. It was also dangerous. Two weeks earlier, a fire had wiped out all of the possessions of at least a couple of families, and resulted in considerable losses for others. That fire had probably been the result of an accident—there'd only been three days of rain all month—but Benjamin was still suspicious that the flames had been "kindled on purpose." Why would anyone do such a thing? "The ignorance, stupidity and mercilessness of the bulk of the collection here," he confided to his journal, "is sufficient to produce such a disastrous event."

More likely, Benjamin's foul feeling about his neighbours was the result of his own exhaustion and frustration. William Morris was spending more and more time away from Roseway, supervising the development of other new communities and leaving Benjamin in charge of the arduous work of laying out the town,[39] often on his own, except for the army of blackflies that constantly conducted dive-and-bite manoeuvres around his head and body. On one occasion, he'd fainted from the heat and hard work. On another, he'd been chased by a bear. On still another, he'd been trapped outside in heavy rain overnight, too far away to make it back to the cover and comfort of his tent. He'd suffered "terrible pains" in his chest, a reminder perhaps of his earlier adventures in the woods after his shipwreck a little over a year ago. He was 53 years old, and now often felt more than every year of it.

Still, he hoped that tomorrow would be fine enough to get back to work. There was much to be done.

David George knew it was another sign that God would provide.[iii] How else to explain such a timely offer of land from a white man, almost a stranger, which came at the very time when the rest of the white men in Port Roseway were telling him to get out of their town now?

David had arrived by ship from Halifax only a few weeks earlier in the company of General Patterson, the commander-in-chief of British forces in Nova Scotia, who'd come to Port Roseway to inspect his troops and get an update on how well the settlers were doing.

David, for his part, had asked to come to Port Roseway in order to save souls. It had been a seven-year journey from Mr. Galphin's plantation on the banks of the Savannah River to

---

39. The process was indeed arduous. First, using a sextant and magnetic compass, Benjamin would establish the exact location and the direction of the lot line. Then someone—often Benjamin himself—would have to clear the lot boundary of any trees or brush. A stake would be driven into one endpoint of the lot line and a sixty-six-foot, one hundred–link chain would be stretched along the compass line, at the end of which another stake would be pounded into the rocky soil. And so on. And so on. Day after day.

this chunk of rocky soil near the banks of the Roseway River. The only constant had been David's faith that he was doing the Lord's will.

Soon after the British captured Savannah at the tail end of 1778, they took ninety of George Galphin's slaves—including David and his family—hostage to "encourage" David's master to persuade his Indian friends to remain neutral during a planned British attack on the new rebel capital of Augusta. The ploy worked and, a month later, the slaves were freed.

By then, however, Galphin had disappeared, so David led forty of the suddenly-no-longer slaves to safety behind the British lines in Savannah. There he'd met up again with his mentor, George Liele, whose anti-revolutionist master had already given him his freedom. The two soon began ministering together in Savannah. In the fall of 1779, however, after a French fleet attacked the city and a stray shell destroyed the stable where they were living, David and his family relocated to Yamacraw, a settlement just west of the protected city where they found shelter in the earthen basement of a house. Phyllis, David's wife, took in washing for the British forces, which helped the family survive.

But then David was stricken with smallpox at about the same time American forces began passing through Yamacraw on their way to launch a counterattack on Savannah. David decided the family should split up. He told Phyllis to take the children back to Savannah, where the British would protect them, while he stayed behind to await whatever God had in store for him. After his family left, David, who by then had the pox so bad he could barely stand, boiled two quarts of Indian corn. He ate a little, he would write later, but then "a dog came up and devoured the rest." David didn't mind. "It pleased God," he told himself. And then he waited to die.

But that didn't happen. Instead, he would recall, "some people who came along the road gave me a little rice. I grew better." When the American troops didn't come as close as he'd expected,

David made his way back to Savannah, where he was reunited with Phyllis and the children.

They eventually made their way to British-controlled Charles Town where they stayed until the British evacuated, at which time they managed to make their escape on a British vessel bound for Halifax. After wintering there, David sought and received permission to accompany the general's vessel to Roseway. (He left his wife and family behind in Halifax.) He'd heard that people of his own colour lived there. He could preach to them. It had been too long.

While General Patterson dined with the local worthies in Benjamin Marston's tent over on Commissary Island, David wandered among the clusters of refugees huddled in tents or lean-tos in the woods, talking with the black refugees. "I began to sing the first night," he would recall, and his singing the Lord's praises quickly attracted crowds. "The black people came from far and near . . . those poor creatures, who had never heard the gospel before, listened to me very attentively."

By the first Sunday morning after he'd arrived, David had found a small valley near a river where he held his first formal church service in Port Roseway.[40] "I was so overjoyed with having an opportunity once more to preach the word of God," he remembered, "that, after I had given out the hymn, I could not speak for tears." That first service was so successful, in fact, he held another that very afternoon. And then another each night after that.

Although his preaching attracted both blacks and whites, it was initially his ministering to the blacks that created problems for him among the other whites. Many had slaves and servants of

40. David George was not the only one interested in the spiritual well-being of the newcomers. He wasn't even the first to visit the new town to preach the gospel. On June 8, 1783, an itinerant 23-year-old white Methodist preacher named William Black had set up a table on some stumps on a lot belonging to Associate Robert Barry and conducted a service that attracted whites and some blacks.

their own who they didn't want stirred up by some troublesome preacher. They eventually informed David he'd better "go out into the woods for I should not stay there."

Which was when the Lord came to his rescue once again. A white man who'd known David in Savannah offered him his own new town lot "to live upon as long as I would, and build a house if I pleased. I then cut down poles, stripped bark and made a smart hut, and the people came flocking to the preaching . . . as though they had come for their supper."

David was happy enough in his new home, except for the fact that he missed his wife and family. But he was certain the Lord would take care of that, too.

If the cheers the Loyalists offered in response to his toasts—*To the king! To the Loyalists! To the town!*—did not seem nearly as heartfelt as those that had greeted his landing on shore earlier that morning, John Parr affected not to notice.[41]

The governor's arrival aboard the British sloop *La Sophie*[41] the day before had been welcomed by cannon salutes fired from the town's new military battery as well as from all of the vessels anchored in the harbour. This morning, as he had stepped ashore for his first official visit to the new town, more salutes had filled the air. Walking up King Street—it had been renamed from the Centre Street of Parr's official Town Plan— he encountered cheering Loyalists lining both sides of the stump-filled street.

Parr's initial destination was one of the town's finest—and first completed—houses. The stately four-storey home— incongruous amid the chaos of construction around it— belonged to Andrew Barclay, a Boston bookbinder who'd been forced to evacuate that city in 1776. He'd ended up sitting out the war in New York where he became a loan officer and, perhaps

41. Among his passengers were David George's wife and children.

not coincidentally, friends with James Robertson, a printer and newspaper publisher, who had been a member of the original Port Roseway Associates.

Standing on Barclay's first-floor balcony fronting King Street, Parr basked in the warm glow of official welcomes from loyalist worthies until he was finally called upon to address the throng himself. He had come to Port Roseway for a number of reasons: to see for himself the progress the Loyalists had made in creating this new city; to appoint the town's first magistrates, justices of the peace, judge of probate, and coroner; and—perhaps most important—to make the announcement that would honour the man who had honoured him with the position of governor.

Henceforth, Parr declared grandly from the Barclay balcony, Port Roseway—née Sawgumgeegum, rechristened Port Razoir and then Port Roseway—would be known as Shelburne in honour of William Petty, the British prime minister, the 2nd Earl of Shelburne.

Shelburne? The Loyalists were stunned. Their loyalist town was to be named after the British prime minister who'd abandoned them, the Whig who'd sold out their interests for precarious peace in Paris, who'd forced them into exile for the crime of being loyal to their king?[42] It couldn't be true. But it was.

Although the official records of the day's proceedings in Port Roseway—suddenly Shelburne—would show that the crowd cheered Parr's subsequent toasts to the king, to the Loyalists, and to their new town of Shelburne (each accompanied by booming cannon fire), those accounts do not capture what must have been going on in the heads of many of the Loyalists as they offered up their hosannas.

Afterwards, Parr—seemingly unmindful of his faux pas—happily adjourned to the new home of James Robinson, a former

---

42. Some of the town's early residents refused to use the name at all.

captain in one of the New York loyalist regiments who was host-
ing a dinner and reception in the governor's honour.

Shelburne!

More than just the city's name had changed. The spring
fleet's first three thousand settlers, the largest single group of
whom were members of the Port Roseway Associates, had been
joined a month later by another twenty-five hundred, many
unconnected to the Associates, who'd sailed in a second flotilla
from New York. More landed every day, in large transports and
small fishing boats. There were now dozens of private vessels
operating what amounted to a shuttle service between New York
and Nova Scotia.[43] Though no one had time to keep an official
count, there were probably close to seventy-five hundred settlers
in Port Roseway by the time Governor Parr arrived to bless the
place with its new name. And still they kept coming. In fact, as if
to highlight the point, three more transports—with ninety more
families—arrived during Parr's visit.

There were no house lots yet surveyed for them, of course.
And no quick prospects for accomplishing that task. Benjamin
Marston was mostly on his own now. One of his assistants had
been dispatched to Annapolis to help with the new arrivals, while
another was busy in the countryside laying out the fifty-acre
farm lots the Loyalists had been promised.

To accommodate the arrivals, subdivisions were already
being grafted to the town's prosaic north and south divisions. To
the south of the original town, Morris had created St. John's division in honour of St. John the Baptist, venerated by the Masonic
orders whose members were prominent among the settlers. To

---

43. Marston believed that many of the vessels were carrying more than Loyalists.
"Under the colour of bringing the effects of loyalists," he wrote, "much smuggling is
carried on of gin, brandy, etc. But," he added with resignation, "these matters will, I
suppose, be better looked into when the bustle of settling is a little over."

the south of that would be Patterson's division, named to mark the visit of General Patterson, and to the north, Parr's division. Streets were being named too; even the captain of *La Sophie*, the vessel that had brought Parr to Shelburne, was venerated with the official naming of Mowat Street.

And the Barclay and Robinson homes weren't the only houses to dot the community-in-progress. Despite Benjamin Marston's grousing, hundreds of new homes had been built since the first lots had been granted two months earlier. Other buildings, including not only houses but also stores, inns, and taverns, were in various stages of construction. A few were fine and already fully framed; most were rough-hewn log homes that could, in time, be transformed into permanent finished structures. Many had been built from the same trees cut down to make room for them. A lot owner would choose some large stones—of which there were plenty—to serve as a fire hearth and construct their new home around it, using other stones for the chimney and for the foundation. Trimmed tree trunks were transformed into outside walls; the roofs were thatched, using dry twigs and hay filled with moss to keep out the rain. Later, the log walls could be framed over to create a more finished look, and the interior subdivided. Most of these first houses were simple one or one-and-a-half storey, New England–style structures with roofs that were higher on one side than the other.

While much work remained to make them into the fine homes many of the refugees recalled from their more prosperous lives in pre-revolutionary America, the simple reality—Benjamin's unkind dismissals of their work ethic notwithstanding—was that they'd made stunning progress in a remarkably short time.

There were parties. And then there were more parties. If Benjamin Marston wasn't much enamoured of the Loyalists' seemingly never-ending need to celebrate this occasion or that event—the king's birthday had been followed later in June by another party, with boxing matches no less, to mark St. John's

Day—he had made an exception for tonight's supper and ball, as well as, of course, for last night's formal dinner aboard *La Sophie*. Benjamin had reason to celebrate. Governor Parr had appointed him one of five justices of the peace for Shelburne.[44]

Once again, he owed thanks to his cousin Edward. Winslow had again interceded on Benjamin's behalf, telling the governor that Benjamin was a man he could rely on and communicate with from time to time, "a gentleman of liberal education, formerly an eminent merchant at Marblehead, in the province of Massachusetts Bay, and employed in various public offices there; distinguished as a magistrate for his zealous and spirited exertions, and one who has always supported the character of a man of integrity." But Winslow, perhaps knowing too well his cousin's provocative proclivities, had also written Benjamin in advance of the governor's arrival, warning him to be on his best behaviour. "Now, my dear friend," he began, "I know you hate all mere matters of ceremony. So do I. But 'tis my maxim that, when I can serve my country or my friends, to make little sacrifices of my own feelings." Winslow no doubt knew that some among the Loyalists were already referring to their officious governor as the "Pasha of Nova Scotia," and wanted to make sure Benjamin kept to himself whatever thoughts he might on the matter. "When the governor arrives," he instructed, "wait on him, offer your services, tell him everything which 'tis necessary to know . . ."

Perhaps thanks to Edward's good advice, Benjamin had leapfrogged over most of the Loyalists' designated captains to win his justice of the peace position. Which only confirmed

---

44. The others were James McEwan, a Loyalist from Boston; James Robertson, the printer, who was already making plans to produce the premiere issue of Shelburne's first newspaper; Joseph Pynchon, the Port Roseway Associates' agent, who'd finally moved with his family to the new community in June; and Joseph Durfee, the first president of the Associates.

Benjamin's low opinion of the lot of them. "Sir Guy Carleton did not reflect that putting . . . illiterate men into commission, without subjecting them to one common head, was at best but contracting the mob," Benjamin confided to his journal after the night of the king's birthday folly, during which two of the captains had almost fought a duel over something or other. "But perhaps he could do no better," Benjamin added tartly. "He might not find among them a fit person to whom to entrust the supreme command."

John Parr was delighted with his first official visit to Shelburne. And optimistic. As he wrote to Guy Carleton from his cabin aboard *La Sophie*, he now had "not a doubt but that [Shelburne] will, in a short time, become the most flourishing town for trade of any in this part of the world, and the country will [be the same] for agriculture."

He also wrote to Lord Shelburne in London, informing his patron of his decision to name the city in his honour. "I flatter myself," he wrote after flattering the man who'd given him the governorship, "that the town will in a very few years be worthy of so fine a harbour."

Perhaps in anticipation of Shelburne's eventual designation as the capital city of Nova Scotia, Parr also ordered a five-hundred-acre lot on the edge of town to be set aside for him. He decided to call this new plot Bowood, in honour of Lord Shelburne's own English country estate. You could never be too grateful.

"We did carefully inspect the aforegoing vessels . . ."[v] The British officer's July 31, 1783, report to his superiors began dryly enough. He and the other three inspectors, including one representing the new American government, had now completed their head count of the 349 black men, women, and children[45] anxiously crowded

---

45. One hundred and forty-four men, 113 women, and 92 children.

aboard the military transport ship *L'Abondance* in the middle of New York harbour. They'd cross-referenced each of those names with the names on the ship's official passenger manifest and then also with the names registered in General Birch's *Book of Negroes.* Check. Cross-check. Confirm. Okay. Ready to sail. Next.

For Boston and Violet King, this time-consuming process was anything but boringly bureaucratic. It was giddily exciting and excruciatingly frightening at the same time. What if one of the inspectors challenged their credentials? What if they were put off the ship? They couldn't be. Their papers were in order. But . . .

The officer's conclusion, written in his best official-ese—"on board the said vessels we found the negroes mentioned in the aforegoing list," which included both of their names—represented yet another hurdle (the last?) they'd had to leap on their daunting, life-altering, lifelong journey to freedom.

In the three months since Sir Guy Carleton had made it plain to George Washington that he would not return to the Americans any former slaves who'd been with the British side for more than a year, three thousand of them, including Boston and Violet, had overcome their doubts about British resolve and obtained their priceless Certificates of Freedom, each one personally signed by Brigadier General Samuel Birch. Their names and basic information had been written up in the *Book of Negroes,* the official ledger Carleton had promised the Americans he would compile in case of future claims for compensation. The entries for Boston and Violet are stark, obscuring much but revealing much too:

VIOLET KING, 35, stout wench. Formerly the property of Col. Young of Wilmington, North Carolina; left him 3 years ago. GBC.[46] BOSTON KING, 23, stout fellow. Formerly the property of Richard Waring of Charles Town, South Carolina; left him 4 years ago. GBC.

---

46. GBC indicated that the person had a Certificate of Freedom from General Birch.

There were similar notations for each of the ship's other passengers, including, intriguingly, Harry Washington, one of George Washington's slaves who'd defected to the British side at the beginning of the war.

There were free blacks aboard, too. Like Stephen Blucke, 31, a well-educated mulatto who'd been born free in Barbados to a black mother and white father and had somehow made his way north. He dressed well—complete with ruffled shirt, cocked hat, wig, and hose—and counted among his friends Stephen Skinner, the former loyalist treasurer of New Jersey who'd escaped to New York after the Americans captured New Jersey, but was now apparently in London. Blucke had married Margaret, a native New Yorker, who'd bought her freedom from her mistress, Mrs. Coventry, twenty-six years earlier when she was just 14. She and Stephen had "adopted" Isabella Gibbons, another of Mrs. Coventry's servants, after Margaret bought her freedom too.

During the revolution, Blucke had been the commander of the most feared brigade in the Black Pioneers, a black loyalist military unit within the British army. The group had first become famous—infamous among the Americans—under the command of a runaway slave known as Colonel Tye,[47] who led lightning raids against his former New Jersey master and other slave-owners, assassinating patriot leaders and seizing rebel supplies for the British. Tye died from wounds he suffered during an attack in 1780, and was succeeded by Blucke, who kept up the fight, mounting successful nighttime raids into New Jersey even after the British defeat at Yorktown and the official cessation of hostilities.

It was obvious that Blucke and his family couldn't stay in New York after the peace, but the Americans would have been hard-pressed to prevent him—a free man who'd never been a

47. He wasn't officially a colonel, since the British never formally named blacks as officers.

slave—from leaving with his family when the British evacuated. Still, although Stephen Blucke's entry noted that the Black Pioneer officer "says he was born free in the Island of Barbados," it also added, perhaps by way of guaranteeing their passage, that he—as well as his wife, and their young ward-servant Isabella— "produces General Birch's Certificate." There was no point in taking any chances.

The passengers aboard *L'Abondance*, the largest vessel in the largest fleet assembled to date in the exodus of black refugees, came from all of the former colonies, most from the slave-holding South but more than a few from the more liberal North. There were single men and women, and generations of families. They ranged in age from two weeks to seventy years, their qualifiers in the *Book of Negroes* designating them as either "stout" or "feeble," "healthy" or "sickly," even, in a few cases, "worn out."

Moses Wilkinson may have been "sickly" but he was—as Boston and Violet would soon discover for themselves—far from worn out. Despite his various physical afflictions—he was blind and crippled—the charismatic, 36-year-old former Virginia slave known as Blind Moses was a man on a mission. His goal was to convert as many of his fellow former slaves as he could to the Wesleyan Methodism he'd already embraced, and *L'Abondance* seemed as good a place as any for him to prose- lytize. Boston King would remain unconvinced. His wife, on the other hand . . .

For the moment, of course, there were more pressing matters for all of them to ponder. Now that the British officer had finally approved the *L'Abondance* passenger list with his standard warning—informing the ship's master that "he would not be per- mitted to land in Nova Scotia any other Negroes than those con- tained in the list," and that if any other blacks were found on board the vessel, he would be severely punished—the crew hoisted anchor and prepared to set sail into a future that was far more hopeful, but no more certain, than the past that the former slaves were leaving behind. They had chosen freedom. But would they find it in Nova Scotia?

The blacks weren't the only ones with certificates attesting to their entitlement. Alexander Watson had one, too.[vi] "The bearer," his note read, "has, from my first knowledge of him three years ago, behaved himself as a loyal subject and, from his losses and sufferings in the rebellion, is most justly entitled to every advantage and emolument accruing to his majesty's suffering subjects." The note, dated August 8, 1783, was signed by General Birch himself.

Both Alexander and his wife, Margaret—who, along with their two young children, Samuel, 3, and Henry, 1, had arrived in Shelburne in September as part of the fall fleet—certainly had endured "losses and sufferings in the rebellion." Margaret especially.

In 1776, Margaret, then a 28-year-old mother of two, had decided to accompany her husband, Joseph Fletcher, a private in the Royal Welch Fusiliers, to New York. His 23rd regiment of foot had just received urgent orders to sail for America to put down a rebellion among the colonials. Margaret told concerned family and friends she would become a nurse or a cook for the troops; the British army always needed women.[48]

They told her she was crazy. Joseph's job was soldiering. Hers was to be at home taking care of their two young boys. The life of a camp follower—for that was the dismissive title she would be given—was harsher than anything even a poor soldier's wife back

---

48. According to *A People's History of the American Revolution*, the British army, much more than its American counterpart, encouraged women to serve in support roles— from cooks and washerwomen to prostitutes—for its troops. In 1777, in fact, there was one woman for every eight British soldiers serving in America. By 1781, that ratio had become 4.5:1. By that point, however, most of the new recruits "were primarily locals . . . refugees with no other means of support . . . not immigrants from abroad."

home could imagine. Trailing the soldiers from one battlefield to the next, "as likely as a regular gunner to be hit by artillery" or to fall victim to any of the many diseases that ravaged the camps; sleeping in tents if she was lucky, or under an open sky heavy with rain, snow, sleet, and wind if she was not; surviving on half rations or none at all; getting no respect from the military brass or even from the soldiers she served; mixing with prostitutes and the rest of the lowest of the low . . . It was no life for her, they insisted, and certainly not for the boys. Besides, they added, America was an ocean away from home and family.

The more they tried to convince her to stay, however, the more determined Margaret became. "I din na marry Josie to stay behint his back," she would insist in an accent still heavy with the Aberdeen of her birth.

But her family and friends had turned out to be more right than they could have imagined. For starters, Joseph had been captured soon after they landed in America. He'd spent much of his first winter in America as a prisoner of war in Albany. It was there that he befriended Alexander Watson, another captured soldier who shared his Scottish roots but had emigrated to America before the revolution, settling in rural New York.

When Burgoyne's army had come marching through in the summer of 1777, Watson had not only supplied them with cattle, sugar, and tobacco—he still carried a document signed by one of Burgoyne's generals, itemizing the more than £22 worth of goods "taken from Alexander Watson at Ticonderoga by General Burgoyne's army, 2 July, 1777"—but also joined the army himself, remaining with them until their defeat, after which he was taken prisoner, too.

During their winter in captivity, Fletcher and Watson made several unsuccessful attempts to get away before finally escaping while supposedly gathering firewood for their captors in a nearby cedar swamp. Watson overpowered their guard while Fletcher gagged him and grabbed his weapon. They then forced the guard, an American soldier named Jonathan, to guide them away from their rebel pursuers in the direction of the British army. After several weeks of surviving on berries and poultry stolen from local farmers, they finally reached a British camp. In return for his help in finding their comrades, Fletcher and Watson offered Jonathan the choice of becoming a British prisoner of war or making a run for it. He chose to flee.

Joseph Fletcher was not so lucky. Soon after rejoining his regiment, he was mortally wounded in battle and brought to the rear of the battlefield where Margaret, who had indeed found employment as a nurse, watched him breathe his last. It wasn't the final time she would experience the death of a family member. Both of her children soon also died in British army camps.

After that, Margaret took a job as a nurse at the Vauxhall military hospital in New York where she'd once again met her late husband's former prison mate Alexander Watson, who'd landed an "honourable and lucrative position" as the ward master and purveyor at Vauxhall. Perhaps it was because of their shared connection to Joseph or because they both came from Scotland, or simply because of the times in which they lived, but they married within the year and, in 1780, had their first child, a son they named Samuel.

Their jobs at the military hospital would end with the end of the British presence in America; like thousands of others, they had to decide what to do next. They chose not to go home to Scotland, a country they hadn't seen in at least a decade. In the end, they settled on New Scotland, a new place to start a new life. Another new life.

For Margaret, there must have been a certain eerie déjà vu about it all. Hadn't she already left her life once and sailed across an ocean with her soldier-husband and their two children? And hadn't they all died? Best not to think of that now.

Better to think of the letter of congratulation her father had sent from Scotland to mark news of her marriage to Alexander, a letter she'd kept among the possessions she'd brought with her to Shelburne. "May God enable you to employ [your life] for the best purpose," Andrew Cowper had written, "and as He hath given you new days and new friends, so may you each be enabled to be a new and better servant for the Glory of God and the good of your immortal souls."

God still had plenty of trials ahead for Margaret—and for plenty of others, too. Their "losses and sufferings" were not over yet.

He was doing his best to complete the evacuation of New York, Sir Guy Carleton had told his friend William Smith, the colony's last chief justice, over dinner one evening late in August.[vii] But the Americans, who were pressuring him to speed things along, also seemed even more eager to do their worst to the Loyalists, making it impossible for him to get this unpleasant business over with.

There were minor irritations. Though Carleton had set up a board of commissioners to consider the claims of slave-owners, and even though his officials had recently removed seven blacks, whose status was in dispute, from one departing fleet, the slave-owners had failed to show up for the hearings. What was he supposed to do about that? And he was also trying to be accommodating when it came to returning homes that the British had taken over during the New York occupation to their rightful owners. He had appointed officers who "will be pleased to cause such estates to be immediately delivered up to the pro-prietors or their attorneys." But many of the owners of the homes and stores in question were now claiming damages as a result of the occupation. Carleton had had to set up yet another board of commissioners to deal with those claims.

Despite all the distractions, Carleton was pushing the evacua-tion forward. Six thousand Hessian troops were scheduled to leave for Europe this coming week, Carleton told Smith, and he had also recently approved a plan drawn up by his commissary, Brook Watson, to contract even more private vessels until November in order to expedite the sailing of all the rest of those who wanted to leave. (The newspapers were full of notices from private companies offering to transport the Loyalists to Nova Scotia. Spaces were in such demand that some, like Daniel Wright, coupled his notice of departure with a threat: "Daniel Wright informs the people who have signed his list for Port Roseway that, if they are not on board this day, before twelve o'clock, their room will be filled with people from the army, as it is not to be expected that the ship should lie by the wharf for no other purpose than to indulge indolent people. It may be depended upon that this is the last notice that may be expected from me.")

The problem—and the opportunity for entrepreneurs like Wright—was that, thanks to the ongoing "violence of the Americans" against them, Loyalists were still streaming into the city from the other colonies, demanding to be evacuated as well.

Carleton had recently written a letter to the president of the American Congress, to make his dilemma plain. He was determined, he wrote, to leave New York "with all possible expedition," but he was constrained by the plight of refugees who found themselves under siege from their former neighbours. "I should show an indifference to the feelings of humanity, as well as to the honour and interest of the nation I serve," he declared, "to leave any of the Loyalists that are desirous to quit the country a prey to the violence they conceive they have so much cause to apprehend."

As a result, he concluded, "it [is] impossible for me to say when the evacuation can be completed."

No, Benjamin Marston told Andrew Barclay's emissary, he had no intention of going to Captain Barclay's house for a meeting this afternoon. If Barclay wanted to come meet with him, he told the man, Benjamin would be at his marquee, his tent office, until ten o'clock that night. "He went off very much disconcerted, in appearance at least," Benjamin noted.

The reality was that Benjamin already knew what Barclay and his friends wanted to talk to him about: the negro lands over on the northwest shore. Parr had designated an area about two miles from Shelburne on a non-navigable inlet of the harbour as the site for the black loyalist settlement. Although the land was worse than that set aside for the whites—the soil was thin and acidic, and even rockier than Shelburne—Colonel Blucke, who seemed to be the leader among the black newcomers, had pronounced himself "well satisfied with it" when he and Marston did an initial walkabout in late August.

In early September, Benjamin had sent his two assistants, Lyman and Tully, off to Birchtown (the name the blacks had chosen for their new settlement in tribute to the British general whose name was on their Certificates of Freedom) to begin work on the survey.

But by this point, everything was behind schedule and much of the rest was in chaos in connection with the distribution of lands. Benjamin more than suspected that some of the captains were making private deals with speculators to add their names to the lists of Loyalists eligible for land grants. He'd already discovered on the list three men from Halifax whom he determined to be "mere adventurers," and invoked his "arbitrary power" to remove their names. More recently, he'd uncovered yet "another piece of villainy." Some of the captains were including minors in their list of those eligible to draw for town, water, and fifty-acre farm lots.

Some were more subtle in their efforts to win advantage. Recently, for example, a Captain McLean had sent Benjamin a seven-pound green turtle as a bribe. "I am obliged to him," Benjamin wrote in his journal. "He is to have a house lot, but this must not blind my eyes. He must run the same chance as his neighbours who have no turtle to send."

The blacks had no turtles to offer. Or much else, for that matter.

Which may explain why Barclay and some of the other white Loyalists seemed to feel they could simply claim the lands set aside for the black Loyalists for themselves. Taking advantage of the slowness and confusion surrounding the survey procedures, they'd hired a man named Sperling to go over to the black area with his pocket compass and a cod line and begin laying out fifty-acre farm lots. Now they wanted to meet with Benjamin, undoubtedly to try to convince him to sign off on the arrangements. He had no intention of doing any such thing. Allowing the white Loyalists to encroach on Birchtown without "even a shadow of a licence," he believed "will utterly ruin it."

Instead, he wrote a letter to his boss, William Morris, informing him not only about the captains' latest ploy of using minors to claim lots but also about "old Sperling's survey and the hobble it had brought the people into."

He would have to spend too much time tomorrow straightening out "that business." And there was so little time to spare.

Boston King wasn't happy when they came to get him. Violet had been over at Mr. Wilkinson's meeting house—she had been spending more and more time with the blind preacher—and had become so agitated by all of his declaiming and proclaiming that she'd collapsed and laid on the ground for two hours, crying out to the Lord for mercy. At first, Boston told the men who'd come to fetch him that he had no intention of going to retrieve his wife, but finally he'd relented. "I went to the house," he would recall later, "and was struck with astonishment at the sight of her agony."

Moses Wilkinson, who was attracting as many as two hundred worshippers to his services and whose meeting house was already becoming central to Birchtown life, was having that effect on people—and on himself. He often "worked himself into such a pitch," one person who watched him had noted, "that I was fearful something would happen to him."

Something clearly had happened to Violet. In the days after her collapse at Wilkinson's, Boston would tell people, "the Lord spoke peace to her soul. She was filled with divine consolation and walked in the light of God's countenance."

Boston was happy for his wife, but he wasn't ready to join

her. Not yet. And, truth to tell, Violet wasn't quite ready to give herself fully to the Lord either. She just didn't know it yet.

Create this new town. Extend that road. Cater to the well connected. Pity the poor. Be solicitous to the old soldiers. Where are the tools the government promised us? The king's bounty isn't enough. Speed up the land grants. Cut the excessive custom house fees. The king's bounty needs to be extended. I want . . . I need . . . Oh, yes, and don't spend any more than absolutely necessary. And, whatever you do spend, be sure to justify, itemize, and account for every single pence to London.

John Parr was doing his best, but he was feeling the full weight of the intense, impossible pressure from every quarter. As he lamented to his patron Lord Shelburne, "there are some not to be pleased or satisfied." Like the Port Roseway Associates down in Shelburne, to take but one example. One of them had even written to Carleton this summer to complain about him. The governor had not only allowed "all sorts and ranks of men" to get grants of town lots that should have been "for us and for us only," James Dole declared, but also had—"to our great surprise"—gobbled up two miles' worth of the town's best land for himself.

That had put Parr on the defensive. Whatever promises of exclusivity might have been made to the Port Roseway Associates at a time when officials expected only a few thousand new arrivals simply could not apply in these dramatically different circumstances. As for the land Parr had set aside for himself, it was "of very little value," he explained in a letter to Lord Shelburne, adding that the property wasn't for his personal use anyway, but merely a hedge in case the province's seat of government relocated there "one day or other."

That day would not come soon, not if Parr had any say in the matter.

The optimism of his summer visit, in fact, had disappeared like the August sun. He'd had to make local magistrates "of men

149

whom God Almighty never intended for the office." The rest were worse. Some Loyalists "refuse to carry the chain in marking their own land without exorbitant pay," he'd noted, while others, "owing to disputes among themselves, quarreling for the same spot, all wishing to be upon the sea coast, great partialities committed by their agents and surveyors . . . [are like] like sharks preying upon each other."

Parr had almost been bitten by some New York loyalist sharks himself this past summer. A group of fifty-five "of the most respectable characters" then still remaining in New York had banded together in July to petition Guy Carleton for 275,000 acres of land in Nova Scotia for themselves, "the deeds to be delivered to us as soon as possible." They included former legislators and such royalist worthies as Charles Inglis, the Anglican clergyman who'd responded to Thomas Paine's "most virulent, artful, and pernicious" *Common Sense* pamphlet with one of his own "at the risk not only of my liberty but also of my life," and George Panton, the chaplain to the British army's Prince of Wales regiment and soon-to-be putative rector at Shelburne. The group claimed special consideration because its members had "constantly had great influence in his majesty's American dominion" and also because their mere presence "will be highly advantageous in diffusing and supporting a spirit of attachment to the British constitution as well as to his majesty's royal person and family" among their lessers in the wilds of Nova Scotia.

Carleton had forwarded their petition to Parr with his own favourable recommendation. And Parr, perhaps without considering the consequences, had dutifully ordered the necessary surveys to begin. Luckily for the governor, however, rumours of this latest land grab had spread quickly through New York's loyalist gossip hothouse that summer. Within weeks, more than six hundred of the remaining Loyalists, who also considered themselves "respectable characters," gathered at Roubalet's Tavern to denounce the fifty-five publicly. They expressed outrage that there could be, among their "fellow sufferers, persons ungenerous enough to attempt ingrossing to themselves so disproportionate a share of what government has allotted for their common benefit," and forcing everyone else to "content themselves with barren or remote lands, or submit to be tenants to those . . . they consider as their superiors in nothing but deeper art and keener policy."

The proposal died soon after that, so Parr didn't have to face the further wrath of the local claims seekers. He'd had more than enough of that already. And everything else. It was difficult to recall now that it had been only a year since, as Nova Scotia's newly arrived governor, he had written that smug first letter back to London: "Your friend Parr is as happy and comfortably seated as you could wish an old friend to be . . ."

The problems Parr faced now were mostly not of his own making. He had, as he put it himself, smacked up against "crises which never happened to any government before."[49] More than fifty thousand people—Loyalists, freed slaves, soldiers, adventurers—were all desperately trying to escape from the same place at one time, and too many of them desired to go to the same place. More than half of them wanted to settle in Nova Scotia, until then a sleepy colonial backwater of a few thousand souls, most concentrated around Halifax. The newcomers had overwhelmed the capital and the other few existing settlements like Annapolis.

Halifax itself was awash in Loyalists, former slaves, troops in transit back to Britain, disbanded soldiers, adventurers, and hangers-on. Those who couldn't afford the exorbitant rents that local landlords were demanding ended up housed in public buildings, warehouses, churches, and even tent cities on Citadel Hill and Point Pleasant Park. Since many had arrived without

---

49. A more dispassionate later observer, Nova Scotia writer Thomas Raddall, put it this way: "Not since the flight of the Huegenots had the western world seen such a large and unhappy migration."

money or resources, the military had had to set up street kitchens—brought ashore from vessels in the harbour—to feed them. "There were many deaths, and all the miseries and unsanitary conditions of an overcrowded town," Parr would write, adding with some pride: "For four months, the bulk of these 10,000 refugees were fed on our streets, and among them were many reared and nurtured in every comfort and luxury in the homes they had to fly from."

The only good news was that Carleton, in the summer, had wisely extended the provision of the king's bounty from six months to a year—until May 1784 "to those whose necessities may require it . . . to carry them through the winter."

Parr had done what he could for them as well as for the thousands of other refugees who'd fanned out into the province's wilderness, hiring teams of surveyors who had miraculously and quickly hacked new cities out of the forests in places like St. John and Shelburne, and then desperately tried to keep up with the never-ending demand for more and more building lots from more and more passengers aboard more and more ships that never stopped arriving from New York.

To complicate matters, there was never enough of anything, including time to plant and harvest the crops that might have helped the newcomers wean themselves more quickly from the teat of the king's bounty. As grateful as they were for Carleton's decision to continue supplying provisions for another six months, no one knew what would happen when the provisions expired at the beginning of planting season in the spring. There had also been no time to complete construction of the thousands of houses needed to shelter people through the fast-approaching winter. Many were now shivering in tents and makeshift huts on shore or huddling below deck aboard ships that had been transformed into overcrowded dormitories for the duration. If this autumn's weather was any predictor, the coming winter would be difficult. "The oldest man in the province does not remember such severe bad weather" as the province had experienced this fall, Parr fretted in one letter to his superiors.

Parr wrote many letters to London. A cautious man who preferred instructions to initiative, he kept begging for direction that never seemed to arrive. In June, he'd written to say that he was doing his best to accommodate the newcomers "notwithstanding I am disagreeably circumstanced in not having had any instructions from government to regulate my conduct." A month later, he tried again: "Government has not yet honoured me with their commands relative to this vast emigration. I have hitherto acted in the dark, to the best of my abilities; and flatter myself that what has been done will be approved of as they have proceeded from the best motives, humanity and justice."

About the only clear instruction he had received from London was to keep a lid on spending. In March, even before the spring fleet had arrived from New York, Lord Frederick North, the new home secretary and the latest in a string of bosses Parr had had to answer to, wrote to admonish him that "every possible degree of economy will be observed" in the settling of the refugees.

Parr had tried to do that. But it wasn't—and wouldn't be—easy. "Though they plague me with complaints and quarrel among themselves," he noted with resignation, "I shall continue to render them every good office in my power."

The feud between George Panton, who claimed to be the one true Anglican rector of Shelburne, and William Walter, who declared himself the same, was, if nothing else, glorious entertainment for cold evenings in the fall of 1783.[viii]

The dispute had its roots in the first meetings of the Port Roseway Associates in New York. On several occasions, the group had debated whether to appoint a Church of England minister to accompany the Associates to their new home. While some, like James Dole, were eager to escape what he called "the hierarchy" of any church at all, others who weren't members of the official British religion—and there were more than a few of those—simply feared any scheme that would give precedence to the Anglicans.

When they couldn't agree on what to do, two of the loyalist worthies took it upon themselves to invite Panton, the former rector of the Anglican church in Trenton, New Jersey, who'd served as the chaplain to the British army's Prince of Wales regiment during the revolution, to accompany the fleet to Port Roseway as their rector. The Society for the Propagation of the Gospel, a British missionary group, added its blessing and promised Panton a small stipend.

Panton was supposed to accompany the first spring fleet to Nova Scotia but had been felled by a fever and forced to wait for the next sailing. By that time, however, Admiral Digby informed Panton he would have company on the voyage. William Walter, the former rector of Trinity Church in Boston who'd done a stint as chaplain to DeLancey's loyalist brigade, was also heading for Nova Scotia in the same fleet with the same intention.

Unluckily for Panton, Walter's ship arrived two days before Panton's, and Walter moved quickly to stake his claim, organizing parishioners into the Vestry of Trinity Church—which physically, of course, didn't yet exist—and then sailing soon afterwards to Britain to inform the Society for the Propagation of the Gospel that Shelburne was without a preacher and offer his services, which the Society, apparently forgetting its earlier endorsement of Panton, gratefully accepted.

Panton, meanwhile, wasn't idle. He'd prevailed upon Governor Parr to induct him as the new rector of St. Patrick's Anglican parish, which, of course, didn't exist either.

When he returned, Walter dismissed Parr's endorsement, claiming that the governor had no power to name anyone until he'd heard the wishes of the people of the community.

While each would-be rector tried to solidify his claim, including by courting the growing community of black Loyalists and servants,[50] he also dispatched a flurry of earnest letters and petitions touting his own many and various virtues while disparaging those of his opponent.

At first blush, the dispute seemed to be one between Shelburne's new establishment and its "people."[51] Panton, for example, accused Walter of "opposing public authority," and argued that no "genuine member of the Church of England and principled loyalist can, consistently and conscientiously, oppose a public establishment by proper authority, which interferes with no person's rights. . . . Such opposition must arise from sinister views." Walter countered by claiming that the local worthies only supported Panton because "they conceive it will please the governor, whose favour in grants of land and public office they may wish." And he didn't hesitate to point out that Panton himself had applied for a grant of five thousand acres.

Supporters of each man were equally vehement, often attending the services of the rival rector simply to disrupt them. The dispute, which would drag on for two years, would ultimately provoke at least one confrontation in the middle of a funeral service.

Perhaps not surprisingly, land had already become a tradeable commodity in Shelburne by the fall of 1783.

On October 13, for example, George Chisholm, a former New York merchant who'd been one of the early Associates, paid

---

50. On November 21, Walter staged a mass baptism for seventy blacks, while Panton, during his first seven months in Shelburne, performed the same ceremony for more than 125 others. James Walker, in his book *Black Loyalists*, suggests that the former slaves may have been eager to find a religion because, "as slaves in the American colonies, they had been discouraged, and sometimes even prevented, from embracing the religion of their owners."

51. In fact, Walter's views were more complex and less populist than they might seem. In one letter, for example, echoing the sentiments of Benjamin Marston, he confided that he believed there were "no men of abilities" among the Loyalists.

Kenneth MacKenzie £30 for his fifty-acre grant and a town plot in Mason's division. That same day, he sold the town plot alone for £10 to Alexander Fraser, a farmer who, like Chisholm, had become an Associate on the recommendation of Alexander Robertson, the brother of printer James Robertson.

Two days later, on October 15, Chisholm bought Fraser's town lot in the North division for £10, then immediately flipped it, selling it to MacKenzie—from whom he'd bought land two days before—for £20 pounds, thus ending up with a fifty-acre plot for just £10.

Not all deals were quite so complex. Alexander Watson and his wife, Margaret, paid fifty guineas for a town lot on King Street and then got one hundred acres of farm and timberland in one of Benjamin Marston's draws. That land, on the east side of the Clyde River south of Shelburne, reminded Alexander of another Clyde River, the famous one in Scotland, beside which he'd spent much of his youth and early manhood. While Margaret and the children remained in Shelburne, Alexander decamped to their new farmland to build a house for them. Once that was completed, they would sell their Shelburne lot and become the lairds of their country manor.

Benjamin Marston was not impressed.[ix] "These people are the very worst yet," he wrote of the hundreds of disbanded soldiers who had begun showing up in Shelburne in mid-September with the first of the thousands of additional refugees who'd been in the fall fleet from New York. "They murmur and grumble because they can't get located as advantageously as those who have been working hard these four months," Benjamin carped, ignoring for the moment his own earlier and similarly disparaging comments about the work ethic of the first arrivals. "They," he concluded of the ex-soldiers, "seem to be the riff-raff of the whole."

The military newcomers were an eclectic mix: veterans of the British army and Royal Navy who had chosen to take their discharge in North America rather than return home to England;

Hessian mercenaries who'd fought on the British side and had now decided to make their home in what was left of the colonies; and thousands of soldiers, most American-born, from the various loyalist regiments. Though some came with wives and families, many did not. Which, as Benjamin himself knew, could pose a problem. There were few marriageable women in Shelburne.[52]

Not that he had much time for such concerns. Or even for writing in his journal. Benjamin's entries this month had been mostly cryptic, and mostly to do with the pressing business of settling the new arrivals before winter. "Located the 43 soldiers mentioned yesterday . . ." "In town Monday, Tuesday and today preparing to draw lots for upwards of 700 persons . . ." "Lyman and Tully in the woods marking out blocks for house lots for the newcomers; myself preparing a list of names to draw . . ." "Today finish rolling up tickets for the Loyalists, who are to draw their lots in the southern part of the town . . ." "Located people on 416 house lots . . ." "Making up tickets today for 383 disbanded soldiers, who are to draw tomorrow . . ."

When he wasn't busy making up lottery tickets, or listening to complaints about poor lots or no lots, or investigating allegations that this child or that black had gotten land he shouldn't, or measuring off the land that the governor had claimed as his

---

52. According to researchers Charles Wetherell and Robert W. Roetger, one of the reasons for Shelburne's rapid decline was the lack of women when compared to men. "Demographically, Shelburne was an anomaly from the start," they wrote in the *Canadian Historical Review*. "Above all else, the sex ratio was seriously unbalanced. Among the 2,774 adult loyalists enumerated in the summer of 1784, the sex ratio was 163 (that is, there were 163 men for every 100 women), and among the 1,316 adults in the companies of disbanded soldiers it was a phenomenal 361. . . . The adult sex ratio in a demographically stable, free population generally ranges between 90 and 110. Collectively in Shelburne it was 205. Given such a dramatic difference between the number of adult men and women, out migration of single men would be predictable."

own, or being confronted at the end of each day with stacks more applications for ever more land grants, or preparing his accounts for the surveyor general, Benjamin tried—without much success—to oversee the construction of his own house.

After the cold weather had set in, he'd moved in with Brinley, the commissary officer, but "his house is so thronged with carpenters, work benches, etc., that I have no lodging room, and he has so much business of his own that it is impossible to find room," so he was bunking now—"on very slender invitation"—with two other single men.

Luckily, Benjamin now had someone to help make his own new house habitable. Three days ago, Lieutenant-Colonel Abraham Van Buskirk and his family had taken up residence in the cellar of the shell of his house and were already gathering stones for the foundation of a chimney.

Van Buskirk had arrived with the fall fleet, but he was definitely not among the "riff-raff of the whole." He was a man of both education and action, a type of which Benjamin believed there were too few in Shelburne. A member of an old Dutch family that could trace its Bergen County, New Jersey, roots to the seventeenth century, Van Buskirk had been a prosperous physician, surgeon, and apothecary before the war. During the war, he'd distinguished himself as the leader of the third battalion of Cortland Skinner's New Jersey Volunteers, leading more than a few church and barn-burning raids on his former neighbours and serving as one of Benedict Arnold's senior commanders during brutal raids on rebel communities up the Connecticut coast. His son Jacob, a captain in the Volunteers, had been badly wounded while fighting with Cornwallis in 1781's failed Southern campaign. After Yorktown, however, the battalion had been forced to bide its time performing garrison duty in New York. By then, discipline had broken down and the battalion, like others, was plagued by desertion and criminal activity. Several soldiers were even sentenced to death for their crimes.

In September, the members of the third battalion were finally discharged from service. Since they had little hope of returning to their former lives, most opted to accept the British offer of half pay for a new life, clothing, provisions, and land in Nova Scotia. While the majority of Van Buskirk's battalion decided to settle near River St. John on the other side of the Bay of Fundy, Abraham had brought his family and thirteen members of his battalion to Shelburne.

Benjamin was glad he had. Shelburne could use a few more like him. And a lot fewer like the 383 ex-soldiers for whom he'd drawn lots today. Poor devils. It was now November 22, so there was no chance they'd finish building houses for themselves before the snow settled in. They'd have to join their fellow latecomers, living either aboard vessels in the harbour, or in temporary huts set up on the common (which was a polite way of describing the still-forested land near the harbour that might possibly, one day, become a public square), or—worst of all—in canvas tents that couldn't keep out the wind and cold.

How many more refugees would Shelburne be able to accommodate?

Thank goodness tomorrow was a day of rest. Or as much rest as Benjamin could expect, knowing that, come Monday, Lyman would be out running property lines for another six hundred people while he worked at home, fielding still more complaints from still more ingrates.

For now, however, he would turn his attention to a more pleasant task: writing a letter to his sister Lucia and her husband. There were some sundries he'd ask them to send him. Shelburne, after all and for all its ambitions, was still in the wilderness.

The breeze—or, more accurately, the lack of one—only added one final embarrassment to Guy Carleton's humiliation. For three days, the *Ceres*, which was to ferry him and the last soldiers, sailors, civilian employees, and Loyalists back to London, had sat, becalmed, in New York Harbor while the victorious

Americans celebrated the end of the British presence with parties, parades, and fireworks that were visible from the deck of the ship.

On the morning of November 25, 1783, American troops had marched down from Harlem to Bowery Lane where the British army still occupied its posts. At one in the afternoon, the British soldiers, led by an "unusually dejected" Guy Carleton, began their march down Wall Street and then left on Broadway to the wharf where the *Ceres* was waiting for them. It was, as Ward Chipman described it in a letter to Benjamin's cousin Edward Winslow, a "mortifying scene" that "occasioned most painful sensations."

Finally, on November 28, the wind came up and the *Ceres* was able to raise its sails and escape this place for good.

By the beginning of the new year, Guy Carleton would be back in London in the house his young wife, Maria, had rented for them in the Queen Anne Street neighbourhood of London. He was 59 years old. Had he just seen his final glimpse of North America?

As he sat down at his desk in Halifax on Tuesday, December 16, 1783,ˣ to pen a short, self-congratulatory, year-end "My Lord" report for his patron in London, John Parr had good reason to be more than a little pleased with himself—and a lot relieved.

"The great emigration of loyalists from New York and other parts of the continent to this province is now at an end, I believe, at least for this winter," he informed Lord Shelburne. "It is impossible to ascertain the exact number [of refugees], but they do not fall short of 30,000 souls, to whom I have rendered every service and paid every attention in my power, which they have gratefully acknowledged, a few worthless characters excepted."

Parr pointed out with becoming pride that, in very short order and in the face of great hardship, several thriving new towns had sprung up where previously there had been nothing but trees. Putting aside his often quarrelsome relationship with residents of Shelburne, Parr happily described it as "the most considerable, most flourishing and most expeditious [city] that ever was built in so short a time . . ."

There was more than a little truth to that. In less than eight months, Shelburne had become the largest city in what remained of the British colonies, and the fourth largest in all of North America. Only New York, Philadelphia, and Boston could boast more than the "upwards of 12,000 inhabitants"[53] Parr reported as Shelburne's population. To put that into the perspective of the times, you could have fitted every man, woman, and child in Montreal and Three Rivers combined into Shelburne. Before it, too, was overwhelmed by Loyalists, Halifax's total population had been barely 1500; even after the influx, it had only about half as many people as Shelburne.

And, Benjamin Marston's criticisms notwithstanding, the Shelburne Loyalists had done much more than just arrive. "Eight hundred houses are already finished," the governor pointed out, "600 more in great forwardness, and several hundred lately begun upon." What passed for architectural style was most likely Georgian, but log houses still outnumbered framed ones by four to one. Even after the first snowfalls, local sawmills continued to operate at more than full capacity, cutting enough boards for another six to ten new homes a week, and the sound of hammering and sawing continued throughout the winter.

Businesses had begun, too. Besides the sawmills, there were shipyards and fish companies, bakers, blacksmiths, and shopkeepers. There were even a number of coffee houses, taverns, and inns, not to mention what one observer described as a "fashionable promenade."

---

53. There is no accepted count for Shelburne's peak population, though estimates range from about ten thousand to fourteen thousand. By the time the first muster was completed in the summer of 1784, many had already left and Shelburne's decline was under way.

There were many "firsts" to report. The town's first newspaper—the *Royal American Gazette*—began publishing on September 8 on a printing press the Robertson brothers had brought with them from New York. The sons of a Scottish printer, James and Alexander Robertson had come to America in the late 1760s to make their fortunes. Their first joint venture was a newspaper called the *New York Chronicle*, which launched and folded in the space of a few months in the winter of 1769–70. A rival publisher named James Parker had dismissed them in a letter to his own silent partner, Benjamin Franklin, as "paper spoilers. . . . They puffed and flourished for a while but the paper is now dropped. They are ignorant blockheads, but have impudence enough." Not everyone had such a low opinion of their skills, however. Sir William Johnston, the colonial superintendent of Indian Affairs, even fronted them the money they needed to buy equipment to set up shop in Albany, where they launched the *Albany Gazette* in 1771. It was the first newspaper in the colony outside New York City. The *Gazette* was only slightly longer-lived than the brothers' New York paper, but after it folded the Robertsons remained in Albany as successful printers, churning out handbills and documents for both the colonial government and the city of Albany, for which they produced 1773's *Laws and Ordinances*.

Even though some of the materials were for the patriotic Committee of Correspondence, the brothers eventually ran afoul of Albany's increasingly arbitrary republican politics. James went into hiding, but Alexander, who'd been crippled from birth and was unable to escape, was captured and thrown in jail. Later, there was a fire in the jail, from which he barely managed to crawl out, burned and bruised.

Reunited in now British-occupied New York, the brothers launched the *Royal American Gazette* in January 1777. While Alexander—with the aid of apprentices—ran the *Gazette*, James followed the British army to Philadelphia and later to Charles Town, setting up local loyalist newspapers that lasted only as long as the British army occupied the city.

Back in New York, Alexander became one of the first members of the Port Roseway Associates. By the time they set sail from New York in the spring fleet of 1783, Alexander had enlisted not only James but also two of their youthful apprentices, James and Thomas Swords, and the Swords family in the adventure.

Within a few months of their arrival, they'd set up their printing press—only the second one in the entire colony—and began publishing under the same name they'd used in New York.

There were other firsts as well. Robert Barry, who'd volunteered his property for Shelburne's first church service back in June, turned part of his log cabin into Shelburne's first school, where his wife taught local children their manners. In December, the governor had approved a bill the House of Assembly had passed to set up Shelburne's first Court of Sessions, which would enforce local law and order, run the jails, maintain roads and bridges, set fees and taxes, organize fire protection, and take care of the poor. It was to hold its first meeting on March 1.

Some things had turned out as the Port Roseway Associates had optimistically expected them to. Fish, for example, were more than plentiful. The first Loyalists had landed just in time for the last of the annual run of alewives[54] into the harbour's shallows. Those were followed almost immediately by salmon, weighing anywhere from nine to thirteen pounds each, and easily scooped from the shallow water. Beyond the shore, haddock was plentiful, as was sturgeon, which often grew to ten or twelve feet long. During the summer, the Loyalists caught skate, mackerel, herring, flounder, eel, and dogfish. The water's bottom crawled with lobster.

The land provided, too: one person reported taking seven hundred rabbits in a single season, another four hundred. The woods overflowed with deer, moose, and black bears, whose meat the settlers would eat fresh, salted, or dried, and whose skins

---

54. A species of shad, more commonly known now in the Maritimes as gaspereau.

they would turn into blankets and clothing. The marshes along the river were alive with ducks and geese; pigeons, doves, hawks, owls, and bald eagles circled in the skies overhead.

The soil, on the other hand, was not nearly as fertile or as easy to plant as they'd been led to believe. The land was rocky, the soil sandy, and where there were not trees there were uncleared stumps. Most of the first gardens were planted around stumps. To make matters worse, few of the early farms were capable of supporting the livestock the settlers had brought with them or bought from traders. They'd had to cut the grass growing in beaver meadows along the banks of the Roseway River and stack it on the edge of town as feed for cattle. The simple truth was that Shelburne could not now—and would not likely ever be able to—feed itself, let alone develop an agricultural export industry.

And Shelburne, though conveniently located for sea travel, was still completely cut off by forests from the rest of Nova Scotia. Early in December, Benjamin Marston's assistant, Lyman, had led a party of more than a dozen Loyalists into the woods "to begin a road through the country to Annapolis" on the other side of the province. Even after that was complete—and who knew how long it might take to cut a path through the impenetrable woods?—it still wouldn't solve the much more serious problem of the lack of a road along the southern shore to Halifax, where most of the important decisions affecting Shelburne would be made.

If many of the white Loyalists were disillusioned, the thousand or so black Loyalists had even more cause for concern. They'd been shuffled off to Birchtown, six miles from Shelburne, and given even worse land than the whites had received. Unlike the whites, they had few resources to fall back on. Some had already been forced to trade their hard-won freedom for lives as indentured servants to the white citizens of Shelburne. That, of course, meant that the blacks had even less time to work on their own homes. Many lived in rocky, dug-out basements, with sticks and moss or canvas for roofs. In exchange for their services to their white employers, they were supposed to be given a small salary plus clothing. But some of the more unscrupulous whites tried to pay them only part of what they were owed, or nothing at all, and provided them with less than their fair share of government rations, too.

Some of the first arrivals—whites, not blacks—had been so disillusioned by Shelburne's pioneer life they'd already left, or were planning to leave as soon as spring came. Some had gone to Halifax, others had returned to the new United States where the weather was better and some of the Southern states had already begun to relax their banishment and confiscation laws in order to lure back their best and brightest.

The American newspapers reported gleefully on the problems the Loyalists were facing. Shelburne's refugees, said the *Boston Gazette*, are "the most miserable set of beings that it is possible to conceive of," and a Philadelphia paper reported that "many of the refugees who have settled at Port Roseway have wrote to their friends in New York [to] by no means . . . come to that place."

Not everyone was as pessimistic. For example, one British naval officer stationed in Shelburne wrote home in October that "this part of the country is almost level and more easy to clear than the generality of it. The small islands and many other parts which have been cultivated some years, are as fertile as it is possible to conceive; and from the excellence of its harbour, its situation for trade and number of inhabitants (many of which are wealthy), there is every reason to believe it will soon be the capital of Nova Scotia."

From the comfort of his office in Halifax, John Parr agreed. It is, he wrote to Lord Shelburne, "a most beautiful situation, the land good, and the fairest and best harbour in the world. I have not a doubt of its being one day or other the first port in this part of America. It is much superior to Halifax in many points. . . .

"I beg my compliments to Lady Shelburne," he concluded, "and have the honour to be, my Lord, Your Lordship's Faithful, Humble Servant, J. PARR."

The war really was over. Gideon White had to accept that and get on with his life. He had stayed behind in New York in the spring even after his fellow Port Roseway Associates had departed for their new homes, waiting for news that his friend Lord Montague[55] had followed through on his plans to establish a private battalion based in Jamaica to continue the fight against the Americans. But Montague's plans had never materialized.

So, in early December, White and 158 other members of Montague's Duke of Cumberland regiment set sail in two ships for Halifax, where they would spend the winter. What then? There was talk of settling in Chedabucto, another new community at the northern end of Nova Scotia being stocked by Loyalists and former soldiers. And, of course, there was still the prospect of joining his friends and fellow Associates in Shelburne.

He'd kept in touch with John Miller, the Associates' secretary, who'd asked for his help in securing house frames to send to Shelburne. And Nat Thomas, a friend from a famous Massachusetts Tory family whose estate had been confiscated during the revolution and who was now in Shelburne, and still interested in the prospect of some joint business ventures. In the meantime, he'd recommended Gideon to the former governor of New Hampshire, John Wentworth, who was now in Nova Scotia as surveyor general. Perhaps Wentworth could find something to tide Gideon over this winter in Halifax. At any rate, there was no point in considering going to Shelburne now. Not with the rest of a Nova Scotia winter ahead.

---

55. Montague died a few months later in February 1784.

"Great Riot today"

Chapter 5.

The new year began much milder than anyone had expected. Especially after the coldest fall in memory. The good weather enabled Benjamin Marston to continue his work. And the Loyalists to continue to build their homes—and to continue to celebrate. On January 19, 1784, about fifty gentlemen and ladies, including the Honourable Edwin Henry Stanhope, the captain of His Majesty's Ship *Mercury*, gathered at McGragh's Tavern for a ball to celebrate the queen's birthday. The evening boasted all of the usual diversions—dancing, cards, and the rest—but for some reason Benjamin seemed less intolerant of this gathering than he had been of some of the Loyalists' earlier excuses for parties. In fact, he was one of the attendees.

Perhaps it was the presence of Stanhope, a "very well bred man," a cousin of the Earl of Chesterfield. Stanhope had arrived in Shelburne in October as the settlement's new senior officer at its fledgling naval station. The British navy considered Shelburne, in the post-revolutionary era, a potentially valuable strategic naval asset. Marston had already designated islands across from the town as Navy Islands, hived off a good chunk of waterfront for a king's wharf and king's slip, and

STEPHEN KIMBER

reserved another island above the falls in the Roseway River for other naval purposes.

Benjamin found Stanhope an interesting character, a "master of the whole etiquette of polite ceremony. His main scope is to appear of importance on every occasion, which unavoidably leads him to make himself a little hero of each tale. Upon the whole he is not a disagreeable man in company," Benjamin concluded, "and may, by a little tickling of his vanity, be induced to serve this settlement very essentially."[56]

But perhaps Benjamin's more benign view of this night's proceedings could have been attributed to the simple fact it took place in a house "where, six months ago there was an almost impenetrable swamp," as he explained in his journal that night. "So great has been the exertions of the settlers in this new world. The room was commodious and warm, though in the rough." He added with uncharacteristic charity that the whole "was conducted with good humour and general satisfaction."

He wasn't worthy. Which was why he was out here again, in the middle of the woods, in the middle of the night, in the snow and the cold, among the beasts of the forest—where he belonged—asking the Lord's mercy.

God and the devil had been struggling for Boston King's soul for as long as he could remember. Sometimes God won. Boston could still recall that day at Mr. Waring's plantation in Carolina when he was only 12, waking from a fiery, apocalyptic dream in which the Lord had come to earth to separate the sinners from His people, and how Boston had promised himself on that day that he would shake off his own badness forever so he, too, could be among God's chosen.

---

56. *Naval Documents of the American Revolution* by William James Morgan offers a less flattering view of Stanhope who, according to one reviewer, "slithered into American history" and "did not receive a fair share of the familial genes controlling manners."

It wouldn't be the last time he would make such a promise. Or the last time he would break it.

Things had become even worse lately, ever since the blind preacher had converted Violet. Her initial euphoria at finding the Lord's blessings had quickly given way to "great darkness and distress" as she, like Boston, struggled with her own human weaknesses. Perhaps it was worse for Violet, who'd been "unacquainted with the corruptions of her own heart" until now. "Indeed, I never saw any person, either before or since, so overwhelmed with anguish of spirit on account of backsliding as she was. The trouble of her soul brought affliction upon her body, which confined her to a bed."

Violet's struggles affected Boston, too. They made him all too aware of what a "miserable, wretched sinner" he had been, and that made sleep even more impossible.

One night, he went to see Joseph Brown, another ex-slave who'd also come to Birchtown aboard *L'Abondance* and become a preacher. Perhaps not surprisingly, given that religion had been denied to so many of them during the long period of slavery, there were already plenty of black preachers mining for converts in these parts. Brown and Wilkinson here in Birchtown, David George over in Shelburne.

Brown did his best to help Boston. "He received me with great kindness and affection," and encouraged him to "seek the Lord with all my heart." The problem was that his kindnesses only made Boston feel worse, "burdened with a load of guilt too heavy for me to bear." When Brown began to pray for him, Boston decided to return home. "I had to pass through a little wood, where I intended to fall down on my knees and pray for mercy," he would explain years later, "but every time I attempted, I was so terrified that I thought my hair stood upright, and that the earth moved beneath my feet. I hastened home in great fear and horror."

But the forest soon became a magnet, a solitary place where Boston could return time and again to try to sort out his own inner turmoil. He'd also begun attending prayer meetings where, each night, another six or seven of his fellow sinners would give themselves up to the Lord. But instead of being delighted for them, Boston only envied them. And that made him realize just how strong the devil must be, and how weak he was. He wasn't worthy to be among the believers, not even his own struggling wife.

So he'd come out here to the forest again tonight. The snow lay in drifts three and four feet deep around him. He cut some spruce bows to make a fire and then sat in front of it, wrapped in a blanket, and tried to listen for whatever it was the Lord was telling him. There were moments when he believed he'd heard the message, had undergone some sort of transformation and could finally rejoice in the Lord himself. But then the moment would pass and he'd fall back into "unbelief, into distracting doubts and fears, and evil-reasonings. The Devil persuaded me that I was the most miserable creature upon the face of the earth, and that I was predestinated to be damned before the foundation of the world. My anguish was so great, that when night appeared, I dreaded it as much as the grave."

Gideon White could only marvel at the transformation. The vast empty harbour and pristine wilderness he remembered from earlier sails past Port Roseway had disappeared, swallowed up by acres of sailing ships loading, unloading, entering, and leaving Shelburne harbour, and the cacophony of hammer, saw, shouts, and curses intended to shape a bustling city out of that former forest.

It was hard to believe it had been only two years since those long evenings in Roubalet's Tavern in New York when Gideon had entertained his fellow Loyalists with descriptions of Port Roseway and its possibilities, and just a year since he'd opted to stay behind in New York to try to find a way to fight on against their American foes rather than abandon the quixotic cause and join them in founding their chosen city.

But he was here now. He'd wintered in Halifax, along with other members of his former Duke of Cumberland regiment, most of whom had since taken up their new promised land in Chedabucto on Nova Scotia's northeast coast. Gideon had considered joining them—he'd even written to friends there telling them he'd be arriving soon—but the lure of Shelburne, old friends, and new opportunities proved too powerful. He'd landed in late spring with three servants and twenty-two members of his regiment, as well as the wife and two daughters of one of his corporals.

Gideon White was 32, a bachelor, and ambitious to make up for lost time. Which is why he didn't stay long in Shelburne that spring. He left for London to lobby officials there to speed up approval of the half pension he was entitled to as a former British army officer, and also to collect on some debts he was owed from his trading days. He already owned a share in one vessel that was bringing rum, sugar, and coffee north from Jamaica in exchange for cargoes of local lumber and fish, but he wanted to use the money he raised in London to broaden his commercial horizons, buying fishing vessels that could supply fish for trade too.

The fishery had turned out to be a mixed blessing for Shelburne's first settlers. The Port Roseway Associates had tried—and failed—to convince Parr to reserve all fish in the neighbouring waters for them alone. But the reality was that there were more than enough fish to go around. On their first day of fishing in the previous year, just five men reported catching eight hundred cod. "Fish," they happily declared, "was never more plenty nor easier to come at than from this place." Unfortunately, they had no idea what to do with the fish after they caught them. Few of the first arrivals had any experience as fishermen; they were merchants and craftsmen who had never cleaned, prepared, salted, dried, and washed fish for market. And they had no boats purpose-built for the fishery. Their first attempts to take commercial advantage of the vast resources of fish were dismal failures. Which is one area where Gideon hoped to make his mark.

He was also extremely interested in prospects in the whaling industry. Before the revolution, fishermen from New York and New England had made fortunes hunting the sperm whale. It had been a valuable colonial export industry for a number of reasons: the sperm whale's clean-burning oil produced a brighter flame than that of other whales; a wax known as spermaceti found in the whale's head could be used to manufacture the finest quality candles; and a substance called ambergris from its intestines was much in demand as a fixative for perfumes for milady. During the revolution, the industry had been decimated by British naval blockades and marauding privateers. After war's end, the American industry had difficulty recovering because Britain slapped expensive duties on American whale oil imports. That, of course, might mean a potential new market for enterprising colonists like Gideon.

Others saw these possibilities. After a whaler visited Shelburne that spring, weighed down with a cargo of whale oil (the head of a single seventy-foot sperm whale can produce a ton of oil), a group of local businessmen quickly set up the Whale Fishing Company, while others—including Benjamin Marston's friend Joshua Watson—fitted out their own ships for the whaling trade.

Gideon bought a one-eighth interest in a vessel. And began thinking about buying up property and commercial lots in and around the new town. His friend Nathaniel Whitworth had told him that so many of the first settlers were already packing up to go elsewhere that he would "probably . . . be able to purchase a store already completed" for less than it had cost to build. While that might be bad news for the town, Gideon saw it as an investment opportunity.

It was a welcome worthy of a governor.[i] On a day in late May 1784, the cannons from the fort at Point Carleton fired off ceremonial greetings as John Wentworth's schooner, under the respectful escort of His Majesty's Ship *Mercury*, slowly made its way to anchor in Shelburne harbour. There were, in fact, more than a few in the crowd of well-wishers at the dock calling out greetings to "Governor Wentworth," fervently wishing he was.

Unlike John Parr, whom they blamed for everything from the slowness of their land grants to the colony's inhospitable climate, Wentworth was one of them: a *real* Loyalist, a former governor of New Hampshire who had paid a price for his loyalty to king and country. Just like them.

Since arriving in Halifax from London the previous fall, Wentworth himself had been at pains—in public at least—to show due deference to his former rival for the Nova Scotia governorship. Wentworth's success in his new position—as surveyor-general of the woods for Britain's remaining American colonies—would depend on Parr's co-operation. His key duty was to identify and reserve valuable stands of white pine forest to make masts for Royal Navy vessels. Since Queen Anne's era, the navy, by law, had first call on any pine tree whose trunk was two feet or more in diameter. In practice, however, the rule was not quite as simple as it sounded. On the one hand, the British navy badly needed the masts for its continuing wars in Europe. On the other hand, the British were trying to encourage development of their remaining colonies. The government didn't want to put any more restrictions than absolutely necessary on where newcomers could settle.

That meant it was critical for Wentworth to designate only the most appropriate white pine forests (many trees were decayed or had been damaged, making them unsuitable for masts), preferably located near rivers or harbours for easy access and shipping, and leave the rest of the land available for development. But in order to do that, Wentworth or a designate personally had to inspect the forests *before* the government could start formalizing large grants to the settlers. So Wentworth, in some measure, was himself responsible for slowing up the process of finalizing the land grants, one of the Loyalists' chief complaints against Parr.

It wasn't the only difference the Loyalists had with Parr for which he wasn't really to blame. Another incendiary issue in the winter and spring of 1784 had been the future of the king's bounty. The previous summer, Carleton had quietly extended his promise to provision the Loyalists from six months to a full year, to take into account the difficulties he knew they would encounter in becoming self-sufficient in their new communities. But that extension was due to run out at the beginning of May. Though General John Campbell, commander-in-chief of British forces on the east coast, had assured the settlers he would continue supplying provisions until he was ordered to do otherwise, the reality was that there was little chance that most of the Loyalists could survive until the fall harvest if London turned off the tap.

Edward Brinley's commissary was still distributing rations[57] to more than eighty-five hundred people in Shelburne, and struggling to keep up with demand. He'd had to supplement his supplies from London by buying additional provisions in Boston and other American ports. Parr and General Campbell had both written to London requesting that the government continue providing rations to the Loyalists beyond May, and Campbell had put in a specific request for additional supplies to be sent over from Britain in the spring. The answer from London had been silence, which did little to ease the anxieties of the Loyalists.

Neither did the continuing controversies over land. The Loyalists, especially those who had arrived in the fall, complained

---

57. As of January 4, 1784, Brinley's records show that he was supplying daily rations to 8645 people: 7160 Loyalists, soldiers, and their dependants, and 1485 freed blacks. To put that in perspective, consider this listing of his inventory from later that same year: 2594 pounds of bread, 213,451 pounds of flour, 3968 pounds of beef, 277,736 pounds of pork, 32,744 pounds of butter, 512 pounds of rice, 3912 pounds of oatmeal, 85 gallons of peas, 333 gallons of vinegar, 3196 gallons of rum, and 7672 gallons of molasses.

that all of the best lots were already gone or had been set aside for the navy and the army. Although they'd been allowed to spend the winter in temporary shelter on the commons, the squatters were now being told they'd have to move from there—not to make way for public buildings but, as one bitterly complained, "for a more valuable end, to accommodate the sons of favour . . . that go to Halifax with pockets full of a mettle well known in Mexico." If the land issues weren't solved and solved soon, the local magistrates declared in a letter to Governor Parr, "this settlement must fall through and the large sums of money already expended shall be sunk. . . . Anarchy and confusion must be the end result."

Though he thought it all much ado about nothing much, Parr did agree to expedite the land grants issue. By the time Wentworth's visit ended, the first grants for water and warehouse lots in the South division—land that Marston had surveyed a full year before—were finally registered. The land now belonged to the grantees on payment of yearly quit-rents of a farthing per lot, first payable after ten years on farm lots and two years on town lots. So much for the promise of free land.

In case Parr's land grants failed to quell the unrest in Shelburne, General Campbell dispatched a regiment to reinforce the local garrison.

By the time Wentworth arrived in Shelburne, he had already surveyed the woods around Halifax and Dartmouth, as well as Windsor and Annapolis Royal. But he knew Shelburne was likely to be more quarrelsome. In fact, the man he'd appointed to be his deputy there—David Thomson, a former shipwright from Philadelphia—had been so intimidated by the protests from the locals that he had achieved almost nothing.

So Wentworth, accompanied by Benjamin Marston, spent two weeks tromping through the boggy, blackfly-infested forests around Shelburne scouting out the best stands of white pine. Although settlement and fire had already taken their toll on the available stocks, Wentworth pronounced himself much impressed with trees he claimed were better than anything available in New England. Although he reserved ten thousand acres for the Crown, he was careful to draw the boundaries so as to interfere with settlement as little as possible. Perhaps because of the respect he'd built up during his years as governor of New Hampshire and perhaps because he'd come to Shelburne to do the work himself, few of the Loyalists questioned Wentworth's decisions about what land to reserve for the Crown or his stern admonition not to cut down any trees he'd put his mark on.

For Benjamin, Wentworth's visit—as hectic as it had been— must have been a welcome respite from his continuing struggles with the locals. Just before Wentworth arrived, in fact, he'd been helping set up a draw for 234 more farm lots when a small rump group, which had already successfully scuttled an earlier draw because it was dissatisfied with the outcome, managed to stop this one as well. "This cursed levelling spirit must be crushed by every means or we shall be for rebellion soon," Benjamin noted in his journal.

It was one more reminder of the price they had paid—and were paying still. In the summer of 1784, Joseph Durfee received a rather curt letter from his stepbrother in Rhode Island, inform- ing him of his stepfather's death three months earlier and demanding he now contribute, "as the law compels," to the final maintenance and burial.

The schisms and tensions that had ripped apart so many families during the war had not ended with the peace. Even as Joseph began to clear the land for the farm he hoped to someday build on the other side of Shelburne harbour—his own promised land—the letter was a painful reminder of the life, and the people, he'd left behind.

It was hard to believe that it had been fifteen years since that day on the beach at Newport when Joseph had watched the mob torch the British sloop *Liberty*. Had that really been the begin- ning of the end? Had his mother, stepfather, and stepbrother been right to support the rebels? Right or wrong, they had certainly been on the winning side. They had not been scattered into exile like Joseph, Anne, and their children, warned never to return to the land of their birth on pain of death.

His stepbrother reminded Joseph of the money he'd once borrowed against his stepfather's house, adding that even signing over his interest in the house wouldn't be enough to cover the costs his stepbrother had paid out to care for his stepfather after Joseph had abandoned the family. And reminded him, too, that the house had almost been confiscated as a result of Joseph's non-payment. "I now request that you will make just proposal, you in good conscience shall think right and justice to be done."

Justice? What was that?

It had seemed like a good idea at the time. William Holmes, who lived in Jones River, twenty miles from Shelburne, had come to see David George. Holmes told David that he and his wife, Deborah, had been converted to the ways of the Lord while reading the scriptures together. Now he wanted David to come with him to his house to help them become better Christians. David did, and then he and the couple made their way north to a town called Liverpool where David preached to a mixed congregation of whites and blacks. "We had a little heaven there," he would recall.

Holmes and his wife returned with David to Shelburne, where the couple testified about their experiences in front of David's congregation and made plans for David to baptize them that Sunday. Which is when the trouble started.

Ever since he'd begun preaching in Shelburne, David's congregation, while mainly black, had always included some white folks as well. And he certainly had white patrons. Including Governor Parr, who'd made sure that David got provisions and a quarter-acre lot in a northern part of town, where he had been able to build a makeshift church.

But that didn't make Deborah Holmes's relatives any happier that she had decided to be baptized by a black man. They gathered a mob, which invaded the service to try to prevent the ceremony from taking place. Deborah's sister, in fact, went so far as to grab Deborah's hair to prevent her from submerging in the water.

That had led to a visit to the local magistrates, who ruled that the couple was entitled to be baptized by a preacher of their own choosing, black or white. While that had resolved the pressing question of the baptism, it did little to ease the racial tensions simmering beneath the surface.

Brigadier-General John Campbell was not seeking the answer to a question historians would puzzle over centuries later: how many people really lived in Shelburne at its peak?[ii] He simply wanted to know how many newcomers to Nova Scotia were entitled to the beneficence of the king's bounty—and who among the rest were taking rations they didn't deserve. That had become an even more critical issue after London finally decided in May to continue supplying provisions to the Loyalists—albeit at two-thirds their original level—for another two years.[58]

The roots of the "General Return of All the Disbanded Troops and Other Loyalists Who Have Lately Become Settlers in the Province of Nova Scotia"—better known as the Muster of 1784—had been planted the previous December when General Campbell wrote to London urgently requesting that officials send him more rations for the suffering settlers. Recognizing the potential for abuse, however, Campbell at the same time had ordered his officials to examine the validity of the claim of each would-be recipient. That preliminary investigation flagged so many instances of fraud that Campbell then ordered a head count of all Loyalists in the province. (The

---

58. It wasn't until June, more than a month after the king's bounty had been scheduled to expire, that word finally reached Nova Scotia that the British would continue to provide rations.

abuse was widespread. Even a worthy such as Benjamin Marston's well-bred cousin Edward Winslow, who was Campbell's military secretary but who'd fallen on hard times after the war's end, wasn't above fiddling with the facts. He'd tried to have one of his infant sons commissioned as an ensign in order to qualify him for half pay and other benefits.)

According to Campbell's muster, in June 1784 there were a total of 14,852 Loyalists in Nova Scotia, 7923 of them in Shelburne. Though the numbers show there were more loyalist newcomers than existing settlers in the province and that Shelburne's population dwarfed Halifax's, both returns also show there were considerably fewer Loyalists than Governor Parr had claimed in his letters to London the previous fall.

There were all sorts of explanations for the discrepancy, including some initial exaggeration on the part of a governor eager to impress his bosses. But it's also fair to point out that the muster masters were told not to include in their lists anyone who was not, at that moment, settled on the lands they'd been granted or who couldn't clearly demonstrate an intention to settle. That eliminated a significant number who ultimately ended up settling their land. It's also true that some among the original refugees had died during that first long winter. And many others, especially those from the poorest classes, had abandoned pioneer settlements like Shelburne for what they hoped would be better prospects in established Halifax. Too often, those prospects weren't better at all. "It is not possible for any pen or tongue to describe the variety of wretchedness that is at this time exhibited in the streets of [Halifax] and, God knows, I am obliged to hear a large proportion of it," Edward Winslow wrote.

Many of those with better prospects, or at least more means, hadn't even waited to draw their lots. If they did get land, they held it only long enough to sell it, collect the proceeds, and run. Close to a thousand people came and went in this fashion in Shelburne alone. A few sailed to Britain. More, including many disbanded soldiers, were swayed by the blandishments from the government of St. John's Island,[59] or the allure of more fertile farmland in Canada. Still others, discouraged by the obstacles to starting over in a new and hostile land, decided to take a chance on what they knew and went back where they'd come from.

That said, there were some non-loyalist, non-soldier newcomers who didn't show up in the official muster but whose presence helped swell the population. Like William Taylor and his wife, London Baptists who'd settled in Shelburne and were using their own resources to support David George's ministry among the locals. And there were also, of course, more than a few adventurers, entrepreneurs, hustlers, and ne'er-do-wells who saw the new settlements as potential opportunities and descended like blackflies in May. To further complicate matters, some British officials had taken advantage of the overall confusion to collect what Edward Winslow described as "a whole shipload of all kinds of vagrants from the streets of London, and sent them out to Nova Scotia. . . . The miserable remnant," who were, of course, ineligible for the king's bounty but who even more desperately needed assistance, "have now no cover but tents. Such as are able to crawl are begging for a proportion of provisions at my door."

Those caveats aside, the muster does offer an intriguing snapshot of Shelburne's population during the summer after the evacuation, including its black population. While the number of white settlers in Shelburne had declined—not only from Parr's optimistic earlier estimates but also from the actual numbers drawing rations in January 1784—the muster shows that the number of freed blacks had increased by close to fifty between Brinley's January 1784 victualing list and Campbell's June muster. Although some of the 1531 blacks lived in Shelburne, most had settled in Birchtown. That shouldn't be surprising. Birchtown was the largest settlement of freed blacks in North America, so it served as a magnet for those who felt unwelcome elsewhere.

59. Now Prince Edward Island.

Their lives were far from comfortable, though. Most had arrived with little money and fewer belongings. They'd been given poor land, and little of it. None of them had yet received farm lots, not that they would have had the time or resources to cultivate them. In order to survive, many worked as labourers in Shelburne, a six-mile walk from Birchtown, where they counted themselves lucky to make half of what a white labourer would ask. Which may explain why some had traded the uncertainties of their new-found freedom for the often more difficult certainty of life as indentured servants to well-to-do white Loyalists. Calling them indentured servants was often just a polite term for slaves.

To get an accurate count of who was entitled to rations, Campbell's commissioners of muster asked each of the blacks for their names and occupations, the names of the companies in which they'd come to Nova Scotia, and to whom, if anyone, they were indentured. They also asked questions about the rations they'd already received. Their findings were shocking.

One man reported that after a full year of indentured servitude, his master had given him only two-and-a-half months' worth of the rations he was entitled to. The master had kept the rest. A female servant reported that she'd received nothing at all from her master after a full year's work, even though he'd listed her as receiving the king's bounty. Others weren't paid even the pittance they were promised, or were cast aside the moment they fell ill. They had little recourse. Though they technically weren't slaves, their masters could go to friendly white magistrates who'd order them punished if they disobeyed. And they were often sold or traded like chattel by their masters, sometimes even passed along to others in wills when their masters died.

Was this really what the British had meant when they had promised them their freedom?

By the summer of 1784, Shelburne finally had a court—and crime—worthy of its status as a major city. When he'd visited

Shelburne the year before, Governor Parr had appointed magistrates and justices of the peace, but there was no actual court and the magistrates could wield little power until the legislature passed bills establishing a new court of sessions and court of common pleas. Parr approved the legislation in early December 1784, but the courts hadn't held their first formal sittings until spring.

The court of sessions—overseen by a justice of the peace and a grand jury drawn by lot from among those with assets of £100 or property worth more than £10 a year—dealt mainly with administrative matters. If, for example, you didn't keep your chimney properly swept and it caught fire, you could be fined a shilling and eight pence. The court of common pleas, on the other hand, was for those accused of assault, fraud, lewd and riotous behaviour, keeping disorderly houses, petty theft, and other minor criminal offences. Given the number of disbanded soldiers and ne'er-do-wells who'd accepted his Majesty's offer of free land and provisions and poured into already overcrowded Shelburne, there was no lack of petty crimes and criminals for the court to deal with.

The problem was that Shelburne had no permanent jail. So one of the court's first orders of business was to consider how to raise the £300[60] it would cost to build one. While the community waited for it to be built,[61] miscreants often ended up in a temporary holding pen on Commissary Island, which was guarded by disbanded soldiers, one of whom was designated to administer the lash, a common punishment for petty criminals of both sexes, often administered at public whipping posts, which officials were also still in the process of having built.

---

60. About $55,000 in 2007 U.S. dollars.

61. For some reason, the jail was never built, even though Stephen Blucke was asked to assemble a team of carpenters and labourers to construct it. Instead, the court eventually rented a house to serve as both courthouse and jail.

While all that was going on, Shelburne experienced yet another unwelcome first. Four men were arrested for robbing a vessel and wounding its captain. After a quick trial presided over by a Supreme Court Justice appointed by Parr, the men were convicted of robbery with violence and sentenced to hang. The day before the sentence was scheduled to be carried out, however, one of the condemned escaped. He was recaptured the next day, but his escape had thrown off the hanging schedule and all of the men were given a reprieve while the governor considered whether to go ahead. In the end, Parr pardoned two of them and ordered the others—identified in their burial records simply as "Shannon and Doyle, two criminals"—hanged.

The sentence was carried out at a gallows on Stanhope's Hill between King and Bulkley streets in what was slated to be a public square. Shelburne had witnessed its first execution.

The truth was that the mob's grievance wasn't with him. But David George was black and he was a preacher, and preaching had given too many of his fellow blacks the wrong idea about their place in the social pecking order, and that was more than enough for this group of white men, mostly disbanded soldiers, who had gathered outside his meeting house with their ship's tackle and a plan to destroy it.

The members of David's congregation had finally completed construction of their church in midsummer, no mean feat when there was so much other building to be done. The previous fall, they'd started by building a simple platform of poles above the ground on David's quarter-acre plot, something they could stand on during the winter's snow. There had been no roof over their heads. In the spring, they'd cut timbers for a building, made shingles, and contributed their few coppers to buy nails to hammer it all together. Though the church was now finally framed in, there was still no pulpit, no pews, and no floor. But there were parishioners. Plenty of them. Close to fifty, in fact, including a few whites like the Taylors and the Holmeses.

183

The controversy in the spring over baptizing Deborah Holmes, and the fact that David had chosen to set up his church in white Shelburne rather than black Birchtown—not to forget that he had allowed other homeless blacks to build shelters on his property—had inadvertently made him a target for the unfocused wrath of many poor whites, including former soldiers.

Like the blacks, the former soldiers had arrived in Shelburne with no money and few skills and had failed to get their promised grants of land, leaving them little choice but to hire themselves out to the well-to-do as labourers. But the ex-soldiers had quickly discovered that jobs that they felt should have been theirs were going to the poorest blacks, who were used to surviving on even less than them and willing to work for lower wages, often one-quarter of what the ex-soldiers asked.

One night, forty or fifty former soldiers hauled down all of the living quarters on David's property, including David's own. They'd almost burned down the church, too, but the mob's ringleader talked them out of that.

When David persisted in preaching despite the violence and threats, however, a number of whites stormed into the church during service one night and warned him what would happen if he continued. Nevertheless, he did. The next day, they returned with sticks and attacked him, driving him off into the swamp. That night, David slipped back into town for his wife and children and they escaped across the water to Birchtown.

Perhaps, David thought, there might be "a greater prospect of doing good" in Birchtown than there was in Shelburne. At least for now.

"Great Riot today." Benjamin Marston looked again at the words in his journal from July 26, 1783, just over a week and a lifetime ago. How could he have known then that the disturbances— caused because "the disbanded soldiers have risen against the free negroes to drive them out of town, because they labour cheaper than they"—would continue for more than a week, and may not be over yet? Or that, even before it was over, the riot would cost him his job, threaten his life, and end forever his dream of settling in Shelburne permanently.

He hadn't seen it coming. He'd spent most of June and half of July working at Point Carleton and Cape Negro, preparing a survey plan for the barracks the army wanted to build there. Back in Shelburne, he was preoccupied with the usual duties. Survey plans for fifteen 200-acre farms on Pell's Road, six more on the east side of the Jordan River. Most recently he'd sent a return of locations on the west side of the Roseway River to the surveyor general. Business as usual. And then . . . nothing usual at all.

The morning after the initial outbreak of violence—against the preacher David George—Marston learned he too was among those in the rioters' crosshairs,[62] probably because they blamed him when they didn't get the land they wanted. But there were by then few in Shelburne who were prepared to defend him. Benjamin had alienated many of the Loyalists with his too-even-handed measurements, his often acerbic tongue, and his always condescending view of them. Not to forget—although beyond his control—the slowness of the government in Halifax in dealing with land grants. And Marston's eagerness to protect the blacks' land in Birchtown. And the suspicion among many that others were getting land they didn't deserve, and were probably paying off Marston to obtain it.

By the afternoon of the second day of the riots, Benjamin, on the advice of his remaining friends, had escaped to the military barracks and been spirited out of Shelburne aboard a boat bound for Halifax. There, he not only heard reports of the continuing

---

62. Benjamin wasn't alone. Thomas and James Courtney, the former Boston tailors who'd managed to get two 500-acre grants on the Roseway River to set up a sawmill, were threatened with violence by the mob. During the disturbances, in fact, guards stood outside Thomas's house to protect it, and him.

chaos in Shelburne[63] but also received confirmation that the threats against him had been more than rumour. Angry rioters had pursued him as far as the barracks. "Had I been found, [I] should have had a bad time among a set of villainous scoundrels—by some subsequent advice, I find I should have been fairly hung."

What Benjamin Marston still didn't realize was that he was about to be hung figuratively for his supposed sins.

By the time Governor John Parr arrived in Shelburne on August 23 to "quiet the minds and apprehensions" of the locals, he'd already decided on how to do it. He announced that he was appointing a who's who of Shelburne's "gentlemen inhabitants" as a board of agents with power to assign all lands "to persons entitled thereto according to his majesty's instructions," and instructed them to investigate any disputes and report them to him.

For Parr, this was an about-face. He'd previously dismissed the idea of such a board as unconstitutional and suggested it "might prove a dangerous tendency." The riots weren't the only thing that had changed his mind. By the time he left for Shelburne, Parr had finally received instructions from Whitehall on how to go about the process of distributing land. Before then, it had been—at best—chaotic. Initially, the Shelburne settlers had used the lottery system as a kind of levelling device. Everyone who had been loyal to the Crown was to be treated equally. "A man who never possessed property of the value of £200 sterling [was considered] as capable of the virtue of loyalty as a man possessed of £10,000." That egalitarian spirit had

---

63. Though there are few first-hand accounts of what happened, Simeon Perkins, a merchant in Liverpool who had contact with many in Shelburne, noted in his diary on July 29 that he'd heard about "an extraordinary mob or riot [that] has happened at Shelburne. Some thousands of people assembled with clubs and drove the negroes out of town."

quickly crumbled as people discovered that some of their number—and some who came later—ended up with more and better land.

Now, finally, London had tried to codify who was entitled to how much land, and why. Parr's instructions covered everything from distributing land to setting up townships. Under the rules, every head of family, man or woman, was entitled to one hundred acres of land, plus an additional fifty for each member of the household, including servants, black or white. Disbanded soldiers were to be given land, the acreage based on their rank. Non-commissioned officers received two hundred acres, privates one hundred; and they were also entitled to the same additional grants for other household members as their civilian counter-parts. Those who'd served in the loyalist regiments did best: a field officer was entitled to one thousand acres, a captain seven hundred, and so on.

During his week in Shelburne and between rounds of wining and dining, Parr met with his new board of agents, whose twenty-two members comprised the majority of the town's most influen-tial residents, including Benjamin Marston's former tenant and soon-to-be Shelburne mayor Abraham Van Buskirk; original Port Roseway Associates Joshua Pell, John Miller, James McEwan, and newspaper publisher Alexander Robertson; and Isaac Wilkins, a one-time New York politician who had recently landed in Shelburne. Even David Thomson, the pleasantly ineffectual former shipwright who'd served as John Wentworth's deputy surveyor of forests for Shelburne, was a member of the board.

Benjamin Marston, however, was not. Governor Parr had decided that Marston was to blame for the riots in Shelburne. Even before leaving for Shelburne, Parr had written to Whitehall in response to its complaints about the high costs of surveying— "My attention to it shall be unremitted," he promised—and described Marston as "a shark trying to prey upon the helpless settlers." Though Marston had probably made a pest of himself, inundating the governor with unsolicited letters full of his usual commentary and advice, there was no evidence he had ever taken a bribe or done anything to enrich himself at the settlers' expense. Not that that mattered now. Governor Parr needed a scapegoat to deflect criticism from both London and the settlers in Shelburne. Marston would do.

In case that didn't work, Parr, upon his return to Halifax, immediately requested that the British navy station a frigate at Shelburne to support the four companies from the 17th regiment who'd already been dispatched to the town to maintain law and order in the immediate aftermath of the riot.

He was only 34, and in what had seemed like the pink of good health, with a new life ahead in a new land. But now he was dead.

Alexander Watson—former prisoner of war, former ward master at Vauxhall military hospital, and now would-be gentleman farmer—had left his wife, Margaret, and their two young boys behind in Shelburne that fall while he completed work on their house and prepared the land at their newly granted farm lot on the Clyde River twenty miles away. Alexander and Margaret had already decided to sell their town lot to help finance their plans.

But then neighbours discovered him dead in his bed in the house he was building. No one knew what had happened. Not that it mattered much anymore.

As Margaret prepared to bury a second husband before his time (unlike her first husband, Joseph, who'd succumbed to his war wounds, Alexander's death was far more troubling for being so inexplicable), she had to ask herself again: What now?

By the beginning of the first snows of the second winter, Shelburne's future was already in its past.[iii] The influx of newcomers had ended, and its population had begun its slow but inexorable decline. No one talked anymore about that inevitable day when Shelburne would replace Halifax as the capital. Now, the local establishment simply contented itself with pressing for representation in the legislature in Halifax as well as for roads to link their still-isolated community with Halifax and Annapolis.[64] Early in December 1784, Parr approved a bill to increase the number of counties, carving out a separate Shelburne County, and providing for both the county and the town to elect their own representatives. But there was no word yet on when the next election would take place.

If Shelburne residents were slowly coming to terms with the reality of their more modest place in Nova Scotia's even more limited universe, that's not to suggest they had totally given up their aspirations to be at least a worldly, sophisticated community within their own borders.

While many Loyalists had lost everything they'd owned in the revolution, others had arrived in Shelburne with substantial personal fortunes and proceeded to spend far too much on building and furnishing fine mansions for themselves. Some would later put the value of the fortunes "dissipated" in this way at £500,000, money that might have been spent more usefully in developing the local economy.

Which is not to suggest there were no businesses in Shelburne. But many of the settlers were in the business of catering to the whims of people spending fortunes they weren't replenishing. You could decorate your new Shelburne home from local shops supplying everything from fancy Scotch carpet (a popular pile-less, reversible woollen double cloth) to imported, brightly flowered calimanco curtains, fluted and plain four-post bedsteads, and brass knobs and locks for your doors—all of it shipped from Britain and all of it expensive.

The mansions had to be fine and finely decorated, for they were focal points of the town's social whirl, which hadn't stopped

---

64. In December 1785, the legislature did set aside £1500 to build a road from Halifax to Shelburne, though it would not be completed for many more years. The province also agreed to offer £200 as inducement to those willing to settle along the proposed road from Annapolis to Shelburne. Few took up the offer and the road was finally abandoned.

since that first ball among the stumps to celebrate the king's birthday in June 1783. Dinners, drinking, dancing, card games. There was now not a royal birthday or saint's day that did not merit a party of one sort or another. If not at a house, then at one of the more than two dozen licensed taverns in the town, or perhaps at one of the many more unlicensed premises whose proprietors had failed—or refused—to pay the five-shilling fee the court of sessions demanded. There were also all manner of fraternal orders—including six Masonic lodges—that staged social events at "Brother Steel's Tavern," also known as the Merchant's Coffee House on Water Street, or at McGragh's on Mason Lane. Even the Friendly Fire Club, an organization of more than two dozen leading citizens, ostensibly established to raise funds to buy fire trucks and "prevent or alleviate the calamity and distress to which we are particularly exposed by fire," also featured frequent convivial gatherings for dinner and discussion.

No wonder some dismissed the townsfolk as "dancing beggars." Or that others did their best to cater to them. Local clothing shops stocked their shelves, as one critic would later put it, "for a clientele in either New York or Philadelphia rather than for [one in] an isolated community in the wilds of Nova Scotia." The advertisements in the city's two—soon to be three—newspapers offered a cornucopia of the latest fashions from London. You could buy English riding habits "made in the newest fashion," camel-hair "superfine camblet cloaks, lined with green baize," not to forget silk and worsted hose. Some shops would even come to you: "Ladies and gentlemen dressed, at their own lodgings, on the shortest notice," boasted one retailer. A hairdresser on Mason Lane promised the best "double distilled lavender water" and Poland hair powder, while Oliver Bruff, the famous New York jeweller who'd re-established himself in a shop at the south end of town under a name similar to his former New York business—this shop was called the Sign of the Tea-pot, Tankard and Cross Swords instead of the Sign of Tea-pot, Tankard and Ear-ring—was still peddling a wide variety of precious jewellery and "trinkets for ladies."

But at the bottom of one of Bruff's ads was another sign of the quickly changing times in Shelburne: "He likewise has for sale a valuable 50-acre lot." Real estate had become a booming, if not always lucrative, business as many of the early settlers, who'd built so optimistically that first year, now tried to get what they could and get out while they could. "To be sold at public auction," read one typical advertisement in the *Royal American Gazette*, "an elegant two story house, a little above the cove, in Carleton Street, corner of Queen Street, 30 x 22 feet and a good kitchen in rear, 18 x 14 feet, with cellar under the whole; there is three fireplaces besides a large fireplace in the kitchen and a good oven."

The chief beneficiaries of all this were the town's newspapers. The *Royal American Gazette*, which the Robertson brothers had transplanted to Shelburne from New York after the evacuation, now had competition. Of a sort. After Alexander, the crippled older brother, died early in 1784 at age 42, his son had joined forces with two of the brothers' young apprentices, Thomas and James Swords, to launch a second newspaper, the *Port Roseway Gazetteer and the Shelburne Advertiser.* The new paper was housed in the same building at the corner of King and Water streets and used the same type, the same design, and mostly the same advertisements. While the *Royal American*, published on Mondays, featured "descriptive essays, letters of opinion, tales and verse" and the *Port Roseway*, published on Thursdays, featured more local and foreign news, they somehow managed to combine to provide a "means of spontaneous rebuttal in the petty but bitter dissensions which flourished in the new settlement of Shelburne."

Both were doing well enough that their success had attracted the attention of another former American newspaper proprietor. As 1784 drew to an end, James Humphreys was preparing to insert a notice in the *Royal American* announcing his plan to launch a third newspaper and expressing his "hopes for the encouragement of the public, not doubting but by constant attention to their interests and amusement, to render his paper worthy of their attention and approbation."

Before the revolution, Humphreys had published the *Pennsylvania Ledger* in Philadelphia. He'd abandoned that venture early on in the war, but returned to resume publication during the British occupation, during which one of his rivals was James Robertson. After British troops evacuated Philadelphia in the spring of 1778, Humphreys escaped to New York where he briefly traded his printer's ink for a merchant's apron. When the British left New York, Humphreys went first to London, where he assembled the materials he needed to restart his printing business, and then returned to America, settling this time in Shelburne. His *Nova Scotia Packet and General Advertiser* would be published on Wednesdays, between the editions of the Robertsons' two papers.

The question was, how long could a town in decline support three newspapers?

Benjamin Marston knew he should be looking ahead. After all, he had landed on his feet, thanks once again to the timely intervention of his guardian angel—cousin Edward Winslow, whose views of Governor Parr ("a man accustomed to dissipation and as competent to the performance of the task assigned as a spider would be to regulate the grand manufactories of Manchester") coincided nicely with Benjamin's own. But it was still difficult for him not to reflect on the end of his days in Shelburne with bitterness. Or to think of Governor Parr without resentment— or anger.

"To answer some purpose with his dear Shelburnites, [Parr] has been pleased to throw a great deal of blame on my conduct," Marston noted angrily in his journal on August 31, the same day Parr returned from Shelburne. A week later, Benjamin went to the governor's office with a memorial requesting a public inquiry into his conduct in order to clear his name. Parr's immediate response was to dismiss Benjamin's request with a sweeping accusation that "everybody accuses [Benjamin] of the most corrupt, partial conduct." But Parr did agree to meet with Benjamin at noon the next day.

When Benjamin arrived for his appointment, however, he was told the governor had left. He tried again a few days later but only got as far as the provincial secretary, Richard Bulkeley, who told him the governor had referred his request to the new board he'd established in Shelburne.

"Am I to look upon that as the governor's final answer?" Benjamin demanded.

"Yes," said Bulkeley.

Benjamin was incredulous. His petition had been referred back to the very people who might have been among those "raisers of the slanders against me. [It is] altogether an *ex parte* business," he wrote, "which I shall not submit to."

Not that it mattered. A few weeks later, he received the official notice that he'd been dismissed from his job. Parr had already written to London singling out Marston as the person responsible for the riots. And the board of agents paid little attention to his petition. They were too busy giving themselves and their friends the best land. Isaac Wilkins, who'd been appointed president of the board, somehow managed to obtain a fifty-acre lot inside Shelburne—ten times the size of a usual grant—and another five thousand acres on the nearby Jordan River.

Benjamin knew that some people in the town still supported him. Gideon White, back from his trip to London, had written a letter to Edward Winslow encouraging him to help find their mutual cousin a new position and lamenting the "injustice done to the reputation of our friend Ben Marston." Benjamin took comfort in that. "I have the satisfaction to know that the best people of that settlement are my friends," he confided to his journal, adding pointedly: "And what a rabble think of me is never my concern—though a governor may be among them."

In Shelburne, it was almost as if the riots had never happened. Only one person was charged in connection with the violence. A man named Ephraim Smith was accused of "disturbing the peace," not for rioting but for "propagating reports of intended opposition to the laws of the province and of cruel punishment determined to be inflicted by riotous persons to the terror of his majesty's subjects."

David George, who'd escaped during the riots, had spent the fall living in Birchtown and preaching from house to house, baptizing close to two dozen more for the cause. But he found that "my own colour persecuted me there," so in December he returned to Shelburne with his family. They discovered that his meeting house had been turned into a tavern in his absence. "The old Negro wanted to make a heaven of this place," the tavern-keeper boasted. "But I'll make a hell of it." Luckily, David was able to reclaim the meeting place. Unluckily, since his home had been destroyed in the riot, he and his family were forced to use the building as both house and church.

As for Benjamin, he'd finally found new employment. John Wentworth, the surveyor of the king's woods, with whom he'd spent those few weeks marking white pine in Shelburne's forests that spring, had appointed him deputy surveyor for the new province of New Brunswick. (That spring, over Governor Parr's objections, the British government had decided to split Nova Scotia in two, carving a new colony out of the northern section west of the Bay of Fundy and naming Guy Carleton's brother, Thomas, as its governor.) Perhaps, thought Benjamin, there was a god after all.

On December 7, 1784, Benjamin Marston closed the Nova Scotia chapter of his life and adventures, leaving its "troubled waters for a place of refuge," setting out on horseback—probably poorer than when he'd arrived—for Saint John and a new beginning.

"A PITIABLE PASSION"

Chapter 6.

A s Jesus passed by, He saw a man blind from his birth,"
began Freeborn Garrettson in a sonorous, compelling
voice. The text for the preacher's sermon was the parable of the blind beggar from the Gospel of John, Chapter Nine.
"And His disciples asked Him, saying, 'Rabbi, who sinned, this
man, or his parents, that he should be born blind?'"

Seated in the congregation of Moses Wilkinson's spare, chilly
chapel in Birchtown, Boston King listened, transfixed by the
charismatic white man at the pulpit. Boston was still grappling
with his demons. And with the meanings of the parables.

Early in January, he thought he'd understood. He'd been one
of sixteen former slaves now working as servants for Mrs.
Robinson, a wealthy white woman in Shelburne. All but Boston
and two others were saved, and they would get together every
morning and evening for prayer meetings. Boston would join
them, hoping he would finally learn their secret. One night in
early January, one of them read from the parable of the sower.
"A sower went out to sow his seed," the man read slowly,
retelling the story from the Gospel of Luke. "And, as he sowed,
some fell by the wayside. And it was trodden down, and the fowls
of the air devoured it. And some fell upon a rock; and as soon as

STEPHEN KIMBER

it was sprung up, it withered away, because it lacked moisture. And some fell among thorns; and the thorns sprang up with it, and choked it. And some fell on good ground, and sprang up, and bore fruit an hundredfold. And when Jesus had said these things, he cried, 'He that hath ears to hear, let him hear.'"

Boston had ears to hear, and he could feel the power of the words in his heart, but what did they really mean? He stood and asked the man to show him the meaning of it. And as he did, Boston realized he himself was one of those "stony-ground hearers." The seed of the Lord had been dropped on him many times now, but he'd failed to let it take root. "I was astonished that the Lord had borne with me so long . . . and resolved by the grace of God to set out afresh for the kingdom of heaven."

That journey, like all the ones before it, had been tortured with as many missteps as steps forward. Once, a few months ago, Boston thought he'd heard a voice speaking to him. "Peace be unto thee," it had said. "I stopped and looked round about to see if anyone was near to me. But finding myself alone, I went forward a little way, when the same words were again powerfully applied to my heart. . . . Yet in the afternoon, doubts and fears again arose in my mind." The next day, after Violet had left their house, Boston locked the door, got down on his knees, and resolved "not to rise from my knees until the Lord fully revealed his pardoning love. I continued in prayer about half an hour, when the Lord again spoke to my heart, 'Peace be unto thee.' All my doubts and fears vanished away: I saw, by faith, heaven opened to my view; and Christ and his holy angels rejoicing over me." His euphoria had lasted for about six weeks before "the enemy assaulted me again . . . and suggested that I was deceiving myself. Then the enemy pursued his advantage, and insulted me with his cruel upbraidings, insinuating, 'What is become of all your joy that you spoke of a few days ago? You see, there is nothing in it.'"

Boston wished he could be more like Violet. Not that his wife hadn't had her struggles, too. In fact, he'd never seen anyone "so

overwhelmed with anguish of spirit on account of backsliding.
. . . The trouble of her soul brought affliction upon her body,"
and she'd ended up sick in bed for a year and a half. Even after the
Lord had finally "brought her out of that horrible pit and set her
soul at perfect liberty," she'd faced other trials. "The joy and
happiness which she now experienced were too great to be concealed and she was enabled to testify on the goodness and living
kindness of the Lord with such liveliness and power that many
were convinced by her testimony, and sincerely sought the
Lord." But not everyone. "She was not a little opposed by some
of our black brethren," Boston would concede years later. But
what amazed him at the time was that Violet had endured those
trials "with the meekness and patience becoming a Christian."

She'd been helped in that by Mr. Freeborn Garrettson, the
preacher who was at Old Moses's pulpit tonight, the preacher
Boston had come to hear.

Garrettson, a white man from a wealthy Maryland family, had
been only 21 when his parents died and left him their entire
estate: a farm, a store, a blacksmith's shop, and twenty servants
and slaves. Two years later, in 1775, after he converted from his
family's traditional Church of England to become a Methodist,
he immediately freed all of his slaves—he called slavery a "crying sin"—and then set out on the road as an itinerant preacher,
determined to bring John Wesley's gospel to sinners all over
Maryland, Virginia, Delaware, and Pennsylvania. Even as the revolution raged around him, Garrettson did his best to maintain
his pacifist neutrality. "It's contrary to my mind and grievous to
my conscience," he told doubting patriots, "to have any hand in
shedding human blood." When the war ended, Wesley dispatched
him to the southern United States where he travelled more than
1200 miles in six weeks to let preachers there know about a conference Wesley had planned for Baltimore in December 1784.

At that Christmas conference, which would later become
famous as the first general conference of the fledgling Methodist
Episcopal Church of the United States, Garrettson had listened

to a heartfelt appeal from William Black, a 24-year-old Methodist evangelist from Nova Scotia. Black, who'd conducted the first church service in Shelburne in June 1783, pleaded with the assembled ministers to dispatch missionaries to help him deal with the flood of Loyalists now filling the province. Garrettson and another preacher, James Oliver Cromwell, agreed to heed his call, and set off for Nova Scotia two months later.

Though Cromwell based himself in Shelburne and Garrettson, who'd set up office in Halifax, only visited occasionally during his frequent proselytizing journeys around the province, it was Garrettson whose influence was greatest—at least for Boston and his wife. Garrettson, whose arched eyebrows and pursed lips lent him a thoughtful, almost quizzical air, had given Violet the courage she needed to "hold fast her confidence and cleave to the Lord with her whole heart," and Boston hoped he could do the same for him.

Garrettson had arrived in Shelburne in early August 1785 to help out Cromwell, whose health was frail. At the time, the local Methodist Society consisted of just sixteen members, whites as well as blacks. Garrettson spent six exhausting weeks in the community during the summer and fall, preaching every morning in Shelburne and then walking to Birchtown where he would hold services at noon before returning to Shelburne for evening services. He quickly arranged to have his adherents build a preaching house in Shelburne to accommodate a hundred whites and a smaller chapel at the north end of Birchtown for the blacks.

Which was where Boston King was now, listening as carefully as he could to the preacher's words, searching the parable of the blind man for the sign he was seeking. In Garrettson's retelling of the story, Jesus explained to his disciples that neither the blind man nor his parents had sinned, he was simply blind, Jesus said, so that "the works of God should be made manifest in him." With that, Jesus had spit on the ground, made a clay of the spittle, covered the blind man's eyes with the mixture, and instructed him to "Go, wash in the pool of Siloam." When he did, the man was able to see. None of his neighbours could understand how this had happened, so they brought him to the Pharisees, who couldn't figure it out either. They only knew that Jesus was a false prophet. "We know that this man is a sinner," they told the blind man.

The blind man, Garrettson told the worshippers, answered the Pharisees simply: "Whether he is a sinner, I know not. One thing I know: that, whereas I was blind, now I see."

Now I see . . . Boston played with the words in his head. It was as if the Lord, through Freeborn Garrettson, was speaking directly to him: "The words were so suitable to my experience." *He saw.* There were no more doubts, only plans. Boston King could see now, and he would help others to do the same. He would "visit my poor ungodly neighbours and exhort them to hear the Lord, and seek Him while He might be found."

William Booth had decided not to accompany his boss, General John Campbell, this morning.ᶦ While the general reviewed the troops of the 17th regiment at the barracks opposite the town of Shelburne, Booth inspected the state of the officers' and soldiers' quarters and settled up with the contractors hired to repair them. Booth was eager to wrap up his business here as quickly as possible in case the general decided to set sail for Halifax the following day. Booth was more than ready to return to Halifax. Who would have guessed it could seem so appealing? Certainly not Booth, who still sometimes wondered how he'd ended up there in the first place.

Could it have had something to do with that unfortunate incident in Gibraltar at the beginning of 1782? Possibly. It was the tail end of the American war and the Spanish, with the connivance of the French, had been trying to take advantage of Britain's preoccupation with events in North America to wrest control of Gibraltar, a tiny British peninsula at the southern edge of their country. For most of the three years of what became known as the Great Siege, William Booth, "much esteemed by everyone," had served with distinction as a first lieutenant in the British Corps of Royal Engineers in Gibraltar.

Reporting directly to the chief engineer, he had been in charge of the men responsible for the dangerous job of discovering and dismantling enemy land mines before they could do their worst to the British forces. But because he was also an accomplished artist and draftsman, General Elliott often ordered him to venture into hostile territory "to take views of the country" as well.

Booth had spent what he would later describe as far too much time "lying so long exposed to heat and rains, [which] brought on a violent fever so as to deprive me of my senses." Diagnosed "insane," he was dispatched to a field hospital where his behaviour became so "outrageous [he was] fastened in his bed," and he was eventually invalided back to Britain. "I will venture to affirm," he would later write cryptically, "that I went through more fatigue of the service during the blockade and siege . . . than any other officer in the place."

Two years later, the Corps dispatched Booth—supposedly recovered, newly married, and wanting nothing more than to be permitted to remain in London where his wife's family were prominent merchants and traders—across the Atlantic to colonial, parochial Halifax. He'd barely begun to find his way around the small, dowdy city when his immediate supervisor, Captain John Cambel, decamped, leaving Booth both to handle his own duties and to assume Cambel's role as the Corps' commander for Nova Scotia. That is how he'd ended up accompanying John Campbell, the general in charge of British forces in what was left of British North America, on this inspection foray through the even wilder colonial wilds of Nova Scotia in the summer of 1785.

When the *Maria* had departed Halifax more than a month ago, the general's intention had been to sail directly to Shelburne, but unfavourable winds had forced them to head in the opposite direction. So they'd stopped first at Charlottetown, where they were lavishly entertained by the governor and where

Booth observed that the soil was fertile and the countryside "remarkably level." Next, they'd visited Cape Breton and an encampment of huts belonging to six companies of the 33rd regiment, which the new governor assured them over dinner would soon be the site of a city called Sydney. Finally, they'd sailed south along the coast of Nova Scotia past Halifax.

Their next stop had been Lunenburg, where they spent a day-and-a-half being entertained by the local customs collector and his wife. The Dutch couple had regaled them with stories, told in heavily accented English that Booth had tried to capture in his diary, about how the man—with gun and sword and grit—had gallantly fought off marauding American privateers who'd attacked their home during the war. The woman, who'd apparently lived in the American colonies before coming to Lunenburg, had known one of the attackers. "Von vas amazingly s'dout and had been von of de servants," Booth wrote, mimicking her voice, "and zed dat he had vaited upon me often but dat I should now vait on him, and did dam and zwear for me to bring dem budding and every ting dat I had in de house." Though the couple's account of the man's courage had been "wonderful and I believe most of us were inclined to credit what [they] had asserted," Booth wrote, other locals soon disabused them of that idea, claiming that the man had actually "hid himself somewhere up the country and in the woods . . . and that he was not seen for three days."

From Lunenburg, they'd made the final, half-day's journey to Shelburne. Sailing past the military base at Point Carleton at the entrance to the harbour at seven knots per hour, Booth would recall, they were greeted with such a loud cannon salute "that the sudden concussion becalmed us."

There wasn't much about Shelburne to put the wind of excitement in Booth's sails. His most striking memory of the city during this visit, in fact, was of the state of the military weaponry in the stores, which included battalion guns, brass and iron howitzers, almost all of it left over from the evacuation of New York nearly two years earlier.

As had happened elsewhere, the principal residents of the town soon showed up to pay their respects to the general, and invite Booth and his fellow officers to join them for dinner. There, Booth met George Drummond, a local doctor and an agreeable sort whose company Booth might have enjoyed if he wasn't so anxious to return to Halifax and his lovely Hannah. And, of course, to begin preparing his letter to the Duke of Richmond, the colonel of the Corps, requesting leave to return to London and a more civilized society.

With luck, this visit to Shelburne would be his first—and last.

The first official handbills announcing a new bylaw "forbidding Negro Dances and Negro Frolicks in this town" began appearing on tree trunks and in public places in Shelburne in the spring of 1785.[ii] Signed by the local magistrates, it warned that blacks caught engaging in "riotous behaviour" could be sentenced to terms in the house of correction, or worse. And they often were.

Although Shelburne's white residents happily continued their own convivial carousing until all hours and at the slightest provocation—no royal birthday was permitted to go uncelebrated—they were not nearly so understanding when it came to partying by their town's black citizens, freed or otherwise. They were especially concerned about what James Cox, a local merchant, described as "bad houses," where their servants might congregate to dance, drink, gamble, socialize, and provide "encouragement to other black people assembling there," as Cox ominously if obliquely described it. There were more than a few such bad houses. The magistrates reprimanded Hysem Leeds and his wife, Silvia Howell, for running a "disorderly house" that was described as "a noisy disturbance to their neighbours." Some of the "houses" were no more than makeshift huts like the one on Charlotte Lane where blacks huddled together out of the elements, but the constables ordered those vacated too.

The white community's fear of just where such frolics might lead—the fear, in fact, of their black neighbours—was perhaps understandable. Most of Shelburne's white residents were no more accustomed to the idea of blacks as anything other than slaves than the blacks themselves were used to their freedom. And for all the lofty talk of freedom during the revolution, the everyday life of most freed blacks in Shelburne remained anything but free—or equal.

Consider what happened in the courts. While whites convicted of petty crimes were most often let off with a fine, blacks were usually sentenced to jail, or hard labour, or the lash—often all three. For the crime of running away from the workhouse, for example, John Windsor was sentenced to the house of correction where he was not only put to hard labour for two months—with a log chained to his leg—but also whipped ten lashes on his bare back each Monday morning for the duration of his jail term.

Public punishments were common. A black woman named Dianna, who'd been convicted on two counts of theft under twelve pence, was sentenced to two hundred lashes "at the Cart's Tail"[65] on a Saturday at noon for the first offence and then another 150 lashes in the same manner on the following Saturday for the second. A thief named Light Horse Jack was sentenced to one hundred lashes—twenty to be administered in front of the jail and twenty each at the corners of Water and King, St. John's, Ann, and George streets.

The truth is that the good burghers of Shelburne would have been just as happy if all those blacks who weren't needed—as slaves, servants, and day labourers—would simply leave. The magistrates did their best to encourage them to do exactly that. Patty Brown, who was convicted of stealing a calico gown to wear to church on Sunday, was sentenced to ten lashes on her bare back with a cat-o'-nine-tails at the public whipping post on Stanhope Hill, and then told to get out of town immediately.

---

65. A common punishment for petty crimes was for the convicted to be tied to the back of a cart and whipped while the cart was paraded through the streets.

After they were whipped for vagrancy, Pompey Donaldson and Thomas Gould were ordered "to go to Birchtown and not be seen in Shelburne."

Though such orders helped solidify Birchtown's growing reputation as the province's only safe haven for blacks—Birchtown residents sheltered many runaway slaves whose masters were trying to reclaim them—it didn't, in the end, prevent the adventurous or the foolhardy from venturing into Shelburne and upsetting the peace and tranquility of the town's whites. A year after those first handbills began appearing, in fact, the magistrates were forced to introduce an even tougher bylaw to try to end the frolicking.

Perhaps not surprisingly, it didn't succeed either.

All things considered, Benjamin Marston thought, the session had not gone badly.[iii] He had prepared for it, of course, carefully assembling all of the necessary documents to prove his case: the 1760 deed of conveyance from Rachel Majery showing that he actually owned his house and property in Marblehead; an inventory of all the furniture he'd been forced to abandon that night twenty-one years ago when he'd escaped from the mob; the May 1782 letter from his nephew informing him that the rebels had sold his property but there was little to show for it; even a copy of his father-in-law's 1744 will that served as the basis for Benjamin's claim to his late wife's interest in one-fifth of a sixty-five-acre farm, along with all its "buildings, stock, utensils etc."

Benjamin had begun his pitch to Commissioner Pemberton with what had become "the indispensable preamble" for all claims seekers, a lofty declaration of his unswerving, unshakeable allegiance to the glorious mother country. Then he'd laid out in detail the price he'd paid for that loyalty. He'd even brought along two character witnesses—Colonel Peter Frye, a Massachusetts magistrate, member of the legislature, and registrar of probate from those halcyon days before the revolution, and Reverend Joshua Wingate Weeks, the former Episcopal rector at St. Michael's in

Marblehead who, like Benjamin, had paid a prisoner's price for his loyalty—to vouch not only for his loyalty but also for his losses.

Those losses were the issue today in Halifax. Three years earlier, in July 1783, the British Parliament had passed the Compensation Act in an attempt to aid former American colonists who'd lost homes, furniture, servants, land, livelihoods, businesses, appointments, and sundry simply because they'd supported the British side in the war. Initially—and overly optimistically—the government had set a deadline of March 25, 1784, for filing claims. But the five claims commissioners didn't even begin to hold hearings until October 1783, and those were all held in Lincoln's Inn Fields, which was conveniently the centre of the legal profession in London but inconveniently a world away from where most of the Loyalists lived. Two years later, Parliament had been forced to renew the legislation, extending the deadline for submissions and dispatching commissioners to North America to hear from the thousands of Loyalists who'd stayed in the United States or settled in the remaining British colonies.[66]

Jeremy Pemberton, the grandson of a British lord chief justice who'd himself become the youngest chief justice of the Supreme Court at 33, was one of two commissioners assigned to British North America. Though he and Colonel Thomas Dundas held hearings in Saint John as well as Shelburne, Montreal, and Québec, Marston chose to appear before Pemberton in Halifax, largely because business had brought him back to the city anyway.

Since his "escape" from Halifax a year and a half earlier—"I never knew that saying farewell can be so pleasant, but it is," he'd written in his diary at the time—Ben's life and career had followed its usual winding path.

---

66. By 1789, when the commission finally completed its Canadian work, it had heard 1401 claims for compensation.

Socially, Saint John—though physically still a "rude little town of frame houses and log cabins scattered amid stumps"—had proved much more to his taste than either Halifax or, certainly, Shelburne. That was largely because, unlike Shelburne, most of Saint John's leading citizens had "numbered among the gentry of the old thirteen colonies."

Marston shared lodgings with the new province's young socialite solicitor general. Ward Chipman—Chippy, as he was known to his friends—had been born in Marblehead and, like Benjamin, was a Harvard grad. He'd spent most of the war in New York as Edward Winslow's deputy muster master and—like Benjamin again—owed his current position to Winslow's support. The two men, along with a young army officer named Harris Hailes, lived in a party house where they often entertained the cream of New Brunswick society. The house was known among lesser locals, somewhat disparagingly, as Felicity Hall.

"Last Wednesday," Marston gushed in one letter to his mentor Winslow, "we 'exhibited' at the Hall under the auspices of General Chippy." The event, declared the man who'd so recently been so disdainful of the excesses of his fellow Shelburnites, had been "a monstrous great ball and fine supper [with] about 36 gentlemen and ladies, such as governors, secretaries, chief justices, chancellors and such kind of people with their wives and daughters. We ate, drank, danced and played cards till about four o'clock in the morning."

When he wasn't entertaining others, he was being entertained. On the occasion of the queen's birthday, for example, Benjamin was a guest at a ball and supper at the Exchange Coffee House hosted by Governor Thomas Carleton and "his handsome and vivacious wife." The thirty to forty female guests "were of the best families only [and] the business was as well conducted as such an entertainment could be."

The problem was that Benjamin's income was no match for his way of life. Unfortunately, there were no fixed salary or benefits attached to his job as Wentworth's deputy surveyor of the woods. Instead, he was supposed to collect fees from each person to whom he issued a grant for Crown-reserved land. To make matters worse, it turned out that Benjamin didn't get along with Wentworth. In most disputes over which lands should be reserved for the Crown, Benjamin sided with his new friend Governor Carleton. Wentworth, for his part, claimed Marston "either negligently or deliberately failed to exert his authority" to preserve the best pine forests for the navy.

So, after just six months in that position, Benjamin quit and moved to Miramichi where he'd landed yet another job for which he was eminently unqualified. With another nudge from his cousin Winslow, Benjamin had been appointed sheriff of Northumberland County, the largest of New Brunswick's eight counties. To stretch his still-too-small salary, Benjamin also took on the task of serving as the local surrogate, probating wills and settling estates, and agreed to act once again as deputy surveyor for the district.

As a place to live, Miramichi turned out to be more similar to Shelburne than Saint John. "A majority of the people are illiterate and ignorant and much given to drunkenness," Marston complained in his diary. The locals were no more pleased with him, some even signing a petition to Saint John complaining about the quality of Marston's survey work. His boss agreed, assigning one important survey to another, "better" deputy surveyor after Benjamin failed to complete his assignment.

Benjamin may have been distracted by his desire to re-establish himself as a businessman. Before he left for Miramichi, he'd talked with Winslow about setting up a trading company to supplement his income. When that failed to materialize, he joined forces with a local Swiss settler named Mark Delesderniers in a new company to buy all manner of goods from Halifax merchants—from guns to crucifixes, gold belt buckles to cheap wine (one shipment of wine was so awful, he wrote, that "a Halifax pig would not have drunk [it]")—and trade them to the local Indians for furs and fish.

Later, the two men joined forces in a more ambitious venture, a proposal to build a sawmill to transform the area's pine forests, which Wentworth himself had described as "the best mast timber in British North America," into masts for the British navy. In February, Marston wrote Governor Carleton, asking for a grant of five hundred acres near the best pine forest on which to build their sawmill. After Carleton gave his government's approval, Marston resigned as sheriff—"being engaged in a plan of business which will wholly engage my time and attention," he wrote in March, "I humbly beg the favour of your Excellency and your Honours to permit me to resign that office"—and left immediately for Halifax. There, he bought some of the materials needed to construct the mill, lobbied Winslow to again use his influence—this time to have the government sign a contract to buy its masts from them—and, finally, organized his own pitch to the British government for compensation for all he'd lost.

His interest in compensation had been sparked by a visit earlier that winter to Edward Winslow's widowed mother, Hannah, in Portland Point near Saint John. Her husband had died soon after the family's arrival in Halifax in 1783, and the family had been "in real distress from the almost certainty of their not recovering anything" from their American estate because they lacked the necessary documentation to make a claim. Benjamin—who had become smitten with Penelope, one of Edward's sisters, during his visit—announced that he would travel to Boston to track down the required paperwork. "To be . . . only a mere instrument in procuring so essential a good will afford a man a very comfortable reflection," Benjamin noted grandly in his journal. But he was as good as his word. Within two weeks of arriving in Boston, he'd tracked down the information Hannah Winslow and her daughters needed to file their claims.[67] And had

---

67. Ironically, the Winslows fared much better with the claims commissioners than Marston himself did. Hannah, who'd asked for £1,725 in compensation, was

begun to think more about his own losses. And what compensation might mean for his future.

The case Benjamin laid before Pemberton on that early May morning was a compelling one. "Case of Benjn. Marsten of Marblehead, Massachusetts," Pemberton's notes began (with a misspelling of Benjamin's surname). "Native of America . . . Resided at Marblehead when Troubles began . . . Declared his sentiments freely and publicly in favour of Brit. Govert . . . Went as soon as he could in an open Boat, which was accompanied with considerable Hazard . . . Continued with the Brit . . ." For his losses, which included his home and store in Marblehead, his library and furniture, his interest in his late wife's farm and other properties, as well as three slaves, Benjamin Marston claimed more than £450 and an additional £25 in rent since the fall of 1775.

Though the claims commissioners had a reputation for asking probing questions and often dismissing supplicants out of hand because of their slowness in filing claims, Pemberton seemed satisfied with Marston's well-documented submission. He even informed Benjamin that he would receive a still-to-be-determined amount in compensation and suggested he appoint an agent in London with power of attorney to collect his money for him.

A new business . . . Compensation for his losses . . . Things, it seemed, were finally looking up for Benjamin.

If Benjamin Marston had been looking for a second, less optimistic opinion about his future prospects, he certainly could have done worse than to talk to Mary Swords, then on her way across the Atlantic to Shelburne from London. She would have told him a thing or two about the loyalist claims commissioners and their arbitrary, niggardly ways.

---

awarded £1100 while each of her daughters received a pension of £33 a year for their losses.

When her teenaged sons had joined their printing masters, the Robertson brothers, in the loyalist exodus to Shelburne in spring of 1783, the feisty Mary had decided to stay behind in New York to press her claim with British army officials for compensation for supplies she'd provided to Burgoyne's soldiers and the damage they'd done to her family's farm during the Battle of Saratoga. After they turned her down—the army had a policy of not paying for damages its soldiers had inflicted during battle— she set sail for London with her two youngest daughters to state her case for compensation directly to the new loyalist claims commission. "I can truly say I don't believe there is one person come from the continent of America that had been a greater sufferer than myself," she would tell the commissioners.

While that was certainly hyperbole, there was no question her family had suffered. She blamed her husband's too-early death in 1779 on the eight months he'd spent in an Albany prison at the not-so-tender mercies of the Americans for refusing to command a rebel militia. His death had left her, she was quick to point out, with six young children to raise on her own. During his imprisonment, the family farm had been overrun by rebels, vandalized by neighbours, used as an operations base by Burgoyne's British soldiers, and finally claimed by the Americans as a spoil of war. After the family was forced to relocate to New Jersey, her new home was also ransacked by marauding rebel soldiers, forcing her to seek shelter with a neighbour and then retreat to New York. Making her misery even deeper, she told the commissioners, she had also lost her oldest son to the conflict. Richard Swords—who looked like his father and was his mother's hope for the future—had died of wounds he suffered fighting for the British at the Battle of Stoney Point in 1781. And, of course, she had not seen her youngest two sons since they had been forced to relocate to Shelburne after the war.

In London, she joined hundreds of other displaced Loyalists, all wanting to plead their cases in person. Mary told the commissioners she wanted compensation for the two-thousand-acre farm, oxen, cattle, and forage she'd lost, plus the cost of supplies taken by Burgoyne's troops, the value of the timber stolen from them by the rebels, and, oh yes, the other many and various sufferings she'd endured as the result of her loyalty to the British Crown.

As with Benjamin Marston's case, the commissioners seemed more than satisfied with her presentation, and with the documents she presented to support her argument that "her husband had a good house."

"No further attendance required," they ruled. But in the end, the commissioners had awarded her just £40 in pension for her losses. Not nearly enough.

Mary had spent the next several years in London trying, unsuccessfully, to change their minds. When she wasn't submitting petitions on her own behalf, she was preparing depositions in support of other claimants, including Simeon Covill, who'd shared a cell with her husband in Albany, and neighbours like Joseph Jessup and Robert Auchmuty, both of whom had also come to London seeking compensation.

Officials told her that her own claim had insufficient official documentation. So, in May of 1786, Mary decided to travel to Shelburne, partly to reunite with her sons, Thomas and James, but also to begin the process of tracking down people who might strengthen her claim. People like Ezekial Ensign, a former neighbour in Saratoga. While her husband was in jail, Thomas Swords had sent Ensign a letter, asking him to safeguard a number of hides Thomas had left in the tanning pit behind his home. Ensign had gone to look, but the hides had already vanished. Stolen. Once Mary found Ensign and got a letter from him testifying to what he remembered . . . and maybe another from Mrs. Brown, the woman who'd taken in Mary and the children after their home in New Jersey was raided by the Americans . . . and perhaps . . .

For the moment, she would settle in Shelburne and rebuild her strength and energy for the battles still to come. In the meantime, she could at least take some comfort in the success of her two remaining sons, who'd become successful publishers in their own right in their new hometown.

Unfortunately, Mary Swords had picked a bad time to visit. Though it was true that they and one of the Robertson sons had launched their own newspaper, the *Port Roseway Gazetteer and the Shelburne Advertiser*, its future was in doubt. In part, its problems reflected the reality that the newspaper business depended on advertising revenue, and while there were still three papers in Shelburne, there were fewer and fewer businesses left to advertise in them, not to mention fewer and fewer readers left to subscribe to them.

But the more immediate threat to the paper was more direct. James Robertson, with whom Thomas and James had come to Shelburne and to whom they'd initially been apprenticed, printed their newspaper as well as his own. Soon after arriving in Shelburne, Robertson had tried to expand his business ventures, going into partnership with William Rigby to open a store on King Street near the printing office. There, he offered everything from Irish linens to ketchup and pickles, all "on the most reasonable terms." The store's immediate success had spawned a second at Milby's Wharf on Dock Street where the items for sale included tea, sugar, powder and shot, and "old high proof rum in excellent flavour." But Robertson's businesses had been among the first victims of Shelburne's economic collapse. The sheriff seized his property to cover his debts. To complicate the situation, he had also been disappointed by the decision on his compensation claim. Like Mary Swords, he had gone to London to present his and his brother's claim for £650; the commissioners eventually awarded him just £200.

As a result, he was now considering an offer from the lieutenant-governor of St. John's Island, Edmund Fanning, to bring his printing press to Charlottetown to print that government's laws, some of which had already been lost to posterity because of the scarcity of manuscript copies. Fanning had promised to recommend Robertson's appointment as King's Printer, with a salary that would allow him to continue publishing his newspaper in a new—and economically more promising—community.

The problem for the Swords brothers, of course, was that they'd no longer have a printing press on which to publish their own newspaper. What would become of their paper then?

Not everyone was leaving Shelburne.[iv] And some who'd left had come back.

Like Margaret Watson. Soon after her husband Alexander's sudden death on their farm on the Clyde River, Margaret had sold it and sailed, with their two sons, to the Bahamas "for the purpose of keeping a boarding house there." Within the year, however, she was back in Shelburne with an inclination to do the same in a house she acquired at the corner of King and Harriet streets. Running an inn for travellers and boarders in Shelburne was obviously a difficult business. She is listed on the town's 1786–87 tax roles as a "poor" widow.

Stephen Skinner was neither a widower nor poor but he, like Margaret Watson, had decided to try to make a go of life in Shelburne even after the sun appeared to have set on its initial promise. Skinner, in fact, cut an impressive figure; he was the kind of entrepreneurial civic leader whose presence might have made a difference in Shelburne's formative days. A member of one of New Jersey's most well-respected colonial families, his father, William, a MacGregor who'd been active in the Stuart cause in Scotland and had changed his name to Skinner after arriving in America, had been the first Anglican minister in Perth Amboy, the capital of East Jersey. Stephen and his brother Cortland were both powerful colonial-era politicians: Cortland serving as attorney general, Stephen as treasurer.

Stephen was best known for his role in the Great East Jersey Treasury Robbery, a political tempest in a teapot that had helped separate that colony's rebels from its Loyalists in the increasingly bitter lead-up to the revolution. The strange and twisted case had its beginnings in the early morning of July 22, 1768, when someone had broken into Skinner's house and stole £6000 belonging to the colony of New Jersey.

The initial investigation into the robbery cleared Skinner of any responsibility for the missing funds. But then two years later, in the fall of 1770, some Whig members of the Assembly decided to reopen the investigation, most likely as a way to embarrass William Franklin, the colony's ultra-royalist governor and a Skinner supporter. This second investigation found Skinner, as treasurer, responsible "for want of that security and care that was necessary to keep [the money] in safety," and demanded that he repay the missing funds. Skinner refused, and the governor supported him.

After two more years of wrangling, the legislature informed Franklin that it wouldn't approve his next annual support bill unless he fired his treasurer. In other words, if Skinner kept his job, no one in government would get paid. Still, Franklin refused to budge. Which was when Skinner decided he had no choice but to resign. Although his decision resolved the immediate issue, the Great East Jersey Treasury Robbery did have long-term consequences for everyone involved. Neither Franklin nor the members of the assembly ever trusted one another again. And Skinner had taken the first baby step on his own long road into exile.

Two years later, following the Declaration of Independence, that step became a giant leap when Skinner joined forces with his brother to form the New Jersey Volunteers, a vaunted loyalist regiment that became known as Skinner's Greens. Stephen served as a major in one of its battalions, but was taken prisoner soon after the revolution began and spent three months in prison in Trenton before the rebels finally allowed him to return to his wife and ten children. A year later, when the British retreated to New York, Stephen followed. By the time the fighting ended, he and his brother had already decamped for London to press their claims for compensation for the loss of their extensive land holdings (Stephen claimed at least five houses and more than twelve thousand acres of farmland, plus cattle and crops).

Three years later—after a gruelling seven-month passage from London, during which his vessel was blown so far off course it had to make a stop in the West Indies, where a cargo of butter Skinner had hoped to peddle spoiled in the heat—Stephen Skinner arrived in his chosen new home of Shelburne, Nova Scotia. He very quickly established himself as an entrepreneur, setting up a paint and hardware store on King Street, buying a schooner to export codfish, speculating in real estate and dabbling in local politics. By July 1786, he was prominent enough that Governor Parr appointed him, along with Joseph Durfee and a few other local worthies, to oversee construction of a lighthouse on the southern tip of McNutts Island. He was the kind of newcomer Shelburne needed far more of.

Soon after he arrived, Skinner also and not coincidentally renewed acquaintances with a few friendly faces from his New Jersey days, including Stephen Blucke, the unofficial mayor of Birchtown whom Skinner had known from the time when Skinner's Greens occasionally teamed up with Colonel Tye's Black Pioneers to stage raids on rebel-held New Jersey.

Like Skinner, Blucke was an entrepreneur, a dealmaker. They would make some deals together.

"I was very sorry to hear about the man from England who has recently been here preaching among you," Freeborn Garrettson began his sermon.[v] "I am here to tell you that this man was not sent by Mr. Wesley's Society, that he was, in truth, sent by Satan."

Freeborn Garrettson knew he hadn't spent enough time of late tending to his Birchtown flock. There'd been so much else to do, so many souls in so many far-flung parts of this vast province, all wanting, needing to hear him preach. But his absence, he realized now, had created an opening for that "negro man," the one who claimed he'd been sent out by Lady Huntingdon to save the souls of his fellow blacks. Garrettson believed he had, in fact, been dispatched by the devil—by whom the Huntingdon woman was almost certainly employed—in order to sow the seeds of confusion "among these poor creatures." Before that man had arrived, Garrettson had written to his boss, John Wesley, "there was a glorious work going on. Now . . ."

That "negro man" was John Marrant, the brother of a black loyalist settler in Birchtown. John had been living in London when his brother wrote him a letter describing the religious excitement he'd seen among his neighbours but also lamenting the lack of what he considered good Christian leaders to channel that excitement into salvation. So John Marrant had come to Birchtown, arriving in December 1785, just four months after Garrettson's first visit.

By then, Marrant, 30, had become an ordained minister and the subject of a bestselling book, *A Narrative of the Lord's Wonderful Dealings with John Marrant, a Black (Now Going to Preach the Gospel in Nova Scotia)*, which had been adapted from the sermon he'd given during his ordination that spring at the Countess Selina of Huntingdon's chapel in Bath.

Born a free black in New York, Marrant had first seen the light as a 15-year-old tradesman and musician living in Charles Town. On a whim, he'd attended one of famous Methodist preacher George Whitefield's revival meetings. Marrant had been mesmerized as Whitefield froze him with a look and declared, "Prepare to meet thy God, O Israel!" Marrant recounted later that he was "struck near dead by the Spirit," and Whitefield announced to the crowd: "Jesus Christ has got thee at last."

Marrant's initial attempts to proselytize among his fellow blacks were short-lived. At the beginning of the revolution, a British press gang scooped him from Charles Town's streets and forced him into service in the Royal Navy. Wounded in a battle with a Dutch warship—he ended up covered "with the blood and brains" of his gunnery partner who'd been killed in action—Marrant became a refugee on the streets of London.

There, he says, he felt his own "call to the ministry clearer and clearer."

He contacted the Countess of Huntingdon, a wealthy widow (she was known to her detractors as Lady Bountiful) who was one of the key figures in what was then a flourishing English religious revival. She was also, and not coincidentally, a key rival to John Wesley, on whose behalf Freeborn Garrettson had journeyed to Nova Scotia.

The countess and Wesley had once been allies, but eventually split over fine points of religious doctrine, most particularly the notion of predestination. Lady Huntingdon believed that, "although the whole world is . . . guilty before God, it hath pleased him to pre-destine some into everlasting life." She and her followers, of course, were among the select. Wesley, on the other hand, opposed the notion of predestination, arguing that it got in the way of encouraging "holy living" among people who might not be predestined for life everlasting.

The countess eventually formed the Countess of Huntingdon's Connexion, a Calvinist missionary offshoot, to take her message to the masses. George Whitefield, who had saved John Marrant's soul in Charles Town, was her personal chaplain. Which may explain why Marrant, after receiving the letter from his brother, sought out Huntingdon, who arranged for his ordination and encouraged him to accept that "Providence" was calling him to go to Nova Scotia to minister to his people there.

Marrant's initial impression of Shelburne was that it was an "uncultivated place" filled with people who "all seemed to be wild. . . . I was obliged to conclude with Abraham, and said, 'Sure the fear of God is not in this place.'" He'd already decided he'd stay no longer than a week when—Providence again—he happened to meet some old friends from America in a Shelburne coffee house. They "talked about old times, which made us shed many tears." They took him to Birchtown where he discovered there was a black community, and that "God had some people in this place." The next day he returned to Shelburne, just long enough to gather up his belongings at the inn. By the next morning, Sunday, December 20, 1785, John Marrant had officially begun his mission.

His first sermon in the Birchtown chapel that had, until now, been Blind Man Wilkinson's private preserve, was from Acts 3: "For Moses truly said unto the fathers, a prophet shall the Lord your God raise up unto you of your brethren." John Marrant had come to be that prophet for them. "Him shall ye hear in all things, whatsoever he shall say unto you." But salvation, he told them, required faith, not only in God but also in the prophet. "Every soul, which will not hear that prophet, shall be destroyed from among the people."

Marrant's speech had its desired impact. Ten members of his audience, he would note later, "were pricked to the heart, and cried out . . . 'What shall we do to be saved?'"

By that afternoon, the crowd was larger, and it included whites and Indians as well as blacks. That night, he told them— quoting John 5—that "the hour is coming . . . they that have done good, unto the resurrection of life; and they that have done evil, unto the resurrection of damnation."

Within the week, he was preaching morning, noon, and night to ever larger audiences. On Christmas Day, he baptized ten and married four couples.

His success did not go unnoticed among the Wesleyans, who quickly lost half of their Birchtown members to the magnetic Marrant, or even among the larger black community, which began to look to Marrant as their secular leader too. In May, some residents asked him to go to Halifax with a petition demanding that the governor honour the British government's commitment to provide them with tools and supplies. They told Marrant that Colonel Blucke, the man who would normally act as their spokesman in such matters, had "gone out of town and left them."

That created a dilemma for Marrant. Stephen Blucke, the former leader of the Black Pioneers, was lieutenant colonel of the Black Militia for the District of Shelburne and had recently been appointed schoolmaster at the newly opened Bray School.[68] He lived in the finest house in Birchtown, which also boasted a flourishing garden. He was not only the most powerful man in Birchtown, but also well connected in the white community. But John Marrant knew that Stephen Blucke was not one of them—not even one of the Wesleyans. He was an Anglican, the only black Anglican in all of Birchtown, perhaps because he was the only one who could afford the twenty shilling per year pew fee at the not-yet-built Christ Church in Shelburne.

Instead of attempting to usurp the powerful Blucke's authority directly, Marrant called a town meeting where the local residents publicly reiterated their desire to have him represent their concerns to Governor Parr. That he was successful—Marrant went to Halifax where he was able to have some of the supplies and tools they'd asked for shipped immediately to Birchtown—not only enhanced his reputation among the residents but also made Moses Wilkinson even more jealous of his rival's success.

Once, while Marrant was out of town preaching, Wilkinson spread a rumour that he had drowned, apparently in hopes of making some of the "weak ones" doubt his claim to be their prophet. That had backfired badly; when Marrant showed up unharmed, his followers were so happy to see him they "would not let my feet touch the ground."

Wilkinson tried again. He confiscated the supplies of pickaxes, spades, hoes, hammers, saws, and files that Marrant had sent back from Halifax, and began to sell them instead. And he announced that he'd sold the town chapel, which Marrant had

---

68. The Bray schools were a project of Reverend Thomas Bray, one of the founders of the Society for the Propagation of the Gospel and an anti-slavery campaigner who'd organized the distribution of books to American blacks before the revolution. After the war, his group launched several charity schools for blacks in Nova Scotia. Blucke, as the most educated member of the community and—perhaps even more important—its only Anglican, was a natural to be schoolmaster.

been using for his services, to the Wesleyan Society for three guineas, which meant that Marrant was no longer welcome to preach there.

The evening Marrant returned from Halifax, his followers showed up at the chapel for services as usual, only to find the doors locked. When they forced their way inside, Wilkinson attempted to grab control of the pulpit to prevent Marrant, who hadn't yet arrived, from preaching. He tried to lead the congregation in a hymn, but no one would sing with him until Marrant arrived—unbeknownst to the blind Wilkinson—and gave the signal for them to commence. It wasn't until after the hymn, when Wilkinson heard Marrant begin to pray, that he knew who the worshippers had responded to. "He crept out," Marrant reported later, "and I saw him no more that night. . . . The devil can never stand against the truth, but will always fly."

When Freeborn Garrettson had left Shelburne at the end of September after his first very successful visit there, he'd appointed Wilkinson and the recently converted Boston King to serve as his pastoral assistants to the black community. But it was now clear that they—certainly not Wilkinson, who'd made himself into an object of ridicule—weren't up to the challenge. So Freeborn Garrettson decided to return to Birchtown to show the people the error of their ways and, more importantly, demonstrate that Marrant was a false prophet. The fact that Marrant was supposedly out of town on his own preaching circuit the day that Garrettson arrived simply made the night's task easier.

After a hymn and a prayer, Garrettson quickly came to the point of his visit. But he'd barely launched into his denunciation of Marrant when, as Marrant himself would recount later, "one of the elders rose up, and told [Garrettson], if he came to preach the gospel of Christ, to preach it; if not, come down out of the pulpit."

"You have no business to rail against a person you have never discoursed with, nor have seen," the man added, alluding—though Garrettson did not know it at the time—to the fact that Marrant had learned of Garrettson's planned visit and returned to town, and was now seated quietly in the audience, listening. "We know that God hears not the prayer of a sinner," the man continued. "I can testify, and several others who are now in the congregation, that God made [John Marrant] the instrument of our soul's conversion, for the devil never converted a soul in his life, nor never can he." He concluded, disingenuously: "I wish Mr. Marrant was here to answer for himself." In truth, Marrant didn't have to answer; every time Garrettson attacked him, one of the congregation would rise to defend him.

How the dispute ended that night depends largely on whose version you believe. Marrant claimed that the next morning Garrettson attended his prayer service and apologized. He "wept much [and] expressed himself hurt for what had happened." Garrettson, on the other hand, would later claim he convinced so many locals of Marrant's blasphemies that Stephen Blucke agreed to have him "put out of town," and added, in a letter to Wesley, that "most of the coloured people whom Marrant drew off have returned" to the Wesleyan fold.

Not that either man would be around to see how it played out. Garrettson returned to the United States in 1787, while Marrant departed for Boston and then London a year later.

While the black Wesleyans feuded with the Huntingdonians in Birchtown and the white Anglicans continued to quarrel amongst themselves in Shelburne, David George quietly went about the business of expanding his Baptist ministry among blacks and whites, within Shelburne and beyond.

In the years following the 1784 race riot, George had travelled all over the Maritimes, usually on foot (he once reported walking eighty miles to baptize fewer than a dozen converts), establishing New Light Baptist congregations in at least seven different communities in Nova Scotia and New Brunswick, including Preston, just outside Halifax.

Not everyone welcomed his proselytizing presence, of course. In Saint John, some of the blacks who wanted to be baptized "were so full of joy that they ran out from waiting on table on their masters with the knives and forks in their hands, to meet me at the waterside." That didn't go down well with their employers, nor did the fact that the mass baptism in the river that day included both blacks and whites. White officials ordered George to cease and desist, insisting he wasn't permitted to preach in their community without a licence. That meant he had to leave and travel more than one hundred miles to Fredericton to obtain one. He did, but the licence that Lieutenant-Governor Carleton issued specifically restricted him to preaching to blacks. Despite that, when he returned to Saint John, George would report later, "our going down to the water seemed to be a pleasing sight to the whole town, white people and black."

He paid a personal price for his incessant itinerancy. During one trip, George's vessel was blown off course in a winter storm and he ended up with such a severe case of frostbite he couldn't walk. When his vessel finally made it back to Shelburne, members of his congregation "met me at the riverside, and carried me home. Afterwards, when I could walk a little, I wanted to speak of the Lord's goodness, and the brethren made a wooden sledge and drew me to meetings."

By that spring, he could walk again, he reported later, "but [I] have never been steady since."

Today's grand wedding in the freshly renovated upstairs of Gideon White's recently purchased home in Shelburne had had its beginnings less than a year earlier in a seemingly innocuous letter of introduction that Gideon's friend and fellow Shelburne businessman Charles Whitworth had written to his brother-in-law John Foxcroft in Cambridge, Massachusetts.

"My most esteemed friend . . . is a gentleman I have known long and am intimately acquainted with," Whitworth wrote, "and from my thorough knowledge of him must beg leave to introduce him to you and my sisters' particular notice and flatter myself that you will find him very deserving of it."

Deborah Whitworth certainly had. Truth be told, however, Charles's unmarried sister was probably as eager at first to escape Boston's bad memories as she was to find romance. She had been just 16 when the bloody Battle of Bunker Hill had unfolded within sight of her home. She'd watched much of it from the roof before British soldiers had forced her inside for her own safety. The battle had been a central event in her young life, and was so even now. Her father, Miles, was a doctor who'd tended to the wounded from both sides of the battle. After Bunker Hill, however, he was arrested by skeptical patriots and thrown into prison for his trouble. Two years later, he died of a fever that swept through his jail. Debbie still mourned his loss, along with the loss of two of her four brothers who'd also died in the revolution.

But in a roundabout way, Bunker Hill had given her a conversational starting point with this handsome stranger with the dimpled chin whom fate—and her brother—had sent her way. Gideon White had been a British volunteer in the Battle of Bunker Hill. That, however, was not their only connection, and not the only link back to her father. During the Seven Years War, Miles Whitworth had accompanied British troops at the siege of Louisbourg, and he delighted in telling his daughter tales of his adventures in the wilds of Nova Scotia. And then, suddenly, another man began regaling her with his stories of that same wild place.

Gideon White was now a man of considerable means in Nova Scotia. He had an appointment as the deputy registrar of the court of vice admiralty in Shelburne, for which he received a small stipend. The rum-for-fish trading venture he'd established with friends from his days in Jamaica was flourishing. He'd not only wisely invested some of his soldier's half-pay pension in farmland around Shelburne but also convinced a few former British officers from his Jamaica days to delegate him to claim other land grants on their behalf. He bought livestock and farming equipment, ordered a wide variety of seeds—apple and peach trees, Windsor beans, savoy cabbage, cucumbers, onions, winter wheat—from suppliers in New York and Halifax, and made deals with eight local black families to become his sharecroppers. They lived on his land, grew his crops, tended his cattle, paid him rent, and shared in the sale of his crops. Within a few years, Gideon had even set up his own grist mill to turn the wheat that his tenant farmers grew into flour he could sell.

Gideon had also taken Whitworth's advice to buy up commercial buildings in and around the town. Thanks to the increasing number of skittish merchants who were eager to escape what they considered to be a doomed settlement, Gideon was able to acquire the buildings for less than they'd cost. The problem, of course, was finding others willing to rent the space, and able to pay for it. He'd already had to take legal action against one tenant, Henry Guest, a jeweller and silversmith from Philadelphia, who'd fallen behind in his rent on a building Gideon had bought from John Miller, one of the original members of the Port Roseway Associates. (Guest's financial problems shouldn't have been surprising; he was one of more than a dozen watchmakers, jewellers, and smiths of various metals competing for limited business in Shelburne.)

Despite Whitworth's sage advice not to be "too hasty in entering into the fishery; rather await the result of other people," both Whitworth, himself a shareholder in Shelburne's Whale Fishing Company, and Gideon, an investor in one of its vessels, were among the locals caught out by the decline of the whaling industry. After some American whaling companies began attempting to circumvent heavy tariffs on foreign whale oil by offloading their cargoes onto Shelburne vessels and then shipping them to Britain, duty free, the British government cracked down, ordering customs officers in Shelburne to obtain documents "truly describing the crew by which the oil imported into your province was taken." Worse, politicians in London began discussing whether to extend the duties on foreign whale oil to the colonies, which could—and would—prove disastrous for the fledgling industry.

In 1786, Gideon White had wisely sold his one-eighth interest in the whaler *Good Hope* but then, despite the ominous signs, immediately—and less wisely—bought a new schooner from

Boston, which he also intended to employ in the whaling industry. It was one of his few business missteps. But it wasn't a complete misstep. It brought him to Boston. And to Debbie. There still weren't many marriageable women in Shelburne, a town where the females were likely to be already married, or children, or of another, altogether less marriageable sort.

For their own good reasons—and for love too, of course—Gideon and Debbie soon decided to marry, settle in Shelburne, and begin their family. She was 26; he was 34. Gideon acquired a fine house that one of the town's founding families had built and abandoned, and fixed it up for his bride. As for Debbie, she had no idea what life in Shelburne would be like. She only knew it was not Boston, and that was enough for now.

Their wedding service on the morning of Tuesday, April 17, 1787, was conducted by Reverend William Walter, who'd been the rector of Boston's Trinity Church before the revolution. The ceremony had to be staged in the cozy second floor of their new house because there was still no Anglican church building in which to hold it. That was because the Anglican congregations were still feuding over which of them was legitimate. George Panton,[69] the pastor of choice among the town's leading Loyalists and Governor Parr, had left Shelburne the year before. Although that should have signalled that Panton's rival, Walter, had won the battle, it turned out that Walter was still fighting a larger war with Parr and with the Society for the Propagation of the Gospel's London headquarters over the future of the church in Shelburne. Consequently, there was still no permanent church building, nor even plans for one. Not that that probably mattered to the happy couple, who soon set off for New England on their honeymoon.

---

69. In 1785, according to the *Dictionary of Canadian Biography*, "a worn out and dispirited Panton gave up the fight and retired from the settlement." He arrived in London in February 1786.

Gideon's own giddily optimistic view of his—and their—future in Shelburne is obvious in the letter he wrote to Charles Whitworth, his new brother-in-law, from Portsmouth, New Hampshire. "This state feels the want of British government," he observed. "This once-business town appears like Selkrig's old house when filled with Methodists on a foggy Sunday morning.[70] Believe me, Charles, Shelburne is a paradise compared with this country in every respect independent of its government. . . . Our soil, business and climate is really superior and we are at Port Roseway inhabitants envied by the people of this country."

Envy was one word for it.

"The inhabitants of Shelburne from the highest to the lowest," James Fraser began starkly, much as he meant to continue, "have a pitiable passion for finery, reveling and dancing and every species of sensual gratification. They vie with one another in making an external appearance in the public eye, as being persuaded that the world will judge of them much more by this than from their internal worth."[vi]

It had been barely five years since the first vessels had spilled their cargo of hopeful, fearful Loyalists onto the rocky shores of Shelburne harbour, and critics were already sifting through the entrails of the settlement's failure to become the new and better New York its founders had imagined, trying to figure out what had gone so wrong so quickly.

James Fraser seemed an unlikely candidate for that task. He was a Scotsman who hadn't even set foot in the new world until 1780, halfway through the American war. He hadn't spent much time in Shelburne either. He'd lived for a while in Halifax and then moved on to Miramichi, New Brunswick, where he ran a general retail store and exported locally caught salmon. His only

---

70. Selkrig's house, in fact, served as Shelburne's jail and courthouse.

exposure to Shelburne was as an occasional visitor during trips to and from Halifax.

But while he was in Halifax, Fraser attended St. Matthew's Protestant Dissenting Church, where Reverend Andrew Brown was the pastor. Brown, a Scottish Presbyterian, was a history buff who had decided to amuse himself while in Nova Scotia by putting together a history of the province based on the writing of "living and reliable sources."[71] And what better source than James Fraser who, like Brown, was a member of the Halifax North British Society? Fraser was certainly living, and he had plenty of opinions, reliable and otherwise, about the residents of Shelburne. Brown himself would later describe Fraser as an "acute, inquisitive man . . . of shrewd understanding, calm passions with nothing of the romantic nature."

Fraser certainly had no intention of romanticizing Shelburne or its inhabitants, whom he dismissed in his vitriolic seven-page manuscript entitled "A Sketch of Shelburnian Manners" as "the dregs of mankind." The problem with Shelburne, Fraser believed, was the Shelburnians themselves. "People brought up in the lap of ease and plenty cannot endure the straits and inconveniences to which inhabitants of a new settlement are subjected," he wrote, adding, "the bulk of the inhabitants . . . contracted an aversion to all kinds of work." To maintain their former lifestyles—not to forget their "extravagant passion for

---

71. When he returned to Scotland in 1795, Reverend Brown took the manuscripts he'd collected, including Fraser's, with him. He never completed his "History of Nova Scotia," however, and the manuscripts were eventually put to other uses. There is even a report that some were used to wrap fish. Luckily, the rest were discovered among a collection acquired by the Public Archives of Canada in 1913. Brown's own view of Shelburne appears to have been not much more positive than Fraser's. After a visit, he wrote: "Every vessel that touched at the harbour carried out, openly or by stealth, whole swarms of the inhabitants. Houses were gutted and abandoned, and streets left without occupant or claimant."

fine cloths and sensual pleasure"—they engaged in "schemes of gainful artifice and commercial speculation [instead of] hard labour and application for gaining a livelihood." If that failed to provide them with the income they needed to keep their good times rolling, they piled mortgage upon attachment on the properties the Crown had granted them, creating a "fertile source of animosities and litigations."

Fraser's Shelburne was indeed a petty, mean-spirited place. He attended at least one evening of dancing organized by "the higher orders of people" in the Long Room at Steel's Tavern in Shelburne, but it's fair to say he didn't have a good time. "Though designed for promoting social and friendly intercourse among neighbours," he wrote, the event became "the occasion of censorious affronts and ill will through the impudence of some forward, pert and gay young people who assume[d] consequential airs by showing themselves reserved, haughty and distant towards those whom they deem[ed] their inferiors and by scoffing at proprieties as well as improprieties in dress and behaviour."

The town was run by disbanded half-pay soldiers and Loyalists who "monopolize . . . almost every public office which is in the gift of government." Those who should have been protecting the community from them were the same, and were mostly corrupt—"the Dispenser of Justice," he wrote of Chief Magistrate Isaac Wilkins, "becomes more terrible than the highwayman"—while the inhabitants themselves, perhaps unsurprising given the rest of Fraser's conclusions, "appear to have a greater zeal for any thing other than religion." Even after five years, he noted, there were no permanent Anglican or Presbyterian churches; their temporary houses of worship were "mean and shabby [and] exhibit no fair emblem of the piety of the inhabitants."

The Shelburnians, Fraser concluded, paraphrasing Saint Paul, were a group of people "whose God is their belly, who glory in their shame."

It is perhaps for the best that Fraser's screed didn't see the light of day for another 125 years.

"The spite of misfortune"

Chapter 7.

William Booth was not feeling well.[i] Again. Perhaps it was another cold coming on. Or just *the* cold. He rubbed his hands together, tried not to allow himself to be distracted by the irritating rash—*exycepelas*, Dr. Drummond had called it—that was playing havoc across his lower back this evening. George Drummond, whom he'd met on his first visit to Shelburne two years earlier and who had now become his friend as well as his doctor, had reassured him it was nothing to be concerned about, just an inevitable consequence of Shelburne's recent spell of cold weather.

Damn this weather!

Damn this place!

Perhaps Captain Cambel was punishing him for something he'd done, or said, or thought. Booth had certainly entertained enough dark thoughts since being posted to these colonies. While his superiors had studiously ignored his requests to return to Britain, Cambel—soon after he'd returned from his own sojourn and taken back his title as commanding officer of the Corps of Engineers in Nova Scotia—had unceremoniously posted Booth to Shelburne for God knew how long.

When Booth had visited Shelburne with General Campbell

two summers ago, he'd remembered it as depressed, and depressing. Now, at the beginning of what promised to be an interminable winter, it was worse. His daily diary entries told the story: "Thick with cool and misty rain all day." "Thick weather and cold, a little sleet today." "Heavy fall of snow during the night." "Thunder at half past four this afternoon." "Windy with appearance of rain." "Snow falling thick." And it was only the beginning of December.

The town was, if possible, gloomier than the weather. There were at least 350 houses sitting vacant in Shelburne, many well built of the best material and design, some still filled with the finest of furniture, all now abandoned as not even worth trying to sell. There weren't any buyers. Booth might have been able to acquire one of those houses for little more than a song (perhaps that bitter local version of the popular ditty "Roslin's Castle"— *On Scotia's barren rocky shore / consigned to labour and be poor*—would have been appropriate), but he had no intention of remaining in this awful place any longer than necessary. For the duration, he and Hannah had decided to rent a house on Water Street from John Aitkens, a local blockmaker who was himself thinking of leaving town.

As an experienced military man, Booth believed he should not be here at all. He had kept a copy of a paper he'd read a few years earlier that grandly tried to explain the difference between the Corps of Artillery, which only had to "manage and direct the guns, and other pieces of ordinance, that are placed upon the works constructed by the Engineers," and the members of his own Corps of Engineers, who, as the paper correctly noted and as Booth was fond of quoting, are "of the utmost importance, the fate of a nation being sometimes dependant upon their skill and abilities."

Booth's duties in Shelburne were certainly beneath his soldierly skills and abilities. He filled his days with haggling over repair bills with carpenters and masons, or preparing yet another drawing the captain would probably not even look at. Cambel certainly hadn't responded to anything Booth had sent him so far.

Booth's task in Shelburne was to survey and make plans of the harbour, the barracks, and every public building in the town. The fate of the nation might not turn on his efforts, but his own health could. To measure the sea line against the harbour, he would have to venture into the icy November water. Dr. Drummond had, thankfully, advised against it.

Last month, Booth had sent a box containing drawings of Point Carleton and a plan for the officers' and soldiers' barracks to Cambel by way of the *Lady*, one of the coastal traders plying the waters between Halifax and Shelburne. No response. Booth couldn't help but agree with the locals who frequently complained that the barracks were poorly located. The stumps and boulders around it had yet to be cleared. For some reason the barracks had been built on the side of the harbour opposite the town, which meant that, during the winter, the ice not only made it impossible for small craft to journey back and forth across the three-quarter-mile width of the harbour but also was usually not thick enough to allow the soldiers to cross on foot. "This the inhabitants say is a great inconvenience, and should be remedied by building other [barracks] nigher the town," Booth had written after his first visit in 1785. What would happen if the soldiers were ever needed in an emergency?[72]

But the officers here seemed not to care much about such matters. Major Edwards, for example, who'd arrived last summer with five companies of the 6th regiment to take over military duties in Shelburne,[73] was still "busily employed in building himself a

---

72. Though the townspeople had written to Lord Sydney with a similar request, General Campbell had advised against it: "The expense of these barracks has been enormous. I do not think it advisable to recommend the incurring of additional expense as I understand the spot was originally fixed by Lt. Col. Morse at their express desire."

73. They'd replaced the 17th regiment, which had been stationed in Shelburne at the time of Booth's first visit.

house" on Crown land without benefit of a licence of any kind. When he wasn't tending his new garden, also on land that wasn't his, or "felling large sticks of lumber for his own private use," Edwards occupied himself by parcelling out patronage—such as the three dwellings Booth had had constructed as hospital huts at a cost to the army of £20—to those whose favour he sought.

Those officials who weren't venal were, most likely, incompetent. The barracks master had "neglected sending my returns for lodging money" while Brinley, the commissary officer, failed to remember to reimburse him for his expenses for fuel even though he'd managed to do so for the other officers. And Brinley had claimed for himself the boat that had previously been for the use of the chief engineer. "Whenever the service required me [to travel] by water, I expected to have it," Booth would later note, "but it has always been either employed by Mr. Brinley, or those he lent it to."

To add to Booth's frustration, he seemed unable to bring the "Wallace affair" to a just conclusion, and that, of course, was upsetting Hannah.

Michael Wallace was one of Halifax's most prominent businessmen, a confidant of the governor, and a pillar of the Roman Catholic church. Who better, Booth had thought—unwisely, as it turned out—to handle a modest business deal involving Hannah's brothers, Edmund and Samuel Proudfoot? Edmund owned Pearl Estate, one of the largest and most profitable plantations on Grenada, while Samuel was a successful merchant in London. They'd asked their brother-in-law to sell a cargo of Edmund's rum, sugar, and Madeira in Halifax and forward the proceeds— expected to be about £1500—to Samuel in London. Booth had obligingly hired Wallace to broker the deal and Wallace had apparently sold the goods, but he'd never paid a penny to Samuel. At one point, Wallace claimed to have sent the money to Samuel by way of one of the vessels sailing to London, but "the *Lyon* arrived in England some time late in June [and] no letters or remittance had arrived at Mr. Proudfoot's." Now that Booth was stuck in

Shelburne instead of Halifax, Wallace wasn't even bothering to answer his letters. Adding to Booth's concern, Dr. Walter, the Anglican minister in Shelburne, had confided recently that he'd heard Wallace's financial affairs were "in a bad way and that, in his opinion, no time should be lost to get a settlement."

After nearly fifteen months of fruitless attempts to get Wallace to honour his obligations, Booth had finally written to a lawyer in Halifax, enclosing all invoices and putting the whole sorry mess in his hands so "that you will please, without any further advice from me, force a settlement and obtain from him a full and clear explanation."

Not that doing so had enabled Booth to put the matter out of his mind. Hannah, of course, fretted continuously about its impact on family relationships. Each new development's "unlucky disappointments fell very heavy on my wife's tender feelings," Booth noted in his journal. Her health, fragile at the best of times, had become even more precarious.

Then, two weeks earlier, on November 22, 1787, he'd received yet another letter from Samuel—dated a month-and-a-half before then—"informing me of his surprise that no remittances have yet been made to him . . . and that he expects me to see it done." Booth had immediately dispatched another letter to his Halifax agent, Lawrence Hartshorne, a Quaker merchant. "I must therefore beg and entreat you will use your utmost on my behalf and to acquaint Mr. Fitzgerald [a lawyer, of the situation]," Booth wrote to Hartshorne, plaintively adding a request for "five dozen bottles and, when there is anything worthwhile, to send me a Halifax newspaper." Halifax wasn't London but it would have to do. For now.

The most exciting event in Shelburne in the fall of 1788 was the brief visit of Prince William Henry, King George's third son.[ii] The prince had already become a fixture on the Halifax social scene, less for the number of his visits—he'd made four stopovers there in two years—than for the gossip each one invariably generated.

In the summer of 1786, the king had dispatched young William Henry's ship across the Atlantic after he learned that the prince was preparing to marry the pretty but unworthy daughter of a Portsmouth naval yard official. William Henry, barely 20, consoled himself by drinking and debauching his way around Halifax—"a very gay and lively place," he wrote, "full of women, and those of the most obliging kind"—falling in love with and proposing marriage to another equally delectable young woman, the sister-in-law of the province's attorney general, and—most notoriously—carrying on a very public affair with Frances Wentworth, the twice-his-age wife of the former loyalist governor and current surveyor general. What made the scandal all the more outrageous—and gossip-worthy—was that the prince had snubbed invitations to dine with Governor Parr and his wife in order to be with his paramour, whose own husband was off in the wilds of Cape Breton, dutifully marking pine forests for his Majesty's masts.

Two years later—after two more brief visits, a recall to Britain in disgrace for his various and sundry actions in America, yet another proposal of marriage to yet another young British woman of whom the king did not approve, and yet another order to sail back to America—Prince William Henry ended up in Halifax again in August 1788.

During that stay, the prince decided to visit British troops in some of the lesser outposts of his father's North American empire, including Shelburne. That no salacious gossip emerged about the prince's activities during his three-day Shelburne stopover may say less about the town's charms, or lack thereof, and more about the prince's state on leaving Halifax.

William Dyott, a British lieutenant stationed in Nova Scotia who'd become one of William Henry's favourite carousing companions, noted in his diary that the night before they sailed for Shelburne at the beginning of October, the prince was "in the greatest spirits I ever saw him in my life." In more ways than one. "Seven of us (the prince included) drank fourteen bottles; that mixed with champagne and claret must have made a pretty fermentation in our stomachs. We all (with stumbling and tumbling) attended his highness to the barge, and parted—I believe?—well satisfied with the evening's entertainment."

This might also explain Dyott's rather unkind description of Shelburne harbour the following day as "desolate" and the town itself as having "as poor an appearance as anything I ever saw." Venturing onto the shore didn't improve his perception. The town site—more than five years after its founding—was "the most wretched I ever beheld. Nothing on the surface of the ground but immense large stones and stumps of trees. Indeed, from the present appearance of the place, you may easily conceive what it must have been; for in the town streets, the stumps of the trees are not taken up." Though there were some "tolerably good houses," he wrote, many were unoccupied, at least according to the commanding engineer, Lieutenant William Booth, with whom he'd spoken and who had recently completed a survey of the town.

Booth had done his best to ingratiate himself with the young prince—you never knew; perhaps the king's son might be of assistance in getting him out of this place—and had showed him some of the watercolour drawings he'd made of the town, including some of its finer homes. The prince had expressed an interest in having some of Booth's drawings for himself, and Booth, of course, said he would be more than happy to oblige.

After the prince dutifully reviewed the 6th regiment—it was so windy that half the soldiers lost their hats—Dyott and a few other soldiers decided to venture through the woods from the barracks to Birchtown[74] to see how the other half lived. Not well.

---

74. Some historians have suggested that the prince may have accompanied Dyott's group to Birchtown, where he was "entertained" by Stephen Blucke "at his big house on the Birchtown Road," but there doesn't appear to be any documentary evidence for this.

"The place is beyond description wretched," Dyott wrote, "their huts miserable to guard against the inclemency of a Nova Scotia winter, and their existence almost depending on what they could lay up in summer. I think I never saw wretchedness and poverty so strongly perceptible in the garb and the countenance of the human species as in these miserable outcasts. I cannot say I was sorry to quit so melancholy a dwelling."

Dyott—and presumably the prince himself—was more than happy to escape such a "melancholy" place. The next morning, after dinner at the barracks with "a Mr. Bruce[75] and a Mr. Skinner, American royalists . . . the only people tolerably decent in Shelburne," they set sail for Cape Breton.

William Booth could only wish to sail away as easily.

Where was Dr. Drummond? Why hadn't he come? William Booth was beside himself with worry and fear and helplessness. Hannah's condition had grown much worse this morning. She could barely breathe. She was coughing blood from her nose and vomiting more of that nasty, yellowish bile. The hard work of vomiting, of coughing, of breathing even, seemed to exhaust her to the point where she could no longer bring herself to a sitting position without her husband's assistance. When he helped her sit up, however, she complained she had no feeling in her hands, her arms, her legs. She needed to lie back down. She was going to die, she told him. Just like her sister Elizabeth. She told him that. Over and over. In her delirium. When would Dr. Drummond get here? How long had it been since Booth had sent Graves to fetch him?

Thank goodness for Dr. Drummond. He had been one of the early settlers of this place, a Loyalist, and he seemed to get along with everyone. He was a surveyor of customs as well as a doctor, and a regular guest at all the best tables in town. Since William

---

75. Bruce, the collector for customs at Shelburne, was also a guest at a dinner for General John Campbell during William Booth's visit to Shelburne in 1785.

and Hannah's arrival, Drummond had become a regular social visitor to their quarters, where he and William would enjoy tea or something stronger, trade books—which reminded Booth that he'd been meaning to lend the doctor the first volume of *Watson's Chemical*—and gossip about the latest news of this doomed town.

The situation had become so bad of late, Drummond had told him, that you could rent a house for an eighth of what it would have cost you last year. Drummond himself had recently bought another house for £25, lot and all. The house alone, he confided to Booth, had probably cost at least £200 to build. Booth couldn't help but wonder why the doctor continued to waste his money on such increasingly worthless— What was that? Another moan? A cry? He wished Drummond would hurry up.

The doctor had been there last night. He'd given Hannah some hawthorn drops in water, along with a little lavender on sugar, which seemed to revive her slightly, briefly. She'd even taken a small amount of clear soup. After Drummond had given "every assistance that time would admit of," he'd left. Booth had stayed with her, but she'd quickly slipped back into her delirium, talking "not sensible" the rest of the night.

This had been going on for close to a month now. Hannah had had her share of bilious complaints in Britain, but they'd become worse since being posted to Halifax, and worse again during the time they'd spent in Shelburne. Early in January, she'd begun waking up once or twice in the night complaining of a tightness in her chest. She soon lost her appetite, and was only able—and then only some of the time—to keep down veal broth, bread, a little calves' feet jelly or whey wine, perhaps some chamomile tea. She'd complain she was chilled, so Booth would wrap hot bricks in flannel and place them at her feet. Then she'd complain she was boiling with fever.

Dr. Drummond had tried everything: hawthorn, lavender, essence of peppermint, mustard poultices on her joints, cream of tartar in her drink, wine sweetened with sugar, even the vigorous application of a fleshbrush to improve her circulation. Though his attentions might relieve her briefly, she never seemed to get better. Still, Booth was inevitably "buoyed up by the doctor's favourable opinion that, with attention to his rules and by using a little exercise in walking about the house . . . that he had not the smallest doubt of my wife getting the better of it." Even last night, Drummond had said before he left that he expected the worst was over now, and that Hannah would soon begin to improve. She hadn't. This morning, she was the worst she'd been.

Thank goodness William had turned down Major Viney's invitation to that dance at the barracks. He hadn't wanted to socialize with that lot anyway. There were tasks he should be doing this morning. He needed to resend his letter to Prince William Henry, for example. Almost immediately after the prince had requested last summer that Booth send him some of his drawings, he had packed a wooden box full of them, added a personal note, and sent it on to Halifax. Soon after, however, he received a note from Commissioner Duncan in Halifax, blithely informing him that he was "sorry to say that a little girl threw [your] letter into the fire" and asking him to send along another copy.

He would also need to follow up on the latest twist in the Wallace business. Before Hannah's illness, he'd written to his brother-in-law in London to let him know that Wallace had apparently decided to pay off his outstanding debt over the three-year-old consignment by shipping a quantity of fresh fish to Proudfoot in London. But Booth's letter had gone astray. He'd put it aboard a brig in Shelburne supposedly bound for London, but had since learned that the captain had changed his mind and was heading for Antigua or St. Vincent instead. Now he'd have to send off another letter. Why was he marooned here in this god-forsaken place from which there was no escape but by sea, and that, as he had discovered, far less than certain?

He couldn't help but wonder how much Hannah's illness was the result of this place, and all the troubles they'd experienced here. "I fear," he noted in a letter to a friend, "the weight fell too heavy on my tender and dearest woman."

He heard a commotion. Was that someone at the door? Drummond? Finally. He only hoped it was not too late.

In 1785, Shelburne had boasted three newspapers.[iii] By early 1789, there were none. In 1787, James Robertson had taken his printing press to Charlottetown, where he'd accepted an appointment as the King's Printer.[76] As for Thomas and James Swords, whose access to a printing press had disappeared when Robertson left, they had returned to New York that same year and launched T&J Swords, Printers. Though barely into their twenties, they quickly carved out a reputation as quality printers of religious materials, and their small shop on Pearl Street had already become known as a centre for the "literate of the city."

The brothers had reunited in New York with their mother and younger sisters. In 1788, Mary Swords, armed with fresh affidavits about her losses and new testimonials to her loyalty, had returned to London from Shelburne to press her case for more compensation once again. But the claims commission had been deaf to her pleas. This time, the commissioners awarded her just £43 more for the oxen, cart, cattle, and forage she said she'd lost while supplying General Burgoyne's forces. It was not even enough to justify the cost and trouble of her trip. Although still angry and frustrated, Mary Swords finally began to accept that, like her sons, she'd have to make her peace with the United States of America.

James Humphreys, the former Philadelphia printer and merchant who'd launched Shelburne's third newspaper, the *Nova Scotia Packet and Advertiser*, early in 1785, had also shut his paper

---

76. London had ultimately turned down the lieutenant-governor's request that a salary accompany the title, so Robertson decided to move back to a Scotland he'd left more than twenty years earlier. He and his brother-in-law opened a shop in Edinburgh as printers and booksellers.

down, preferring the precarious uncertainties of the shopkeeper's life in Shelburne (he now sold fine shoes and beaver gloves from a store at the corner of George and Water streets) to the dismal certainty of being a publisher in a city that was collapsing on itself. How dismal? Fewer than 100 of the 441 original Port Roseway Associates deemed eligible to draw lots for a precious piece of Shelburne six years earlier were still listed as owning real estate in Shelburne County in 1789.

Not everyone left, of course. Some of those who stayed even thrived. It helped if you had a government appointment, or two, or three.

Besides his many and various private business interests, Gideon White, for example, also served at one time or another—often at the same time—as deputy registrar of the vice-admiralty court, justice of the peace, sheriff, customs collector, justice of the inferior court of common pleas, major of the 22nd battalion of the militia, *custos rotulorum* (the highest-ranking civil authority in the county), and—most recently—an elected member of the provincial House of Assembly.

Joseph Durfee, another of the original Port Roseway Associates, had fared almost as well. In addition to being chosen—along with Benjamin Marston—as one of the community's first justices of the peace, Durfee had served as the fisheries overseer for Birchtown and Roseway River and the official surveyor of all locally built vessels. He'd also supervised Shelburne's harbour pilots, a group of black Loyalists who lived on McNutts Island at the mouth of the harbour, from where they guided vessels into and out of the port. In 1786, after much lobbying from locals, who wanted a lighthouse to guard the entrance to the harbour—like the one on Sambro Island near Halifax—Governor Parr had asked Durfee (along with Stephen Skinner and others) to help supervise its construction.

That task was now complete, which was more than all right with Joseph Durfee. He'd had enough of all-consuming undertakings, such as leading British warships past enemy fire into Charles Town harbour during the war, or controlling thousands of small craft traffic in occupied New York harbour, or founding a new city in the wilderness. He was 54 years old now and keen to settle with his wife, Ann, and their five grown children into a new and more relaxed life as a gentleman farmer. Soon after arriving in the first fleet, he'd been granted 550 acres on the western shore of Shelburne harbour, which he'd since partially cleared and where he now raised cattle, horses, sheep, and hogs. By 1788, the family was living in a farmhouse he'd constructed on a hill commanding a clear view of the harbour entrance. The original house—a wood-framed building above a deep cellar kitchen walled with fieldstone—had recently been expanded to include a ground-level kitchen with its own bell-shaped gambrel roof. Durfee's only son, Robert, 30, worked with his father on the farm whenever he wasn't busy following in his father's footsteps as a master mariner.

But Durfee's happy experience wasn't typical. Joseph Pynchon's experience was. Pynchon, the advance scout who'd so enthusiastically reported back from Halifax to Durfee and the rest of the Associates in the winter of 1783 that Port Roseway offered "the best situation in the province for trade, fishing and farming," had himself stayed only eighteen months before returning to Connecticut. His fellow scout, James Dole, had also returned to the United States, re-establishing his retail business in Albany. According to Anglican minister William Walter, in fact, four-fifths of the original settlers had returned to the United States, where the laws against Loyalists had finally been relaxed. They left behind "hundreds of cellars with their stone walls and granite partitions . . . like uncovered monuments to the dead, [telling] a tale of sorrow and sadness that overpowered the heart."

They left for all sorts of reasons, of course: business or personal, and often a combination of the two. Gideon White's brother-in-law Charles Whitworth, for example, had formed a trading business with his London-based brother, Nathan, but the venture collapsed, largely due to British government regulation. His wife then left him and took their children back to New York.

After moving in briefly with Gideon and Debbie, Charles decamped permanently to Jamaica.

Margaret Blucke returned to New York too, leaving her ten-years-younger husband, Stephen (whom she now referred to distantly in her letters as Mr. Blucke), and her twenty-years-younger servant girl Isabella (whom she described as that "poor unhappy girl") behind in Birchtown. Stephen and Isabella would later have their daughter baptized at the Anglican church in Shelburne.

Many of those who did remain in Shelburne lived very different lives than they had before the revolution—and certainly than they'd imagined for themselves when they'd sailed out of New York harbour six years before.

Consider the case of Oliver Bruff. He had been a skilled jeweller to the elite in New York before the war; now, in a city with more smiths than customers, he billed himself much more prosaically as a mere tinker. In New York, he'd advertised for workers with the promise that he not only paid the highest wages in the city but also offered the bonus of a "quart of grog a day." In Shelburne, he quickly lost all of his eight servants—freed blacks—who'd accompanied him from New York. They left after he tried to keep part of their government-assigned rations for himself. Within two years of landing in Shelburne, Bruff was in such dire financial straits that he was forced to sell both his farm lot and his picket-fenced town lot with its storey-and-a-half log house for just a few guineas. To add to his humiliation, he'd had to dramatically reduce his initial claim for compensation for his American losses—he maintained his Maryland property was worth £48,000—after officials warned him of the penalties for perjury. In the end, the commission completely rejected his much more modest £4000 claim.

Perhaps not surprisingly, there were rumours that Bruff had begun drinking much more than he should.

William Booth woke with a start. He was freezing cold. He was soaking wet. What was it? Sweat? No, he realized in a dull kind of daze, the floor around him was covered with still-rising water. Where had this flood come from? And why? Not that it mattered. Nothing mattered.

Hannah was dead! She'd been delirious, totally insensible for much of the past two days, and then, at 4:40 on the afternoon of Sunday, February 22, 1789, he'd heard her scream out. Once. And then silence. She was 38 years old. They had been married for just a few years, and almost all of it had been spent here, far away from friends and family and familiarity. Booth was not ready for her to be gone.

Hannah had not been his only recent loss. He'd just received a letter from his sister informing him that their mother had died. He would have to write back to his sister now, tell her his own latest awful news. And inform his brothers-in-law, of course.

But not yet. He was exhausted. He'd needed to sleep first. But not in the bedchamber they'd shared. He couldn't, wouldn't. He'd asked one of Hannah's maidservants to place some bedding on the floor in the lower room and gone to sleep there. Which is where he was now. Soaking wet. He tried to make sense of it all. There must have been a thaw—the weather here was so unpredictable—melting the snow piled against the foundation of the house and filling this lower room with water.

Booth struggled to his feet and made his way to the fire still burning in the fireplace. He wrapped himself in dry blankets, quickly poured and drank two glasses of Madeira and then found the fleshbrush. He rubbed himself with it for half an hour, trying to warm his body, trying to clear his head, trying to stop coughing. He began to compose the letters in his head, the ones to his family, of course, but also the urgent one he would now write to the Duke of Richmond, the commander of the Corps of Engineers. "Had I," he would begin, "been so fortunate as to have obtained my request and which no man on the face of the earth could have thought in the least unreasonable, I am sure . . . I should have saved my dear partner . . ." He was sure of that.

Sure, too, that the duke could not deny his latest request for "relief . . . in order to settle my affairs at home."

Boston King slowly, awkwardly plowed through the waist-high snow along what, in summer, was the well-worn path between Birchtown and Shelburne.[iv] Under each arm he carried a small handmade wooden chest. In one hand he held the saw he'd used to make them. Just in case, he told himself, just in case.

As he walked, he prayed: prayed that Captain Selex would approve of his effort this time, prayed that he'd be able to return home with something—anything—that would allow him to feed himself and Violet. Boston didn't need to remind himself that they were down to their last pint of Indian meal. "Lord," Boston pleaded as he trudged through the silent forest, "give me a prosperous journey."

It had been an awful winter, and not just for Boston King. All of British North America was suffering the effects of a continuing famine, but Nova Scotia had been especially devastated. Since the arrival of the Loyalists, the province had been unable to produce enough food to feed itself, and last year the British had cut off the king's bounty for the newcomers.

The provincial government had recently had to pass special legislation to allow it to import essentials from the hated United States, but even that did little to improve the situation. In Halifax, at one point, bakers reported that they were down to just four days' supply of flour. No wonder even the locals had taken to disparaging their homeland as "Nova Scarcity."

The situation was worse in Shelburne. The local merchants had sent a petition to London, blaming their current problems on everything from the government's decision to eliminate the royal provisions before the settlement could become firmly established, to trade restrictions with the United States, to the lack of roads and infrastructure needed to make Shelburne a trading city.

For his part, Boston King blamed the white inhabitants for Shelburne's "very distressing" situation, "owing to their great imprudence in building large houses, and striving to excel one another in this piece of vanity. When their money was almost expended, they began to build small fishing vessels but, alas, it was too late to repair their error. Had they been wise enough at first to have turned their attention to the fishery instead of fine houses, the place would soon have been in a flourishing condition; whereas it was reduced in a short time to a heap of ruins, and its inhabitants were compelled to flee to other parts of the continent for sustenance."

The situation for the blacks of Birchtown was worse. They had no place to flee to. By the time Britain cut off the royal provisions, most still hadn't received their promised farmland, and the town lots they had been given weren't fertile enough to grow vegetables or raise cattle. Some had been forced to kill and eat their cats and dogs for food. Others traded their best clothing, even their blankets, for a little flour to keep them going. Some didn't make it. Boston himself had watched as several of his fellow citizens "fell down dead in the streets through hunger."

Or from disease. Smallpox swept through the area, briefly felling even John Marrant, the man who claimed he'd been sent by God to save them. One day while he tried to preach his regular sermon, he reported, "the blood came running out of my nose and mouth, so that the people were all frightened. They took me out of the pulpit and carried me to my house." Marrant had survived, another sign—or so some suggested—that he really had been sent by God.

Boston and Violet, for their part, continued to support Mr. Garretson, the Methodist preacher who'd saved them both, and Boston had done his best to act as Garretson's pastoral assistant when he wasn't in Birchtown. It wasn't a role he wanted: "I found great reluctance to officiate as an exhorter among the people, and had many doubts and fears respecting my call to that duty," he explained, "because I was conscious of my great ignorance and insufficiency for a work of such importance."

Boston, in truth, had been almost relieved when circumstances forced him to leave Birchtown—and his pastoral obligations—to search for employment. He had wandered from place to place—Annapolis, Digby, Chebucto—but there was no work to be had anywhere. Finally, back in Shelburne, he had tried offering his carpentry skills on the town's streets where he'd met up with a Captain Selex, who hired him to build him a storage chest. Boston had immediately hurried back to Birchtown where he worked through the night to complete the project. Selex had rejected it, but encouraged Boston to try again and offered clearer instructions on what he wanted.

Dejectedly, Boston had trudged back to Birchtown. "Being pinched with hunger and cold," he wrote, "I fell down several times, through weakness, and expected to die upon the spot."

Others did die on that same path. John Marrant claimed he'd encountered two women on the outskirts of Birchtown who'd gone to Shelburne to beg for food, but hadn't the strength to make it all the way back home. One was already dead when Marrant discovered her, the other "partly chilled with the cold, the snow being four feet on the earth." Marrant, himself still weak from his bout of smallpox, took some rum from his knapsack, made her drink a little, and then rubbed the rest over her face, hoping to revive her. It did. Together, they stumbled back to Birchtown. "Sometimes we both fell down together . . . but by the help of the Almighty God, I got her a mile nearer town."

Boston, too, was convinced the Lord had "delivered me from all murmurings and discontent" that day. Back in Birchtown, he had set about building another chest. The next day, his prayers were answered again when, "to the joy of my heart," Selex agreed to buy it. He paid for it in Indian corn. Boston was also able to sell the other chest to someone else for cash, as well as the saw, which he'd brought with him to sell in case nothing else found a taker. "I was exceeding thankful to procure a reprieve from the dreadful anguish of perishing by famine," he would write later. He was thankful, too, that he lived in a Christian country. For reasons he didn't quite understand, Boston had lately been thinking more and more about Africa, the land his father had been stolen from so many years before. Now that he himself was saved, Boston couldn't help but imagine "what a wretched condition . . . must those poor creatures be in who never heard the word of God or of Christ, nor had an instruction afforded them with respect to a future judgment."

Unfortunately, there didn't seem to be much Boston could do about that. "As I had not the least prospect at that time of ever seeing Africa, I contented myself with pitying and praying for the poor benighted inhabitants of that country which gave birth to my forefathers."

Though he couldn't know it at the time, others elsewhere were already hatching ambitious plans that would dramatically alter Boston's "prospect" for seeing Africa.

Still no reply from Cambel! William Booth could not believe the effrontery of the man. It had been more than two months since he'd received the letter from the Duke of Richmond in response to his request to return to London. "It will not suit with my other arrangements to send an officer to relieve you immediately," the duke had written, "but I shall have no objection to your coming to England upon leave of absence for six months with the approbation of the commander in chief and Captain Cambel, to whom you will make application for this purpose."

It was not exactly what he'd hoped for, but Booth would make the most of his six months. With luck, he'd be able to convince whoever needed convincing to allow him to stay in Britain. As per the duke's instructions, Booth had sent off letters to both General Campbell, the military commander-in-chief for Nova Scotia, and Captain Cambel, his immediate superior in the Corps. Campbell had quickly approved his request. Cambel, however, still hadn't given him a definitive answer and seemed, in fact, to be doing his best to ignore him. What was he up to?

It had been more than six months since his dear Hannah's death, and Booth had spent much of that time suffering from the cough he'd picked up that night on the wet floor, a cough that had only become worse after the funeral.

Soon after her death, Booth had moved out of their rented house—too many memories—and taken lodgings in the home of Mrs. Holderness, whose husband, a merchant and shipbuilder, was currently in the West Indies on business. The Holdernesses lived in a large house with a fine garden, the second- or third-most impressive residence in the whole town. Mrs. Holderness had confided to Booth that it had cost them £1100 to build when they'd arrived with the first settlers. Thanks to the abundance of cheap labour, it had, like many buildings in town, been built considerably larger than even a family of eight—the Holdernesses had six children, three boys and three girls—would require. But, as Booth was quick to note, the Holderness house, "like all the buildings [in Shelburne was] not complete, three rooms remaining to be ceilinged and plastered."

It didn't matter to Booth. He had rented three finished rooms in the house, including a bedchamber upstairs and a downstairs front parlour with use of the kitchen and a garret for his servants. The rent of £18 per annum—plus supplying the kitchen with fuel—was probably more than he needed to pay in Shelburne in 1789. One of the houses he and Hannah had considered renting for £30 per year when they'd arrived in town two years ago was now being advertised for £10. It seemed that even the speculators had given up buying. When a Mr. Harvey, who was leaving for Philadelphia, had put up his house and garden lot for auction this spring at £100, it had attracted not a single bid. Two years ago, Mrs. Holderness confided, the man had turned down £500 for the house alone. Even Booth's former landlord, John Atkins, was leaving. He had arrived in Shelburne with £8000, but was now so broke he'd couldn't pay his own mortgage. He was currently asking, and not getting, £5 for the space Booth and Hannah had been renting for £22. His situation was so bad he'd had to ask Booth for a loan of £10 to pay for his passage to New Providence in the Bahamas, where he hoped to start anew.[77]

Still, living with Mrs. Holderness and her young family had seemed like the best circumstance for Booth in the immediate aftermath of his loss. She was solicitous, sending along "a small and very good" pudding she'd made from the fruit he'd given her one day, an apple tart and three custards a few days later. And she'd often offer him some white wine whey for his cough, which persisted in spite of her attentions.

Mrs. Holderness was also a good storyteller and gossip. Apparently, she and her husband had not got along well with the deputy surveyor, a Mr. Marston, so when Mr. Holderness had tried to enter his name for a draw for some water lots, Marston had removed his name from the draw, decreeing that he already "had land enough." In fact, Mrs. Holderness confided, "none but those who tipped Mr. Marston were allowed the chance of ground."

Booth had done his best to respond in kind, offering his own tidbits about military personnel they'd both known. Her family had been in a "very good way of business" during the British occupation of New York, she'd told him, and sold to the military as well as civilians, so she knew many of the soldiers who'd been garrisoned there.

Booth was also pleased to respond favourably one day when Mrs. Holderness sent two of the older daughters to ask if she

---

77. By 1789, the exodus of Loyalists had become so great that the provincial legislature passed a law requiring anyone wanting to leave to obtain a pass. The government made sure that those departing had paid all back taxes before they were permitted to take their leave.

could borrow his copy of Duché's *Sermons*.[78] The girls were wearing dresses their mother had made from some curtains of Hannah's she had admired, and which Booth had been pleased to give her. The girls thanked him politely for the dresses. "They are very genteel girls," Booth noted that day in his diary, "and constantly do much credit to the school mistress of the place." Unfortunately, Mrs. Holderness told him, the schoolmistress was closing down her school and moving to Halifax. When she'd first set up in Shelburne, she'd had forty pupils; today there were only twenty, not enough to make it worth her while.

When he wasn't socializing with Mrs. Holderness and her family, Booth visited with his small circle of friends, most of whom seemed to have some connection to his wife's death. He'd become friends with Colonel Abraham Van Buskirk, for example, whose own wife had died a week after Hannah. And Dr. Drummond still called regularly. They talked occasionally of Hannah; Drummond's eventual conclusion was that she had died of the nervous fevers.[79] Reverend Walter, the Anglican minister who, along with Reverend John Rowland, had presided at Hannah's funeral, was another frequent visitor. Which reminded Booth: last month, John Taylor, the mason he'd hired to cut and build a pedestal on Hannah's grave, had presented him with a detailed bill for £25 for the work he intended to do but still hadn't begun. Booth would have to prod him.

Thinking about her tomb made Booth remember, as he often did, Hannah's funeral. It had been—sad as it was—a fine and fitting occasion. Being military, Booth had worn his uniform coat, black waistcoat, and breeches. The coffin had been draped with black cloth, as was the custom at home. Since black silk was not

---

78. Jacob Duché was a famous Anglican chaplain to the first and second Continental Congress who later turned against the revolution and was forced into exile in England, where he became a follower of Emanuel Swendenborg, a scientist-mystic.
79. Typhoid.

available, the mourners had worn white hatbands, which Booth had discovered was the custom in America. In the two days between Hannah's death and internment, Booth had had a vault built for her at the church burying ground next door to the spot where they were now building the new Christ Church and where—soon, he hoped—she would have her appropriate memorial. The officers of the 6th regiment, whatever else Booth may have thought of them, had attended the service in number, as did the barrack master; Mr. Bruce, the collector of customs; and many of Shelburne's most important citizens and merchants, including Stephen Skinner, who'd also become a friend.

When Skinner would stop by for tea or wine, they'd often talk about Hannah's asthma, which Booth was convinced had been made worse by Shelburne's cold, damp climate. Skinner didn't disagree, but said that the climate had been a godsend for his gout. He'd been a "martyr" to the affliction before settling in Shelburne, he said, but had suffered "no fit as of this year."

Skinner had been sympathetic, too, when Booth had complained, as he did more and more often these days, about Captain Cambel. In May, he'd become so frustrated with his commander's high-handedness he'd even written a list of the six reasons "I think sufficient for my not proceeding with another drawing of Shelburne harbour" as Cambel had requested. They ranged from "my health will not admit of my sitting down to drawing" to "I was not put on this station as Captain Cambel's draughtsman. . . . In support of [my] rank as captain lieutenant in the corps," he added with more than a little indignation, "I conceive that I have an undoubted right to object to doing the drudgery of a draughtsman." Besides which, he had already "sent plans of all public buildings here showing the ground and the whole of the environs in the best manner I was able."

He believed he had more than earned his right to return home, especially given the circumstances of his wife's death. So why was Cambel ignoring him? He'd written to Cambel a second time, on July 24, giving him the benefit of the doubt. "I am inclined to think, sir, that by some accident or other, my letter to you might have miscarried. Otherwise I could not doubt of your reply, as I had therein given you a copy of His Grace the Duke of Richmond's letter to me, mentioning His Grace's leave for my returning to England on my private affairs."

Still nothing for another month and a half and then, finally, yesterday—September 2—a letter had arrived from Halifax aboard the *Stag*. In it, Cambel claimed that he hadn't received Booth's first letter at all, and that his July 12 letter hadn't reached him for nearly a month. "No letter of mine, to him, has ever miscarried before," a skeptical Booth complained to his diary, "and I never remember a three week's passage from Shelburne to Halifax." Worse, Cambel, "not trusting my word," had demanded that Booth send along another copy of the duke's letter before he would proceed with the request for leave.

What was really going on? Booth had heard rumours that Cambel was in some trouble in Halifax, something about a court martial, but he couldn't get any details. And what could that have to do with him? More likely, Cambel was just as eager to return to Britain as Booth, and thought his chances might be diminished if there was no one in the province to take his place. Why else had he waited so long to finally answer his letter? Booth thought he knew. "As soon as he hears that the ship had sailed for England from Shelburne, which is the only one and which I certainly could have had a passage, he writes me. . . . This has every appearance of intent to retard my getting to England."

And now Booth had even more reason to want to be there. He'd recently learned that Michael Wallace, who'd never sent the cargo of fish to his brother-in-law in London as promised, was now in Britain himself. Perhaps he could finally track him down, force him to pay his now three-year-old debts. Would this never end?

Shelburne's Anglicans had much to celebrate.ᵛ It was December 25, 1789, and for the first time since the settlement's founding, all of the town's Anglicans were able to worship together in their own permanent church building. Three days earlier, the wardens of the new Christ Church, "in due form of law, by receiving at the hands of [architect Isaac] Hildreth and [master builder] Aaron White, the key to the great west door of the church, turning out the said builders and locking the door upon them, and then immediately opening the door again," had ceremoniously taken possession of the building. Perhaps more important, the Christmas service, jointly conducted by Shelburne's two Anglican ministers, signalled a final, formal end to the debate over who should be the real leader of what was still, by far, the dominant denomination among white Loyalists.[80]

During Shelburne's first two years, Reverend George Panton, the choice of the governor and the church establishment, and Reverend William Walter, his more popular rival, had competed in unseemly contests over which one would conduct baptisms, marriages, and funerals. In 1785, Panton had ended the "classes-and-masses" phase of the dispute by quietly retiring and returning to Britain.

Despite that, Governor Parr initially refused to acknowledge Walter, whom he continued to regard as a democratic interloper in the proper functioning of the Church of England. He only reluctantly agreed to a compromise with local authorities a year later. The agreement was that, henceforth, there would be two Anglican parishes: St. George's under Walter, and St. Patrick's under a new minister, Reverend John Rowland.

Like Walter and Panton, Rowland had been a loyalist chaplain during the revolution but, unlike them, he'd decided to remain in the United States at the end of the conflict to help organize the Protestant Episcopal Church, the necessary new name for the old Church of England in freshly independent America. Though he was well liked—"If you know [him]," said

---

80. In 1788, there had been "about 800 inhabitants in St. Patrick's parish" and probably the same number in St. George's parish.

one fellow preacher, "you could not but *love* [him]"—and could probably have continued to conduct services at St. Andrew's Church on Staten Island where he'd lived with his family since the mid-1770s, the reality was that he couldn't continue to receive his clerical pensions from Britain while he lived in the United States.

So Rowland had travelled to Halifax in the summer of 1786 to present his own case for compensation to the loyalist claims commission and, not coincidentally, to meet with Governor Parr to determine whether there might be any openings for a man of his background in Nova Scotia. By the time Rowland appeared before Commissioner Jeremy Pemberton on July 2, he was able to announce that he planned to settle in Shelburne after receiving "a very favourable response" from Parr to his request for a ministerial position there.

Even before he finally moved with his family to Shelburne nearly two years later, Rowland—who had a reputation as a "tactful peacemaker" and who knew Walter from their time together in occupied New York—had taken the first tentative steps toward reconciling Shelburne's warring factions. He met with Walter and reported he'd been "well received." Walter, for his part, wrote that he and Rowland "have been old acquaintances and have lived in the habits of friendship. It is therefore probable we shall continue in those habits."

Though they initially continued to operate as separate parishes, Walter, Rowland, and their respective vestries met on May 1, 1788, to agree on a message of thanks to the Society for the Preservation of the Gospel in London, which had agreed to fund both ministries, for its "munificence and condescension in granting to the town a mission for each of the gentlemen . . . by means of which those differences which formerly did exist among the members of the church are happily done away, and union and harmony restored." That Sunday, they held their first joint service in a temporary church building, during which Rowland delivered a sermon based on Psalm 55: "It is you, a man my equal, my companion and my familiar friend. We who had sweet fellowship together, walked in the house of God in the throng."

The problem was to find a permanent house of God. Partly because of the feud, the various factions had ended up renting space for their services in a variety of venues, including a temporary Anglican church building, Freeborn Garrettson's Methodist Chapel, the Presbyterian Church, and even the courthouse.

Just more than a month after sharing "sweet fellowship together," the two ministers and their church wardens jointly agreed to hire a bright young local architect named Isaac Hildreth[81] to create a permanent church that both parishes could share. The British government agreed to fund up to £400 of Hildreth's £620 estimate. Parishioners, setting aside their previous differences, quickly joined forces to raise the balance.

With construction completed "in a handsome and workmanlike manner, and of excellent materials," hundreds of Anglicans filled the pews of their cavernous new church on Christmas Day. In the continuing spirit of co-operation, Reverend Rowland read the prayers and Reverend Walter preached the sermon.

All was well, except for the fact that the new church had been built for a growing city. And Shelburne was no longer growing; it was shrinking. Quickly.

It had been the best winter Boston King had spent in Birchtown. Soon after he'd sold his wooden chests, a man from Shelburne had hired him to build three flat-bottomed salmon fishing boats. The man said he'd pay Boston £1 per boat and even gave him two baskets of Indian corn as an advance on his fee. Later, the man engaged Boston again, first to build him more boats and a new

---

81. A decade later, then Nova Scotia Governor John Wentworth hired Hildreth to design the new Government House in Halifax, which historian Brian Cuthbertson would later describe as "an architectural achievement unequally by any other governor in the history of Canada."

house for his family on Chedabucto Bay near Cape Breton and then as a crew member on one of his fishing vessels.

Although leaving Birchtown meant he'd had to give up his duties as one of Freeborn Garrettson's pastoral assistants, Boston King had not stopped proselytizing. He even attempted, without much success, to convince his employer, who "was as horrible a swearer as I ever met with," to stop taking the Lord's name in vain. His employer, luckily, didn't take offence, even thanking Boston at the end of one trip. "I believe if you had not been with me, I should not have made half a voyage this season." The previous fall, when it came time to pay his crew, the man had given each member £15 in wages, "and my master gave me two barrels of fish."

Back in Birchtown, Boston—who had so recently been down to his last pint of Indian meal—"was enabled to clothe my wife and myself, and my winter store consisted of one barrel of flour, three bushels of corn, nine gallons of treacle, 20 bushels of potatoes, which my wife had set in my absence, and two barrels of fish."

As always, Boston King thanked the Lord for his blessings.

Benjamin Marston gazed wistfully at the letter his sister Lucia had sent him from Marblehead, carefully considered once again her hopeful proposition, then finally took up his pen. "As gratifying your wish in making my native country [my] residence for the remainder of my days," he wrote, "it is not in my power to do for lack of means."

Not in my power . . . Little, in fact, seemed to be in Benjamin Marston's power anymore. He was adrift in London—jobless, penniless, prospect-less—thanks to Mr. Pitt and all those favour-seekers the British prime minister had favoured over him.

Benjamin had to acknowledge he had created some of his own problems, of course. Coming here, for starters. Or was that for enders? Had his first mistake—his big one, the one from which all the others flowed—occurred when he had decided to support the wrong side in the revolution? He tried not to think of that now. Instead, he looked again at the words he had just written.

Lack of means . . . How had it come to this?

When Benjamin had decided in the summer of 1786 to sail to England to press his compensation claim in person, he had been giddily optimistic. "How much [I'll get] I don't know, for they don't divulge," he'd confided to a friend, "but I am sure it will be agreeable." Given the reception when he'd presented his claim in Halifax, Benjamin was certain he'd collect at least enough to allow him to pay off his many debts, including, of course, the cash he'd had to borrow from his friend Ward Chipman for his trip to London.

Since he'd been expecting to be gone only a short time, he'd left his trunk—containing two decades' worth of journals, letters, assorted papers, and surveying instruments—with Chippy in Saint John. But that wasn't all he'd left behind. There was the still-unfinished Miramichi sawmill project and a pile of unpaid bills he'd run up with any number of Halifax merchants from whom he'd bought goods to trade with the Indians. He'd also left that business venture in a shambles.

None of these missteps would have mattered had the British government simply lived up to Pemberton's promise to compensate Benjamin reasonably for his losses from the revolution. To be fair, Pemberton hadn't set a sum when Benjamin had appeared before the loyalist claims commissioner in Halifax in May 1786. But Judge Pemberton had encouraged him to appoint a London agent to collect his money. Partly because of that, Benjamin had dared to imagine he would receive at least something close to the £475 he'd asked for.

But Prime Minister William Pitt—ostensibly concerned about the total amount his government would have to hand out once all claims were filed—had decided to make only partial payments on each claim until he had a final tally. Even so, Benjamin had expected an initial payment of at least £300. Instead, the government gave him £45—not even enough to return to New Brunswick, let alone do all the other things he had hoped to do with the money. To add insult to injury, as he wrote bitterly to

Winslow, Benjamin could name any number of others less worthy who'd received considerably more than him, thanks to their good political connections.

Edward Winslow's connections, it turned out, no longer connected quite so well, at least not in London. His influence there had actually begun to wane after Pitt wrested political power from Lord North and Charles Fox in 1783.[82] Winslow did suggest that Benjamin contact Brook Watson, an old friend who'd been Guy Carleton's commissary officer in New York and was now the lord mayor of London, but Watson had turned out to be less than helpful. "Brooky may be a good factor in all matters to which percents are annexed," Benjamin wrote to Winslow, "but, as to anything through mere friendship, it must not be expected."

Benjamin had tried to find work and ways to get himself back to New Brunswick, but they all came to naught. In 1788, he was hired as a companion to a London merchant heading for St. John's, but the merchant changed his mind at the last moment and decided to travel alone. That same merchant then offered to recommend Benjamin as an agent to another company, which was considering a fishing venture in either Nova Scotia or Newfoundland. The company eventually decided on Newfoundland, where it already had an agent, so Benjamin was out of luck again. The third time was not a charm either; he was recruited as the salesperson for a company bidding on a mast contract in New Brunswick, but the company didn't win the contract so Benjamin didn't get the job.

---

82. Winslow's living circumstances mirrored his declining influence. Having grown up in "a great mansion overlooking Plymouth Rock, which his father had built to entertain the social élite of Massachusetts," in the late 1780s he'd ended up living in Granville, near Annapolis Royal in Nova Scotia, in a two-room log house—known as Mount Necessity—with his wife, five sons, six daughters, widowed mother, and three unmarried sisters.

Meanwhile, compensation officials continued to encourage him to remain in London to wait for the rest of his money, but it never arrived. "Daily delays," he lamented in a letter to Ward Chipman, "still keeps that pittance at a distance. . . . [83] It seems," he added sadly, "as if I had ceased to be the sport and become the spite of misfortune."

Still, Benjamin did his best to "weather [misfortune's] malice," even touting another money-making scheme in his letter to Chipman. "I have invented an improvement to Hadley's Quadrant," he wrote of the instrument mariners use to figure out where they are by measuring the altitude of the sun. He'd hired an optician to produce a prototype. "This invention, I hope, will bring me sufficient to discharge the few debts I owe."

Though his invention—like his other ventures—ultimately came to nothing, Benjamin not only refused to be discouraged, but did his best to keep up the flagging spirits of friends like Edward Winslow, who had managed to land prestigious but poorly paying appointments in the colonies while a "pack of heavy ass'd pensioners living in England" siphoned off the most rewarding positions.

"My dear Ned," Benjamin had written at one point, "don't let misfortune depress your spirits. He who feeds the moose and caribou, the wild ducks and geese, the shad, gaspereaux and salmon, takes care of you and me also, and though we may sometimes be pinched, we shall be recompensed by an ample allowance of smart money." Despite that seemingly Pollyannaish sentiment, Benjamin was quick to add that he didn't want to "cultivate in you any liking to misfortune." Instead, he urged Winslow to "fight, scratch, kick, bite, throw stones, do anything to [misfortune]. I hate the very name of the toad."

---

83. By the time he finally received the rest of his compensation three years later, that pittance had become pitiful. The British government awarded Marston just £105 in total, less than a quarter of the amount he'd claimed.

Benjamin's own mood now was careening wildly from frequent frustration and anger to nostalgia, even occasionally to hopefulness. In today's letter to Lucia, for example, he wrote of his vision for his future. "I hope now, after my return from England, that my ramblings will be at an end, and that I shall be able to spend the rest of my life in the enjoyment of domestic tranquility by a fireside of my own, with some kind, fair, female companion sitting on the opposite chimney corner." He even had a certain someone in mind: Edward Winslow's oldest sister, Penelope, with whom he'd become smitten during his visit to her mother in New Brunswick before embarking on this latest misadventure. "I am sure I shall enjoy such a piece of good fortune when it comes, with a double relish," he added. "The long want of everything which deserves the name of comfortable has given me a very keen appetite for every enjoyment in which peace and tranquility and regularity make any part."

Whenever he imagined this idyllic future, he couldn't help but reflect on the turbulent past that had brought him to this sorry present—and the choices he had made during the revolution. "There is not remaining in my mind the least resentment to the country because the party whose side I took in the late great revolution did not succeed," Benjamin told his sister, "for I am now fairly convinced it is better for the world that they have not." That said, he wasn't yet ready to praise those who'd fomented it. "I should as soon think of erecting monuments to Judas Iscariot, Pontius Pilate and the Jewish Sanhedrin for betraying the Lord of Life because that even was so important and universally beneficial . . ."

"Cannot do worse, massa"

Chapter 8.

Governor," the young man said, smiling, bowing slightly, offering his long, elegant hand in greeting.[i]

"Mr. Clarkson," John Parr responded formally, stiffly, awkwardly extending his own hand to the stranger who had come to call on him. "Welcome to Nova Scotia."

Parr had known John Clarkson was coming, of course, and well before his ship had tied up at the dock this morning. He knew, too, why he was here. And he didn't like it. He'd already refused to meet with the black, Peters, when he'd attempted to call on him earlier. But that had been easy. Clarkson was another matter entirely. He was white and British, a naval officer—had he really quit the service or simply taken a leave of absence?—and he obviously had the ear of the British government. Or did he? There were John Parr's orders, and they were clear enough. But then there was that *other* letter, the mysterious one that seemed at odds with the first. Parr would have to tread carefully.

"Come in and sit down," he said, gesturing to his inner office.

On the surface, the two men could not have been more unlike. Parr was 66, short, fat, blustering; Clarkson, just 27, was tall, thin, charming in a shy sort of way. They did share one trait, however. Both men were agonizing self-doubters. But while John Parr was a man of few fixed convictions, simply eager to please his political masters if only he could figure out what it was they wanted of him, John Clarkson was a man of unshakeable, singular conviction whose endless anxiety came from questioning whether his actions were the best way to achieve "the Mission."

There could be no doubt that John Clarkson was a man on a mission. Some said he'd resigned his commission as a lieutenant in the Royal Navy because it conflicted with the principles of the gospel; others said he'd simply asked for a leave of absence to assist his brother. Whichever version was true mattered less than the reality that Clarkson had thrown himself completely and totally into this mission.

His older brother Thomas, a clergyman, was one of the leading lights in the anti-slavery movement that was slowly gaining support in Britain. His group, which included activists like Granville Sharp and William Wilberforce, had set up a company whose goal was to establish a free settlement in Africa for blacks who'd been stolen from their homes and made slaves. Though their initial efforts—resettling London's poorest blacks in Africa—had ended in dismal failure, they were undeterred. In fact, they'd recently joined forces with a black loyalist ex-soldier named Thomas Peters who'd convinced them—or had they convinced themselves?—that Nova Scotia, with its thousands of frustrated but hard-working black Loyalists, would prove fertile recruiting ground for their next back-to-Africa expedition.

Peters, who was rumoured to have been born of noble lineage in Africa and stolen into slavery as a young man, had travelled to London from Nova Scotia the year before, carrying a petition from his fellow blacks seeking redress for their many and various grievances against the British government. Peters, a slave who'd earned his freedom as a guide for the British army, had settled in Brindley Town near Digby at the mouth of the Bay of Fundy in Nova Scotia after the revolution because Shelburne was already overrun with black settlers. He and his group of sixty Black Pioneers and their families—like their fellow blacks in Birchtown and Shelburne—had quickly discovered the hollowness of the British promises of land and freedom. But unlike those in Birchtown and Shelburne—whose leader, Stephen Blucke, had ingratiated himself with the white power structure—the blacks in Brindley Town had an angry champion in Peters. When he failed to get satisfaction on this side of the Atlantic, Peters set off for London. And now, a year later, in October 1791, he had returned with a new dream: he would lead his people back to Africa to establish their own free settlement in Sierra Leone.

John Clarkson agreed to go to Nova Scotia with Peters, partly to handle the logistics of the relocation on behalf of the London-based Sierra Leone Company and partly to assist in dealings with what Clarkson anticipated would be reticent, perhaps even obstructionist white officials. Like John Parr.

Unfortunately, Peters—who didn't completely trust the Englishman and bristled at the suggestion he required his assistance—had landed in Halifax before Clarkson, been rebuffed in his attempt to meet with Parr, and already left Halifax to begin soliciting settlers for Africa in his old haunts at Brindley Town and Saint John.

So Clarkson was on his own in his dealings with Parr, though he was not without leverage. With the help of the British abolitionists, Peters had been able to tell his story to Henry Dundas, the British secretary of state, who'd already written to Parr, ordering him to investigate Peters' complaints of unfairness in doling out land grants. If the black Loyalists had been badly treated, he instructed Parr to make sure they got land "in a situation so advantageous as may make them some atonement for the injury they have suffered by this unaccountable delay." Dundas also suggested two other alternatives for satisfying the settlers' grievances. The British government, he said, would underwrite the costs for those blacks who wanted to relocate to Sierra Leone with Clarkson's company. Black veterans could also choose to re-enlist in the West Indian Black Carolina Corps, which was in need of soldiers.

Dundas's letter put John Parr in an uncomfortable quandary. What if an inquiry determined that the black Loyalists hadn't received the Nova Scotia land they'd been promised? Whose fault would that be? And if they chose to leave for Sierra Leone or the West Indies instead of remaining in the province, whose administration would that reflect badly on?

Parr knew that Clarkson knew all about the Dundas letter; Parr suspected Clarkson's group may have even had a hand in its drafting. But he was certain that Clarkson didn't know about the other message, the one from "E.N.," an official in the minister's office, that seemed to countermand the first.

John Parr wasn't at all certain what he should do, so he acted as he always did when faced with such a dilemma. He equivocated. He patiently explained to the earnest young man seated across from him that he did indeed intend to set up an inquiry to look into Peters' complaints (neglecting to mention that he'd already written to Dundas, dismissing Peters' allegations as "a misrepresentation. . . . I have at all times peculiarly attended to their settlements," he informed his political master, adding somewhat haughtily, "I think I may with safety say that these people were put on lands and in a situation then much envied") and assured Clarkson he would appoint agents in each section of the province who would explain each of the various options being offered to the black settlers (without, of course, pointing out that all of the commissioners he planned to appoint would be white and, for the most part, hostile to the idea that such a rich source of cheap labour might choose to leave the province).

Not that Clarkson was fooled. He "could plainly see," as he confided to his diary later, "the governor would rather I should not succeed." Still, he was smart enough to know it would not be wise to antagonize needlessly such a powerful figure so, when Parr invited Clarkson to a dinner the next night with a group of local worthies, he was quick to accept. Who knew? Perhaps he would find more sympathetic companions at dinner.

Africa! Boston King rolled the word around in his mind once more, heard the faintly familiar-yet-mysterious sound of it. Strange. Over the past several years, he'd often thought about the land of his father's birth, imagining what a continent filled with black people might look like, fretting that its inhabitants had not had the opportunity he'd had to hear the word of the Lord, wishing there was some way he could bring its blessings to them, but knowing he couldn't.

And now, suddenly, here was this tall, reed-thin white man meandering from hut to cabin to lean-to in Boston's new village of Preston, talking animatedly about the possibility that he and his fellow black Loyalists might really return to the land of their fathers and establish their own free town there, a Christian place where all men really would be equal. It seemed impossible, but . . . nothing was impossible with faith. Had the Lord come to guide him again? To Africa this time?

Two years earlier, the Lord, with a little help from Mr. Black, had led him from Birchtown to Preston. A community of about a hundred families near Halifax, Preston was yet another poor black community on the edge of a more prosperous white city. William Black, the young Methodist missionary, had become the society's general superintendent for eastern British North America after Freeborn Garrettson returned to the United States. In 1789, Black had invited Boston and Violet to relocate to Preston to take charge of the society's work among the blacks there.

Boston had done his best, though he was still uncomfortable in the role of a preacher, and it had taken him many frustrating months to feel like he was reaching anyone. But then one day, near the end of one of his sermons, he finally felt a divine presence in the little chapel he and his fellow Methodists shared with David George's Baptists and the local Huntingdon followers. Some in the congregation that day "fell flat upon the ground, as if they were dead, and others cried aloud for mercy," Boston would remember. After that, he became more confident, except, of course, whenever white people came to hear him speak. Then, "I was greatly embarrassed because I had no learning, and I knew they had."

But the white man who'd come to Preston today had put Boston at ease with his disarming charm and his boyish enthusiasm for an idea Boston suspected was a heaven-sent answer to prayers he hadn't quite articulated.

John Clarkson explained that he was part of a group whose members wanted, "as far as possible in their power, to put a stop to the abominable slave trade." They had organized a company, and he had come to Nova Scotia to find a group of "Adventurers," blacks of "honesty, sobriety and industry" who wanted to start new—and truly free—lives for themselves in Africa. The company would assist with the sale of whatever property they had in Nova Scotia, provide free passage to Sierra Leone, and guarantee them land and provisions on arrival, all in exchange for a share of the foodstuffs their new farms would soon produce. Best of all, slavery would be expressly forbidden, and "the civil, military and commercial rights and duties of blacks and whites shall be the same and secured in the same manner."

As obviously enthusiastic as Clarkson was about his plan, he was also quick to leaven his encouragement with cautions and caveats, as if worried that his own optimism might lead them astray. Pioneering in Africa would undoubtedly be hard, he told Boston. Those whose lives in Nova Scotia had become tolerably comfortable should probably remain where they were and build on what they had.

Boston King listened carefully to all that Clarkson had to say. He had, he had to admit, "just gotten into a comfortable way." In addition to his role in the local church, he'd landed a job with a "gentleman who gave me two shillings per day, with victuals and lodging." He could easily stay here and build on what he had, as Clarkson had suggested. And yet . . . And yet, there were so many Africans who needed to know what he now knew.

After considering a while, Boston approached Lawrence Hartshorne, a Quaker businessman from Halifax who'd accompanied Clarkson to Preston today, and told him that he wanted to go to Africa. Hartshorne brought him to Clarkson who was, at first, reluctant to encourage Boston to leave his "comfortable way. . . . But when I told them that it was not for the sake of the advantages I hope to reap in Africa which induced me to undertake the voyage, but from a desire that had long possessed my mind, of contributing to the best of my poor ability, in spreading the knowledge of Christianity in that country . . . they approved of my intention, and encouraged me to persevere in it."

Boston King had become one of the first, but certainly not the last, Sierra Leone "Adventurers."

John Parr hesitantly swung his legs out from the coverless bed on which he'd spent another fitful night, painfully raised his body to a sitting position, and gingerly prepared to stand up by delicately placing one foot and then the other on the cold floor of his bedchamber.[ii] The pain was excruciating. And it was not just in his big toe any longer, though that appendage was certainly red and swollen. The searing, hot-poker agony had now spread to other joints as well.

It should have helped to know he was in good company, that Benjamin Franklin and Thomas Jefferson were fellow gout sufferers, and that many people referred to this affliction as "the disease of kings" because of its association with too much good food and drink, but Parr could find little comfort even in that knowledge. Only agony. Worse, his disease of kings seemed to be flaring up more and more often these days.

Parr didn't have time for gout; he had important business to attend to. Not the least of which was nipping this Sierra Leone business in the bud before it could flower into something more significant and dangerous. He wasn't doing this simply in his own political self-interest, he told himself. He was doing the bidding of his superiors in London, even if they couldn't acknowledge publicly what they wanted him to do. While Dundas's official letter to Parr, which had been printed in the local press, spoke benevolently of "atonement," Parr had received a second, cryptic but clear, and contradictory instruction from inside the secretary of state's office. The private note, sent at the same time as the public letter, was signed by "E.N."—which could only be Evan Nepean, Dundas's ambitious undersecretary of state—and it encouraged Parr to "do all in [your] power to retard" the Sierra Leone venture. What did the note mean? Was Nepean relaying private instructions from his boss, instructions he didn't want known? Parr couldn't be sure, but he did know that putting an early end to Clarkson's mischief-making would almost certainly be in *his* best interest.

He'd been busy since he'd met young Clarkson two weeks ago. As per Dundas's official instructions, he had set up a commission to investigate Thomas Peters' complaints but tightly constricted its terms of reference. It could look only into Peters' specific allegation that he'd been denied property in the Annapolis-Digby area and not his more general criticisms about the way in which Parr's government had parcelled out, or failed to parcel out, land to its black settlers. As a result, it seemed exceedingly unlikely that the commissioners could find fault with the governor himself for any injustices.

To make that even less likely, Parr had appointed two allies, members in good standing of the white establishment in Annapolis—Alexander Howe, an "old settler" Member of the Legislative Assembly and ardent anti-Loyalist, and Job Bennett Clark, a local businessman—to conduct the investigation.[84]

---

84. Not surprisingly, the final report declared that Peters was the author of his own misfortune for having left Annapolis in frustration too soon. "It appears that every attention was paid to this man, and his people in general, and that they had lands granted to them wherever they chose to settle in this province—and that if he had not hastily quitted it, he would have received his full share of provisions and lands with the others."

He'd also handed Howe a related patronage plum—along with his own thinly veiled instructions. Howe would serve as one of the agents whose ostensible job was to inform the local black communities about the option to emigrate to Sierra Leone and then gather the names of any who wanted to take it. "My motive [in appointing you]," Parr had indiscreetly explained in his letter to Howe, "was to give you a little employment and put a little cash in your pocket. You need not be over-anxious in procuring or persuading the blacks to remove." Nor, presumably, need Howe be overanxious about determining whether Thomas Peters had, in fact, been poorly treated.

Parr's other agent appointees were, with one notable exception, men of equally dubious devotion to the cause. The exception was Lawrence Hartshorne,[85] the Quaker businessman who'd served as William Booth's agent in Halifax and become something of a zealous convert to the Clarkson cause, having met with the Englishman soon after his ship first docked in Halifax and then accompanying him on his rounds of meetings with blacks in both Halifax and Preston. Parr had heard reports that, on the first day Clarkson had set aside to interview prospective emigrants, Hartshorne had signed up seventy-nine of them. And that there were at least a hundred, maybe more, waiting for the chance to join them.

Luckily, Parr had chosen his other agents more wisely. James Putnam, like Howe a Member of the Legislative Assembly, was responsible for informing residents of the black communities along the eastern shore and in Guysborough of the government's relocation offer. So far, Putnam had—impossibly—not discovered a single soul in any of those communities who was the least

---

85. It's not clear why Parr chose Hartshorne, a successful hardware merchant and influential man in local business and political circles, but also a Quaker and abolitionist. Even more surprising, Hartshorne was a supporter of Parr's political rival, John Wentworth. After Wentworth assumed the lieutenant-governorship, Hartshorne became an MLA and, eventually, a member of Wentworth's ruling council.

interested in going to far-off Sierra Leone. Parr felt certain Putnam would be no more successful in the weeks ahead.

The pseudonymous author of a letter to the Halifax newspapers attacking the project turned out to be the father of Job Bennett Clark, another of the agents Parr had appointed. "Philanthropos's" letter warned that if the blacks were lucky enough to escape being returned to slavery, they would almost certainly die in the steaming, unfamiliar, unhealthy African jungles. The letter was read aloud in black communities across the province, as was part of a report from the Society for the Propagation of the Gospel describing the deaths of earlier would-be settlers in Sierra Leone.

To cover the largest and most important black communities, Shelburne and Birchtown, Parr had appointed Stephen Skinner, the influential former New Jersey politician, local businessman, and political fixer who quite obviously knew what was expected of him. Skinner was already quietly lobbying his old friend Stephen Blucke, the unelected mayor of the Birchtown blacks, to use his influence to discourage residents there from getting caught up in Clarkson's wild scheme.

Parr's most pressing concern this morning, however, was that Clarkson himself was on his way to Shelburne. Would he be as successful there as he had been in Halifax? Was there anything Parr could do to "retard" his progress? Perhaps a letter to Skinner, instructing him not to enlist anyone? But on what grounds?

Damn! This gout made it difficult for him to think clearly. Perhaps a glass of port would ease the pain.

John Clarkson began, as he inevitably did, by carefully testing the older black gentleman seated across from him. "Well, my friend," he said, "I suppose you are thoroughly acquainted with the nature of the proposals offered to you by his majesty."

It was October 25, 1791. For the past three mornings, Clarkson had turned this room in the Shelburne Inn into a processing centre where he could meet face to face with those who wanted to go to Sierra Leone and determine for himself their suitability. The line outside his door formed early, and was always long. Young, old, men, women, even children. It was exhausting, and distressing. He'd listened to horrendous story after horrific tale about the brutality these "poor creatures" had had to endure, not only as slaves but also—worse—as supposedly free British citizens here in Nova Scotia. Some of them had apparently given up hoping for themselves, and asked only that Clarkson allow their children to join the Sierra Leone expedition so they could seek new and better lives in the continent of their forefathers. Clarkson found their intensity overwhelming, their sincerity poignant.

The ill-dressed man in front of him today had been born in Africa and still spoke English in an awkward, stuttering, almost singsong way. In response to Clarkson's question, the man allowed that, while he had not heard the specifics of what Clarkson had told the gathering at Moses Wilkinson's chapel two days earlier, it didn't make any difference.

"No massa," he began earnestly. "Me no hear. Nor no mind. Me work like slave. Cannot do worse, massa . . . Am determined to go with you, massa . . . If you please."

Listening quietly, Clarkson was overcome again by the enormity of the task he had taken on, and by the absolute rightness of this mission.

His new friend David George[86] might call it providence. Their first encounter five days earlier had certainly been providential; the black preacher had been standing on the dock in Shelburne harbour preparing to board a vessel bound for Halifax in order to look for Clarkson when his schooner miraculously—providentially—tied up at the same wharf. George explained to Clarkson that his parishioners had heard rumours about the Englishman's African adventure, and were curious to learn more.

---

86. George named his youngest child John in honour of Clarkson.

They weren't alone. Before Clarkson had left Halifax, Hartshorne passed along a letter he'd received from a Mr. Blucke, representing, he claimed, another group from Birchtown who were also eager to join the exodus and wanted more information.

Clarkson knew better now. About Blucke. And about Stephen Skinner, the man seated beside him this morning. As the official agent Parr had appointed in Shelburne, Skinner was supposed to be assisting him in enlisting blacks for Sierra Leone, but he was also Blucke's ally—or was it the other way around?—in attempting to thwart his efforts.

Everyone in Shelburne, it seemed, had heard of the Sierra Leone project, and everyone had an opinion on it. Some land speculators, "actuated by the vilest motives, [tried to] persuade [the blacks] to go [so] that they may purchase their property on the most shameful terms," he noted, but most of the white employers in Shelburne adamantly opposed the idea, fearing the loss of their main source of cheap labour. They were especially concerned that the "wrong" blacks might decide to leave. Clarkson's strict insistence that prospective settlers provide him with proof of their good character and industry, they fretted, would drain the already troubled community of its most productive and useful black citizens, leaving only "the shiftless, the sick and the disabled."

Even before Clarkson arrived in Shelburne, emotions had begun to bubble over. Some whites were offering bribes to their black workers to convince them not to leave. Others were concocting more nefarious schemes—inventing debts, withholding wages, refusing to sign the statements attesting to their good character that Clarkson required—to dissuade their servants, slaves, sharecroppers, and employees from abandoning them. A few, even more ominously, threatened physical violence. In fact, George had confided to Clarkson that if anyone found out he had met privately with the Englishman, "my life would not be safe." Clarkson, George added, should be careful too. As Clarkson wrote later, "he cautioned us from appearing in the town or the country after it was dark for—as some of the inhabitants were men of the vilest principles—our business in this port might probably induce them to do us an injury."

As a result of his discussions with George, Clarkson decided not to continue with his intended itinerary, which would have taken him to the black communities in Digby and Annapolis, but to return to Halifax immediately after meeting with as many potential recruits as he could find in Shelburne and Birchtown.

After meeting with George's Shelburne congregation—to a person, they expressed the desire to go to Sierra Leone—Clarkson travelled the next day to nearby Birchtown. There, he addressed an even more enthusiastic gathering of close to four hundred people of all ages and denominations who'd crowded into—and around—Moses Wilkinson's chapel to hear the promise of yet another promised land.

Well aware that "the future happiness, welfare and perhaps the life of these poor creatures" turned on his words, Clarkson had deliberately chosen to be as neutral as possible. Standing at the chapel pulpit, he read aloud, word for official bureaucratic word, the British secretary of state's August letter to Governor Parr, not only explaining the British promise to relocate the black Loyalists to Africa if they so chose, but also outlining the offer to enlist them in the British army in the West Indies. Clarkson also read out the British politician's clear orders to their governor to investigate Thomas Peters' complaints and, if justified, to rectify the wrongs done. Clarkson didn't have to explain to this skeptical audience how much faith they should place in Parr on that score.

As he'd done in Halifax, Preston, and Shelburne, Clarkson was careful to warn his audience that attempting to create a new community for themselves in the wilds of Africa was not an undertaking for the faint of heart, and he suggested that those who had somehow managed to begin to make lives for themselves in Nova Scotia would be best served by choosing to stay and build on that foundation.

While Clarkson did his best to refute some of the most ludi-
crous of the false rumours the mischief-makers were spreading—
that he was really a slave trader in disguise; that they'd all die in
the steaming jungles of disease or marauding beasts; that they'd
have to pay huge quit-rents just to get title to their promised
land—he kept returning to his mantra. They should, he
repeated, "weigh it well in your minds and not suffer yourselves
to be led away, on the one hand, by exaggerated accounts of the
fertility of the soil or, on the other, by representations of the
badness of the climate."

Nothing he said, however, appeared to discourage anyone.
After he'd finished speaking, the locals mobbed him, assuring
him "they were unanimous in their desire for embarking for
Africa, telling me their labour was lost upon the land in this
country and their utmost efforts would barely keep them . . . and
as they had made up their mind for quitting this country, they
would not be diverted from their resolution though disease, and
even death, were the consequence."

The next morning, back in Shelburne, Clarkson began interviewing each of those who wanted to leave. Skinner sat beside
him, carefully making a list of the names of each successful
applicant.

On the surface, Skinner appeared to be an enthusiastic if
unlikely convert to Clarkson's cause. Over dinner one night, he'd
even complimented Clarkson on his hard work and even-
handedness in his dealings with the blacks. Behind Clarkson's
back, however, Skinner was among those doing his best to undermine him. He encouraged his friend Blucke to collect signatures
on an anti–Sierra Leone petition. The petition, which Blucke cir-
culated even during Clarkson's visit, disparaged those among
their fellow citizens who were "so infatuated" as to go along with
his scheme and called on the government to provide each of those
who stayed in Nova Scotia with a grant equal to the amount it
would pay to ship their fellow citizens off to a place "we conceive
to be their utter annihilation."

Although Blucke did manage to convince fifty-two of his neighbours to sign his petition—which was to be forwarded to Governor Parr—more than five times that number signed up for the Sierra Leone expedition in just the first three days after Clarkson's speech. And many more were waiting to add their names to the list.

Such success heaped yet another anxiety on John Clarkson's already full plate. When he and Peters had left London for Nova Scotia three months earlier, the Sierra Leone Company had anticipated its two agents, between them, might, with luck, attract a few hundred hardy souls to their banner. That was the basis on which they'd convinced the British government to underwrite the blacks' transport to Africa. Given the dramatically increased numbers, would the government now change its mind and renege on that offer? Even if it didn't, where would Clarkson find enough vessels to transport all these people from Shelburne to Halifax, and then to Africa.

But even in his most self-doubting moments—and there were many—meeting people like the determined old man sitting opposite him this morning kept Clarkson focused on the real mission. When he began to trot out his usual cautions—"You must consider that this is a new settlement and, should you keep your health, you must expect to meet with many difficulties . . ." the man didn't even wait for him to finish.

"Me will know that, massa," he said quickly. "Me can work much. Me care not for climate. If one die, had rather me die in my own country than in this cold place."

There was nothing more to say. Clarkson nodded at Stephen Skinner, who added the man's name to his ever-lengthening list.

Dead! No one had expected that![iii] On November 25, 1791, Governor John Parr died, the victim of a sudden, especially virulent attack of gout. He was 66.

Although everyone who was anyone in Nova Scotia politics, business, and religion attended his funeral four days later, and although they would all, publicly at least, pay proper deference to the man who had presided over the affairs of their colony for nine tumultuous years, there seemed a curious lack of sadness at his passing.

Or perhaps not so curious. John Parr, a career military man of modest accomplishment accustomed to following clear orders and being obeyed without question when he relayed those orders down the line, had had the misfortune to land his appointment at a time when it called for someone entirely different. He had tried. When it became clear the Nova Scotia governorship was not to be the soft sinecure he had expected, Parr had thrown himself into doing whatever it was he thought his political masters in London wanted him to do. His problem was that they, too, often, didn't know what they wanted or, just as important, didn't make it clear to him. He had also tried to accommodate the Loyalists, but their demands never ended. And there were too many of them, all wanting both the same things and too many different things. Parr had become convinced that no one—not even their sainted leader-in-waiting, "Governor" John Wentworth—could have satisfied them.

It didn't help, of course, that Parr wasn't one of them. And it didn't help either that he had begun his tenure by renaming their new city after his patron, who just happened to be their nemesis. They'd lobbied unsuccessfully for years to get rid of Parr, and now gout had finally done what letters and petitions could not.

What now?

John Wentworth, the one-time loyalist governor of New Hampshire and current unhappy surveyor general of his Majesty's forests, happened to be in London at the time of Parr's death. As soon as he heard, he wrote to Lady Rockingham, urging his former patron's widow to use whatever influence she had to win him the rightful place that Parr's appointment had denied him. "The government of Nova Scotia has been the particular object of my expectation," he wrote pleadingly, adding that landing such a prestigious position would allow him to "continue my [family] name in that line of respectability that it has ever possessed since its settlement in America in the year 1628."

Wentworth certainly was not the only one whose first thought, on hearing of Parr's death, was what it might mean for John Wentworth.

James Dole, one of the original Port Roseway Associates who'd long since abandoned Shelburne and returned to his home in Albany, wrote to his friend Gideon White, exulting that "the enemy of Shelburne has moved to his grave, and its friend [Wentworth would soon move] to the helm."

According to Wentworth's wife, Fanny, at least forty other Nova Scotia Loyalists wrote letters to them in London, urging John to seek the governorship. And the day after news of Parr's death reached London, the house where they were staying "was filled with a levee of merchants from the city of London . . . all advocating that [John] ask for Nova Scotia."

It seemed only a matter of time before the job would be his.

But John Wentworth's near future mattered far less to John Clarkson than his own immediate present. He had finally returned from Shelburne, excited but, as usual, anxious. Having seen and experienced first-hand the suffering the black Loyalists had endured and the hostility they—and he—had faced from the white settlers, Clarkson was no longer quite so doubtful about the wisdom of their relocating to Africa. However, he was now extremely concerned about whether he could accommodate all of those who'd signed up. Besides the ever-expanding group in Shelburne, it turned out that virtually everyone in Preston—250 people—had decided to join the exodus. Where would they find enough vessels? And what kind of seagoing accommodations could he provide them with? In London, Clarkson had heard horrific tales of life aboard the overcrowded, filthy slave ships, and he was determined that these settlers—close to a third of whom had made that dreadful journey from Africa to America—not have to endure anything even remotely similar on their return trip to Africa.

But how to prevent it? Clarkson was dependent on yet another local agent, Michael Wallace, a prominent Halifax businessman (the man who'd caused William Booth such aggravation) who'd been chosen by John Parr and contracted by the British government—which was paying for transportation—to line up the necessary ships and supplies for the voyage. Was Wallace up to the task? Was he even supportive of the mission? Judging by the quality of Parr's other appointments, Clarkson wasn't encouraged.

Clarkson, in fact, wasn't especially despondent at the news that the governor had died. Despite the fact that he was a Christian and a charitable sort, his conclusion, which he confided to his diary, was that Parr was a man of "inferior abilities . . . not calculated for the position he filled."

The fact was that Parr, almost to his last breath, had done his best to undermine Clarkson. Two weeks earlier, soon after Clarkson had returned from Shelburne, Parr had blithely informed him over dinner one night that he'd already ordered Skinner not to enrol anyone else for the Sierra Leone expedition. He'd done it for the blacks' own good, Parr told Clarkson, because they had become too "infatuated with the notion of a change of situation, which he thought would be the means of sending them to their graves." Clarkson had tried to argue, but the governor was adamant. At least, Clarkson thought now, Parr would no longer be an impediment.

While Wentworth jockeyed for position in London, Clarkson would have to deal with Richard Bulkeley, the long-time president of the province's governing council who would now take over as acting governor. Would he be more accommodating to Clarkson's mission, or at least less obstructionist?

Clarkson would find out soon enough, as he would need to call on the acting governor for assistance almost immediately. On the very day of Governor Parr's funeral, Thomas Peters had returned to already overcrowded Halifax leading a bedraggled group of more than ninety people whom he'd signed up during his journey to Annapolis, Digby, and New Brunswick. Many had brought with them little more than the often inadequate clothes they wore on their backs. Where would they live until the boats arrived?

"David George!" John Clarkson stood ramrod straight on the ship's deck in the middle of Halifax harbour, calling out the names of each of its confirmed passengers—"not slaves," as he was at pains to reassure them. As he announced their names, each head of family stepped forward in the gathering darkness to receive a copy of a certificate Clarkson had specially printed for the occasion. "The bearer," the unofficial but symbolic certificate read, "having produced to us a satisfactory certificate of character as required by the Company . . . shall receive free of expense" a specified number of acres in Sierra Leone in accordance with the "printed proposals of the Company."

Although the certificates declared it to be December 31, 1791, it was already January 10, 1792. And Clarkson had initially assured the Adventurers they'd be leaving Halifax on December 20, 1791. It was yet another indication of just how unpredictable, chaotic, and tumultuous the last month and a half had been for John Clarkson, and especially for the 1196 men, women, and children who would finally set sail for Africa tomorrow morning.

No one had anticipated that so many of what one Halifax newspaper dismissed as the "sooty brotherhood" would choose to leave Nova Scotia. Not the provincial government, which had done its best to discourage their flight. Not the British government, which had committed to pay for their relocation but was now having second thoughts. Not the officials of the Sierra Leone Company in London, who were expected to manage their resettlement in Africa. And certainly not John Clarkson, who had been left largely on his own to make it all happen.

The would-be emigrants had been streaming into Halifax since early December. They came by ship and by foot, some having walked a hundred miles or more through knee-deep snow carrying little more than the clothes on their backs.

In addition to the 90 people Thomas Peters had brought with him to Halifax, another 220 had made their way by land or by sea from New Brunswick, while 250 more—virtually every man, woman, and child in the community—had left Preston a ghost town.

The largest group, of course, came from Shelburne and Birchtown. "Almost all the blacks went," David George would recall, "except for a few of the sisters who were inclined to go back to New York, and sister Lizzie, a Quebec Indian, and Brother Lewis, her husband, who was half an Indian, both of whom had been converted under my ministry and had been baptized by me." Birchtown lost all of its black religious leaders—Moses Wilkinson; Cato Perkins, who'd taken over when John Marrant left for the United States; and John Ball, a former member of Wilkinson's congregation who, like Boston King, had become a preacher in his own right—and almost all of their congregations.

In total, 544 people had arrived in Halifax from Shelburne aboard twenty-two vessels of every shape and size. They were hungry and tired; they'd packed two days' provisions but their weather-delayed trip had lasted five. Only David George seemed unperturbed. He'd managed to preach a farewell sermon during a stopover in Liverpool, where the wife of one of the locals who "was very kind to me" gave him some salted herring he hoped would last him and his family all the way to Sierra Leone. David seemed equally sanguine amid the overcrowded craziness of Halifax, putting the long weeks of waiting to good use by preaching from house to house in the city.

John Clarkson's days—and nights—had been far more frenzied. If he wasn't haranguing Michael Wallace, trying to have the agent act more expeditiously to contract the fifteen ships needed to transport the Adventurers to Africa so they could arrive before the onset of Sierra Leone's rainy season, he was negotiating for warehouse space, stoves, and bedding to accommodate the seemingly never-ending influx of refugees. The first warehouse he'd rented, the Sugar House Barracks, had quickly become so overcrowded he'd had to find another to prevent an outbreak of disease. Even so, eight would-be Adventurers had died waiting for their ship to sail. Clarkson not only had to find places for the new arrivals to stay; he also had to beg Bulkeley, Parr's interim successor, for donations of warm clothing because "more than half the people from Shelburne are entirely naked."

Clarkson was also spending money he didn't know for certain he had—though he'd been writing frequent letters to Company officials explaining the situation in Halifax, he'd received no replies or instructions—to refit the fleet of motley vessels Wallace had probably already paid too much to hire.

He and Thomas Peters had minutely inspected each ship, making sure there was sufficient space for each passenger and adequate ventilation for the journey. If not, they hired carpenters to complete renovations. Clarkson was keenly aware that many of those making this voyage had already endured the reverse journey in the overcrowded, stinking hold of a slave ship, and he was determined that nothing on these ships would remind them of that horror. He drew up rules for the ships' masters covering everything from on-board cleanliness to the security of the passengers' supplies. He always referred to the Adventurers that way, insisting that the ships' captains treat them always as "passengers who have paid the price demanded by the owners for their accommodation."

At the same time—and to the chagrin of Thomas Peters—Clarkson drew up equally strict if patronizing rules for the blacks, demanding "modest and decent behaviour towards the officers of the ship [and] particular attention to divine worship in the best way you are capable of, constantly remembering with humble gratitude the goodness and power of God, and that if you conduct yourself in such a manner as to have His approbation, you must be happy."

Tonight, Clarkson was travelling in a small boat from vessel to vessel, reading aloud his codes of conduct one more time, offering encouraging words for the journey, and dramatically presenting his special certificates to each and every family.

David George carefully examined the document Clarkson had given him. There was a time not that long ago—though it sometimes must have seemed like forever—when he could not have read the words on the paper, when he could not have spelled let alone dreamed of obtaining freedom. For more than fifteen years now, he and his fellow black Loyalists had been chasing the elusive British promise of freedom. For a brief moment, David had thought he'd found it in Shelburne, but that had proved illusory. Now he had sold his meeting house lot and all of his land in Shelburne, perhaps half an acre in total, to a local merchant for £7, had packed up his wife and six children, and was preparing to set sail one more time, leaving behind this cold, rocky, and unfriendly place in search of a reality that would finally match the vision in his head. Would Sierra Leone provide that? And what would happen to Birchtown—and Shelburne—now that so many of them were leaving it?

David George and John Clarkson shared a brief farewell embrace before Clarkson scrambled into the small craft that would take him to the next vessel. There were still more ships to visit and certificates to present tonight before he could rest. Tomorrow, they would sail for a place they called Freetown in the Province of Freedom, where everyone would finally be free and all would be equal.

And now this! Gideon White had been convinced he had weathered the worst Shelburne had to offer: the end of the royal provisions; the collapse of the whale fishery in which he'd personally invested so heavily; the British trade deals with the Americans that had effectively cut off Britain's still-struggling North American colonies from much-needed trade advantages; the years of famine; and, of course, the continuing exodus.[iv] First, so many of his fellow Port Roseway Associates, who'd once shared the dashed dream of building a new and better New York, had left. Then the other would-be settlers, adventurers, and ne'er-do-wells who'd tried and then abandoned the place as hopeless had followed. Finally, this past winter had seen the departure of the black backbone of the community—the servants and labourers and, oh yes, tenant farmers who'd done the hard work no one else wanted to do, and done it better and for less than anyone else.

Gideon knew more about that last point than he cared to. Since his marriage to Deborah five years earlier, he'd invested heavily in his farming operations. He'd returned from his honeymoon with two oxen, two cows, and a horse. Later that same year, he'd ordered another six "fat" oxen, a cow, a milk cow, half a dozen sheep, seventy-six bushels of oats, ten bags for the oats, two hundred clover feed, and a cart. Followed the next year by another fourteen oxen. Eight black families had run his various farms as sharecroppers, and every single one of them had now left him for the African darkness.

There were rumours in Halifax that the entire fleet had been destroyed, and that no more than a dozen of the poor, deluded emigrants had actually arrived in their promised land. Not that that made it any easier on those, like Gideon White, whom they'd abandoned. The departure of the blacks, as he wrote to his brother-in-law Nathaniel Whitworth in London, was "a serious loss—but more so to me than anyone."

Despite that, Gideon had somehow managed to maintain the sunny optimism that had helped him survive all those earlier crises himself, and that he would now need in order to nurture his distressed fellow citizens as their recently elected representative in the provincial House of Assembly.

Gideon and Deborah spent much of that winter in Boston, resting, visiting family and friends, and preparing for the spring sitting of the legislature in Halifax. Gideon found new reason for hope in a letter he received from an old friend in Shelburne who was urgently requesting "as many garden seeds as you can beg for me. We have had the most pleasant winter I ever knew," Nicholas Ogden wrote, "and the spring is very forward. Many have begun their gardens." Could this, finally, be Shelburne's new beginning?

Gideon received his answer in another letter that reached him a month later, shortly after he and Deborah returned to Halifax. It told of a drought in Shelburne County that had "ruined the hay harvest and most of the crops in the ground. . . . The grass has been burnt the same as if it had been cut and dried . . . the whole of the oats is scorched and I am afraid ruined beyond recovery. . . . Forage will not be had."

Gideon was still reeling from that news when, five days later, he received another letter. "Amazing fires" were sweeping through Shelburne County, wiping out everything in their destructive path.

Gideon hurried back to Shelburne to see for himself. It was even worse than he'd expected. In fifteen days, the fire had destroyed more than fifty homes, not to mention barns, mills, and outbuildings. Gideon's grist mill was one of the fire's victims. His house had only been saved "owing to the great exertions of my friends," who'd covered the roof with wet blankets to keep it from catching fire and spent three days spraying it with water from the town's two fire engines.

"Providence has no doubt some great cause for the repeated judgments against this very settlement," Gideon wrote bleakly to his brother-in-law a few days later. "God's will be done. This last stroke has completely knocked down this settlement. The 800 negroes who were carried to Sierra Leone was a serious loss, but the most serious matter is my grist mill. No grist . . ."

Gideon stopped, almost as if he didn't want to let that thought take him where it might. "Enough of disagreeables," he wrote. "I will make the best of it."

"The high mountains at some distance from Freetown appeared like a cloud to us," David George later would write of that optimistic day in early March 1792 when the vessel carrying him and his flock finally dropped anchor in the harbour overlooking their new homeland. It was, he said, "a great joy to see the land."

That joy could only have been compounded by the horrific

journey they'd survived to get there. Thanks to the vagaries of the weather, they hadn't actually sailed out of icy Halifax harbour until five days after John Clarkson's farewell tour of the ships. And then the fleet—many of the assembled vessels were small coastal schooners ill-suited to an ocean crossing—had been battered by a raging, mid-Atlantic storm that began soon after they left and did not abate for more than two weeks.

Boston King had watched helplessly as one man—who'd "died as he had lived, without any appearance of religion"—had been swept overboard, leaving a wife and four children to fend for themselves. "I was on the deck at the same time that he met with his misfortune," Boston recalled, "but the Lord wonderfully preserved me." The Lord answered his prayers to preserve Violet, too. She'd been "exceeding ill most of the voyage. . . . I expected to see her die before we could reach land, and had an unaccountable aversion to bury her in the sea. In the simplicity of my heart, I entreated the Lord to spare her, at least till we reached the shore. . . . The Lord looked upon my sincerity, and restored her to perfect health."

Many others were not so blessed. At least sixty-five of the emigrants, including three of David George's elders and many of the youngest, oldest, and weakest among them, succumbed to a fever that ran rampant through the fleet during the voyage. Many more fell ill, including Clarkson himself.

Finally, after more than six weeks at sea, the first of the bedraggled vessels limped into the safety of Freetown harbour.

At first glimpse, their future appeared promising. Freetown was located in a lush tropical paradise. There were plenty of fish for catching in the river, much game for shooting in the forests, and—unlike in Shelburne—acres of wild trees weighted down with all manner of tropical fruit for them to eat. Beyond the townsite, the mountains offered forests filled with trees they could fell for the lumber they would need to build their settlement.

On the first Sunday, the 1100 who'd survived the journey gathered under a hastily built, canvas-sail roof to remember those who had not made it and to offer thanks and celebration for those who had. While there was much to celebrate, it soon became obvious that this was not the promised land—or even the land they'd been promised.

In theory, the new town was to be laid out in much the same fashion as Shelburne, with nine wide streets running parallel to the river and three cross streets, thus dividing the town into convenient blocks for further subdivision into building lots.[87] In reality, as in Shelburne, nothing had been done to prepare for the newcomers' arrival. Even though a group of more than a hundred white company officials, including surveyors, had arrived the month before from London, they'd done almost no work in laying out the town.

The Nova Scotians quickly organized themselves into companies to begin clearing the land, but they were assaulted by nature: temperatures that reached more than 40 degrees Celsius by midday, tornadoes, plagues of insects, animal attacks, and the too-quick onset of the rainy season that Clarkson had worried about back in Halifax. The rain began soon after they arrived and continued, virtually without pause, for four months. Provisions ran short, and the settlers' promised rations soon became half rations.

There was a malarial epidemic. Eight hundred—nearly four in five of their number—fell ill, as did the Company's alcoholic, London-sent doctor, who suddenly expired one day, either of the effects of malaria or from the results of a drinking binge, leaving them with no one qualified to look after the sick. Another forty settlers died within a few months of landing in Sierra Leone. "The people died so fast," Boston King remembered, "that it was difficult to procure a burial for them."

Violet King, who'd been spared the indignity of a burial at sea, was one of those who died of "the putrid fever" soon after

---

87. Each of the twelve streets was named after a director of the Sierra Leone Company.

arriving in Sierra Leone. One Friday in early April, Boston reported, "she suddenly rose up, and said, 'I am well: I only wait for the coming of the Lord. Glory be to his Name, I am prepared to meet him, and that will be in a short time.'" Two days later, surrounded by friends singing a prophetic hymn—"Lo! He comes, with clouds descending"—Violet sang along until the final verse before she "expired in a rapture of love."

In the summer of 1792, love was in short supply in Freetown, where the natural disasters and calamities were, in some ways, less troubling than the man-made mess the Sierra Leone Company seemed to be making of its noble intentions.

Part of the problem was that there were clearly different views of the Company's goals. While the Company's directors were united in their desire to abolish the slave trade, they were not as clear on the role they wanted Sierra Leone to play in that campaign. While John Clarkson and some of the others conceived of the new settlement as a shining example of what a free and equal community of blacks and whites could accomplish together, others saw the community as a way to demonstrate to a skeptical business and political world that there was a profitable alternative to the hated slave trade. They wanted to establish plantations—worked by free rather than enslaved blacks—that could survive and prosper by trading with England. As such, they were much less concerned with—and certainly less support- ive of—the idea of the black settlers running their own affairs.

During the months John Clarkson had been in Nova Scotia promising the would-be Adventurers their own land "free of expense" in a community rooted in the fundamental belief that the rights and duties of blacks and whites "shall be the same," the Company's directors in London were approving a constitu- tion that established an appointed council of eight white over- seers, including a superintendent, to govern the colony; required the settlers to sell their produce exclusively through the Company; and set out rules governing landholding, including a quit-rent of one shilling per acre and a tax of 2 percent on all produce generated by the settlers on their land. So much for land "free of expense."

To make matters worse, the councillors sent by the Company turned out not to be much harder working than their white loyalist counterparts in Shelburne had been and, thanks to the "democratic" way in which the council had been set up—with everyone, including the superintendent, having an equal say—they spent most of their time arguing among themselves. One can only imagine how Benjamin Marston might have described them.

Thomas Peters was outraged, and said so to anyone who'd listen. Many did, especially those from Annapolis, Digby, and Saint John, to whom Peters remained the charismatic leader who'd convinced them to join the expedition in the first place. The settlers from Shelburne, Birchtown, and Preston, though no less disillusioned by the broken promises, still seemed prepared to give Clarkson the benefit of the doubt. Peters' occasionally personal attacks against Clarkson soon brought David George, who called Clarkson "Honoured Sir" and considered him one of his closest friends, into the fray. After preaching against Peters, George received death threats from some on the other side.

The frustrations on all sides finally boiled over on April 7, the day on which the councillors decided they would need to reduce the settlers' promised rations by half. One faction among the settlers met to elect Peters as their speaker-general and began circulating a petition to confirm his role as their official spokesperson with the Company.

By the time reports of the gathering reached Clarkson, who had reluctantly agreed to act as the Company's superintendent though he desperately wanted nothing more than to return to England and finally marry the fiancée he had left behind to take on this mission, the relatively mundane factional meeting had been transformed by the magic of gossip and innuendo into a planned coup, whose goal was nothing less than to depose Clarkson and install Peters as governor in his place.

A distraught Clarkson immediately called an emergency town meeting for the next night—Easter Sunday—during which he confronted Peters directly. "It is probable that one or the other of us will be hanged before this palaver is settled," he began ominously. He then proceeded to harangue the assembled multitudes with a catalogue of all that the Company had already done for them, "although they were perfect strangers," and also reminded them of "the many sacrifices I had made and am daily making to promote [your] happiness." And he promised to do what he could to speed up the laying out of their lots of land. But then, denouncing the "criminality" of what he supposed they were plotting, he offered dire predictions for the future of the settlement should they allow the "demon of discord" into their community. He ended with a ringing demand that they choose between him and Peters.

No one did. Instead, they tried to explain that their intention had simply been to ease the Honoured Sir's burden by choosing one of their own to act as their spokesperson in dealings with him. It turned out, in fact, that even David George had signed the petition.

The fact that Clarkson had overreacted to the settlers' frustrations, which, in truth, Clarkson himself shared, probably said more about his own resentment of Company officials in London than his feelings about the settlers themselves. After he followed their urgings "not to expose myself any longer to the evening air as they observed I was much fatigued with talking to them and they feared it would materially injure me," Clarkson retired to his own quarters to try to sort out his feelings. "The Nova Scotians," he wrote, "if left to themselves, would fully come up to the character I have invariably given them, but they have not had fair play."

They certainly hadn't.

Ironically, Benjamin Marston also ended up in Africa, and not far from where the former Birchtown residents were trying to establish their new lives.

In January 1792, in the middle of the deepest depths of his London despondency, he had unexpectedly landed a job—as the surveyor for the Boolam Island Company. The company was headed by Henry Hew Dalrymple, an English abolitionist who had been slated to become the governor of Sierra Leone until a falling out with Thomas Clarkson led him to establish a rival venture: a settlement on the island of Bullom,[88] barely twenty miles from Sierra Leone.

Benjamin was less interested in the reasons why Dalrymple had decided to establish his colony than in the reality that it offered him a "door to escape out of England. I have embraced the opportunity," he wrote to his friend Chipman in March 1792, "with as much joy as I ever did to get out from the worst prison I was ever in."

More than just escape, Benjamin was convinced that Bullom also represented a chance for him to atone for his own very modest and distant role in "that most wicked traffic" as the owner of a few slaves, as well as an opportunity to participate in the "Robinson-Crusoe kind" of adventure he'd discovered he now preferred to ordinary employment. Perhaps most important to the relentlessly optimistic Benjamin, Bullom offered one last chance for financial independence.

Though his salary (£60 a year) was "no great thing," he explained to Chipman, the position came with a grant of five hundred acres of land, and Benjamin was already imagining its value in a few years. "The land will soon be worth £500 if the settlement should succeed, and should it prosper greatly, much more, and that in a short time," he wrote, even suggesting the possibility that he and Chipman might start a business together in Saint John to export house frames and building materials to the new settlement.

It was not to be. On August 10, 1792, barely two months after he'd arrived in Bullom, Benjamin Marston died of an outbreak of

---

88. Near the border between Sierra Leone and the Republic of Guinea.

the same African fever—malaria—that decimated his colony and the Nova Scotians' settlement in Freetown.

News of his death didn't reach his friends in North America for another year and half. On May 14, 1794, Ward Chipman—who'd long since given up hope Benjamin would repay him the costs of his trip to England "unless the good fellow had met with that good fortune which he so richly deserved"—conveyed the sad news to Edward Winslow. "Being at length satisfied that our worthy unfortunate friend Marston was really dead," he wrote, "I the other day opened his chest. The uppermost thing was a tin case enclosing some papers, all of which I now send you . . ."

What went wrong? The short answer is everything. Though historians still quibble, and parse, and dissect—one concluding that Shelburne's demise was "as much a failure of expectations as economics;" another suggesting that its founders had "failed to see that Shelburne lacked a natural hinterland;" still another arguing that the cause of its collapse "was neither social nor economic but demographic. Shelburne had too many single men"—the simple fact is that everything that could possibly go wrong in Shelburne's early years did go wrong.

That probably shouldn't have been surprising. Shelburne was born out of the anger, fear, bitterness and chaos—especially chaos—of the tail end of the American revolution when more than 30,000 disillusioned, displaced persons were all desperately seeking at the same time a new place they could call home. They did not choose Nova Scotia so much as circumstances chose it for them; it was British and it was close at hand. But they did choose Shelburne. They might have settled instead in Halifax; for all its many and various faults and lacks, Halifax was at least an actual garrison town the newcomers could overwhelm and eventually absorb even as it absorbed them.

There was no Shelburne in Shelburne. No one had even been sent ahead to survey the townsite or lay out the lots; Benjamin Marston and the other surveyors arrived just days ahead of the first 3,000 clamouring refugees. Shelburne was an idea, an improbable dream of a new and better New York that would become "an ornament to the British Empire," a beacon of hope in a bleak time. But hope blinded them to the reality that their Mecca was nothing more than a spit of rocky shoreline bordered by impenetrable forest and icy water. The would-be settlers were selective too in who they listened to, selective even in what they heard. They heard the province's surveyor-general, for example, when he told them Shelburne offered "the best situation in the province for trade, fishing and farming," but they closed their ears when he qualified that with the fact that they should "expect indifferent land in every part of the province."

Shelburne's attractions were often illusive. It did boast a wonderful harbour, but it was at least partially frozen over during the winter months. The forests could provide a bountiful harvest of timber but there were no rivers to float them to market. And there were no roads linking Shelburne to other major settlements like Halifax or Annapolis.

As one early loyalist wrote, Shelburne "has few equals . . . for bleakness, barrenness and rockiness, yet here . . . these town-bred men—merchants, tailors, carpenters and joiners, bricklayers, glaziers, tinsmiths, cabinet-makers, stationers, millwrights, goldsmiths, cutlers, wheelwrights and engravers—were set down to scratch a living from the soil or wrest it from the sea."

That, of course, was another reason for Shelburne's failure to prosper: it attracted the wrong sort of people for the job at hand. Most of the original Port Roseway Associates were not the pioneering sort, and there were few strong leaders among them. The Wentworths and the Winslows chose to live elsewhere. Those who followed, like the disbanded soldiers, not only didn't include many potential leaders but they also helped skew the new settlement's ratio of men to women even more dramatically than it was. By 1787, there were two men for every woman in Shelburne. And most of the women were either married or not of marriageable age. Those among the male settlers who wanted to find a mate, settle down and build a community soon found themselves looking elsewhere.

While those who conceived Shelburne may have had a dream, they failed to understand what it would take to transform their vision into reality. And they made some lousy decisions. "In their initial enthusiasm, they imagined the town becoming a new metropolis that would rival New York and Philadelphia," wrote historian Brian Cuthbertson, so "they poured their rapidly evaporating wealth into building fine houses rather than into industry."

That didn't matter as long as they were able to enjoy the benefits of the royal bounty; as soon as the British stopped providing provisions in the summer of 1787, however, many more were forced to go elsewhere to find paying work to support their lifestyles, often abandoning their fine houses in the rush to escape.

Those entrepreneurs who did hope to take advantage of their location—and their demonstrated loyalty to the crown—in order to make Shelburne the pivotal trading port between Britain's West Indian colonies and the mother country quickly discovered, to their surprise and chagrin, that London was not only prepared to forgive and forget its past differences with the United States in the interests of prosperity, but also that it was unprepared to favour its remaining colonies with the trade protections and tariff barriers they needed to succeed.

It may have taken a little longer but many of the Shelburne loyalists, faced with their own bleak prospects, discovered they could forgive and forget too. "On their arrival," notes historian Neil MacKinnon, "the rhetoric was that of a morality play, their world seemingly divided into loyalists and rebels, the virtuous and the villains, their fondest ambition to make Nova Scotia the envy of their enemy . . . With tempered realism, the loyalists came to accept the results of the revolution, and to set about arranging the rest of their days within the limitations of this reality."

For many, that meant swallowing their bile and their pride and returning to America. Though there are no accurate statistics, it appears that the majority of those who abandoned Shelburne in its first years went to the new United States. By the late 1780s, the mood in America had shifted too. The new country needed their skills and their wisdom. When William Walter, the Anglican minister who served as a British army chaplain during the war, finally returned to Boston in 1791, for example, one newspaper reported that "he has been invited to officiate in several of our meeting houses and met with universal approbation."

Add to all of that the natural disasters—drought and fire— that beset the town in its first decade, not to forget the decision by so many in the black communities in Shelburne and Birchtown to seek the freedom in Sierra Leone they'd been promised, and denied, in Nova Scotia, and you begin to understand just how much went wrong.

In some ways, all the reasons matter less than the reality. By 1816, the city that had once, if incredibly briefly, rivaled Boston and New York and Philadelphia, was a ghost town with just 374 settlers. Writer Thomas Chandler Haliburton, who visited Shelburne in 1826, wrote that "the houses were still standing, though untenanted. It was difficult to imagine that the place was deserted. The idea of repose more readily suggested itself than decay."

The government eventually compiled a list of all those properties whose owners had disappeared. Those with taxes unpaid were offered for sale. If they didn't sell—and most didn't—the houses on them were ordered demolished as fire hazards. Marion Robertson, who wrote *King's Bounty*, the definitive local history of Shelburne, concluded: "Strangers who stood beside the ruins 30 and 40 years later wrote of its grass-grown streets, its broken cellar holes, its wharves falling into the water, and marveled that these ruins existed within a few years of their first erection— tragic proof that towns are not built without careful forethought and resolution."

Stephen Blucke: After the exodus of most of Birchtown's blacks to Sierra Leone over his objections, Blucke's stature and influence declined. His ultimate fate is still a matter of mystery and legend. In 1795, the Bray school, where he'd been the schoolmaster for a decade, closed its doors for want of black students amid rumours Blucke had been fiddling the accounts, claiming more students than attended so he could get more funding. Blucke swore an oath before local magistrate Gideon White, insisting he'd told the truth, and the Bray Associates in London reluctantly paid up. But soon after, Blucke himself disappeared. His torn clothes were later discovered on a road near town. Some speculated he'd been killed by wild animals, but no body was ever found.

William Booth: Booth, who left Shelburne for London on his six-month leave of absence sometime late in 1789, got his wish and never returned. We know little about his later life, except that he remained in the Corps of Engineers. He was promoted to major in 1795 and lieutenant-colonel in 1800. He died in London in 1826 at the age of 78. He left behind five volumes—450 closely written pages—of diaries and correspondence, much from his time in Shelburne, and three known watercolours and drawings, documenting his two years in Shelburne.

Oliver Bruff: Though officially eulogized as a loyalist who had "suffered much persecution at New York, where he finally quitted a very comfortable situation and sought asylum in this country," the unofficial version is sadder. In 1793, he left Shelburne and settled in nearby Liverpool, N.S.. After his wife left him, he ended up, according to one researcher, "a penniless drunk surrounded by a couple of bottles." He died in 1817. The only known surviving example of his handiwork is in the collection of the Nova Scotia Museum.

Guy Carleton: Carleton returned to North America in 1786 as the Governor-in-Chief of his majesty's remaining colonies but he wasn't able to convince London to make his dream of creating one central government a reality. After close to 10 years as governor-in-chief, he resigned and returned to England in 1796. He died in 1808. He was then 84.

John Clarkson: In December 1792, Clarkson left Sierra Leone for what was supposed to be a short vacation in England, but he never returned. He had come to London "full of righteous indignation," and informed the Company directors that "their general way of doing things is so disgusting that I really could not keep my temper and very often flew out in abuse . . . They were highly displeased at my openness." Perhaps not surprisingly, they fired him. He subsequently went into private business in Essex, but never lost his zeal for the abolition of slavery. He became a founder of the Society for the Promotion of Universal Peace. He died in 1828.

Joseph Durfee: The first president of the Port Roseway Associates died in 1801 at his farm overlooking Shelburne Harbour. He was 66. In the words of his obituary, he had "removed to Shelburne with his family and the wreck of his property and sat himself down upon a tract of uncultivated land. The same industry and perseverance which had uniformly distinguished him soon rendered him an example to that infant settlement. Few men possessed a more manly and independent mind, exhibited more striking traits of industry, or have quitted life more generally and universally regretted."

David George: During the voyage from Halifax to Sierra Leone, David George had asked Clarkson "if I might not hereafter go to England . . . I told him I wished to see the Baptist brethren who live in his country." He accompanied Clarkson to London in December 1892, carrying a petition to the directors of the Sierra

Leone Company, expressing their thanks for Clarkson's efforts on their behalf and urging his return as permanent governor of their colony. Later, he and Clarkson had a falling out. George returned to Sierra Leone where he became the father of the African Baptist Church in Africa. He died in 1802.

Boston King: After his wife's death, King convinced Clarkson to allow him to establish a church and school for 20 students at a company plantation on Bullom Shore along the Sierra Leone River. In 1784, at the company's suggestion, Boston came to England and studied at the Methodist's Kingswood School to improve his own teaching skills. There, he also "found a more cordial love to the white people than I had ever experienced before." While at Kingswood, he wrote "Memoirs of the Life of Boston King, Black Preacher." In 1796, he returned to Sierra Leone where he served as a company agent at Sherbo, 100 miles south of Freetown. He died there in 1802.

Stephen Skinner: Though he'd led the rear-guard action to prevent Shelburne's black loyalist exodus to Sierra Leone, Skinner was also its main beneficiary. He bought 45 town lots, two five-acre lots, three 10-acre lots and 11 40-acre lots from departing blacks at bargain basement prices. For six town lots, for example, he paid a total of just 10 shillings. Skinner continued to be one of Shelburne's most powerful and influential citizens, serving as the county's member of the legislature from 1793–99. He died in 1808 at the age of 73.

Thomas Peters: Soon after his confrontation with John Clarkson in Sierra Leone, Peters found himself accused, tried and convicted by a jury of his fellow blacks of stealing money from the trunk of a dead man. He claimed the man owed him the money, which may explain why his punishment was simply a public reprimand and a promise to make restitution to the man's widow. Within two months, however, Peters was dead too, another victim of malaria.

Reverend William Walter: The Anglican clergyman at the centre of the religious feud among the white Anglican loyalists in the city's early years, left Shelburne in 1791 for Boston where he became the rector of the Christ Church there.

Margaret Watson: Margaret's career as a boarding house operator didn't prove lucrative enough to save her eldest son Samuel from being bound out as an indentured servant to Barrington businessman Joseph Harding from the age of 13 to 21. Her younger son Henry managed to get employment in Halifax when he turned 16 but he died three years later of consumption. That same year, 1799, Margaret's third Scottish-born husband—James Cutt, a disbanded soldier from the 76th regiment who'd become a tailor— also died. Margaret eventually moved in with her own widowed son, Samuel, who had by then moved to Halifax. Margaret, who took care of Samuel's two sons, was known as an eccentric disciplinarian. She wouldn't let the boys eat solid foods, made them stand for meals and kept a bundle of rods over the mantle to use as needed. She died in 1825 at the age of 78.

John Wentworth: Wentworth did get his wish; he succeeded Parr as Governor of Nova Scotia, and served for 16 years. Despite the fond hopes of some of his Shelburne supporters, he could do nothing to prevent the town's decline, and he certainly never considered changing its name or making it, as some had dreamed, the colony's capital.

Gideon White: White lived out his days in Shelburne, but it wasn't always easy, perhaps especially for his wife, Deborah. "Madame had rather be envied than pitied," he wrote at one point, "and the fact is our situation here is by no means the most eligible . . ." All nine of their children had to leave Shelburne for their education, or to find work, or a marriage partner. "It is a hard matter for Mama to part with her," Gideon noted when one of his daughters left for school in Boston, "but she appears to think it will be for her advantage, therefore she submits." Gideon's own ambivalence about his relationship with the land of his birth became evident in 1821 when the Pilgrim Society of Plymouth, Massachusetts, elected him an honourary member. In his letter of acceptance, he wrote: "I beg you will acknowledge to its members the heartfelt delight I feel in being enrolled as a descendant of the first born child of New England. The pride of my life had ever been to know I was born in the Old Colony of Plymouth, and no distance or change of things will ever or can alter the highest regard I have for every descendant of our forefathers."

Edward Winslow: Though he never truly recovered from the devastating impact of the revolution on his family and income, Winslow is remembered as one of New Brunswick's founding fathers. In 1804, he was appointed to the New Brunswick Supreme Court. He died in 1815, "pursued to the grave by his twin nemeses, debt and gout."

ACKNOWLEDGEMENTS

Anyone who sets out to write the story of a place begins with local histories, and local historians. When it comes to Shelburne, the late Marion Robertson, a Massachusetts-born Shelburne teacher, researcher, and folklorist, is still *the* historian. Her *King's Bounty*, the fruit of more than twenty years of poking through musty official minutes, court documents, church records, and family histories, established the firm foundation on which I was able to construct my own narrative. And I am grateful for all her hard work.

She isn't the only local historian to whom I owe a debt. Eleanor Robertson Smith, an enthusiastic and indefatigable volunteer at the Shelburne County Genealogical Society and the author of *Loyalist Foods in Today's Recipes*, introduced me to William Booth's incredible diaries and agreed to share them with me. She also told me as much as could be discovered about Margaret Watson and the fate of Oliver Bruff.

Mary Archibald, a teacher and amateur historian, authored insightful biographies of some of the town's founding fathers, including Gideon White and Joseph Durfee, as well as providing thumbnail sketches of all of Shelburne's leading citizens in her *Rules and Orders of the Friendly Fire Club, Shelburne 1784*. She is also the co-author of a Shelburne County Museum booklet, *Loyalist Dress in Nova Scotia*, that helped me imagine how the Loyalists might have looked during this period. Mary Mackay Harvey's article "Gardens of Shelburne" provided insight into what would have been growing in their yards and fields, while Laird Niven's reports of his archaeological expeditions in and around Birchtown helped me understand what that community must have looked like in its heyday.

No one who attempts to write about the journey of the black Loyalists from slavery to Shelburne to Sierra Leone can fail to acknowledge the seminal work done by two historians: Ellen Gibson Wilson, author of *The Loyal Blacks*, and James W. St. G.

Walker, author of *The Black Loyalists*. Both of these works were originally published in 1976 and both are still the definitive works on the subject.

The Loyalists, white and black, who travelled to Shelburne were part of a larger and historically significant migration. I am indebted to the work of many historians—including Neil MacKinnon, Christopher Moore, and Esther Clark Wright—whose work helped me better understand that relationship.

I am grateful, too, to the University of New Brunswick's Electronic Text Centre for fortuitously choosing its Benjamin Marston Diary Project as a prototype in a long-range plan to make important historical documents available electronically. And grateful to Benjamin himself, of course, for being worthy of such attention.

As with any project, this one endured its share of bumps and changes of direction over time. Meg Taylor, my editor on my previous book of non-fiction, *Sailors, Slackers and Blind Pigs: Halifax at War*, conceived of the original idea for this project and was its first editor. She will probably not recognize the story it has become, but I am grateful to her for convincing me not to be afraid to tackle an historical narrative.

There have been other editors along the way: Martha Kanya-Forstner, Amy Black, and Tim Rostron. Each has made this a better book and I am grateful to all of them. As I am to Maya Mavjee, Doubleday Canada's publisher, whose faith in this project never wavered.

Many thanks also to eagle-eyed copy editor Susan Broadhurst.

I would like to acknowledge the support of the Canada Council in providing research assistance as I developed this project.

As has been the case since 1995, I want to thank Anne McDermid, my agent, for making my job as a writer an easier one.

Finally, of course and always, my sincere thanks and gratitude to my wife, Jeanie, for her patience and support.

Writing a narrative account of historical events involves assimilating a lot of similar material from many different sources and then trying to combine all of those disparate pieces into a seamless narrative.

Perhaps an example will help clarify my storytelling technique.

In his after-the-fact memoir, David George describes a youthful incident in which he experienced a crisis of faith:

> I lived a bad life and had no serious thoughts about my soul, but after my wife was delivered of our first child a man of my own colour, named Cyrus, who came from Charleston, S.C. to Silver Bluff, told me one day in the woods, that if I lived so I should never see the face of God in Glory (whether he himself was converted man or not, I do not know). This was the first thing that disturbed me, gave me much concern. I thought then that I must be saved by prayer. I used to say the Lord's Prayer that It might make me better, but I feared that I grew worse, and I continued worse and worse as long as I thought I would do something to make me better, till at last it seemed as if there was no possibility of relief, and that I must go to hell.

I reimagined that episode as a scene in which an anguished David is repeating the Lord's Prayer, hoping it will "make me better" but already understanding that it has not. There's nothing in the scene I wrote that isn't true to David's description in his memoir. When I describe David as "taken aback" by what Cyrus had said to him, for example, that is my I-think-not-unreasonable interpretation of his words. There's more to the scene than simply David's dark moment of self-doubt, of course. In non-fiction narratives, scenes often serve a secondary purpose of allowing the author to unobtrusively slip in context and background. The scene, as I wrote it, also introduces David to the reader and recounts the story of his life to date. In his own account, David wrote about the day he asked "Mr. Gaulfin," [*sic*] the owner of the Silver Bluff Plantation, to allow him to become one of his slaves. That strange request becomes less puzzling when you learn more about the life and times of George Galphin and his treatment of his slaves. That information is not in David's memoir, but it is well documented elsewhere.

Separating a story from my narrative back into its constituent elements can sometimes be complicated. Often there are many sources for the same incident, with different authors contributing new details or unique insights to the larger picture. I've tried to signal those contributions in these endnotes. But I've also attempted not to make these notes exhausting. If it's clear from the context—especially as the stories develop—that a section is based on the diaries, journals, or correspondence of a particular character, I haven't referenced those sources every time they're used. In cases where that material has been supplemented with information from other sources, however, I have attempted to mention those other sources below.

PROLOGUE

i   *First, you had to meet with Joseph Durfee at his home on Water Street . . .*
The beginnings of the Port Roseway Associates is well documented. I've taken details from such sources as Kenneth Scott's "Rivington's New York Newspapers," Hazel Mathews' *The Mark of Honour*, Barnet Schecter's *The Battle for New York*, Robert Apuzzo's *New York's Buried Past*, Oscar Theodore Barck, Jr.'s *New York City during the War of Independence*, and Claude Van Tyne's *Loyalists in the American Revolution*.

CHAPTER I

i   *Joseph Durfee stood alone on some rocks at the far end of the beach . . .* This account of the scuttling of HMS *Liberty* comes primarily from *Crowd Action in Revolutionary Massachusetts 1765–1780* by Hoerder Dirk (see Bibliography) while most of the details about Joseph Durfee's life and ancestry come from *Eleven Exiles: Accounts of Loyalists of the American*

Revolution, edited by Phyllis R. Blakeley and John Grant. Much of the broader context about relations between England and her North American colonies is drawn from *The Long Fuse: How England Lost the American Colonies, 1760–1785* by Don Cook.

ii   *"Our Father, who art in heaven . . ."* David George left an account of his life as a slave and his conversion to Christianity in interviews he gave in England to two Christian Brothers in 1792. The information on George Galphin comes from a number of sources, including Edward J. Cashin's *The King's Ranger* and the *New Georgia Encyclopedia* (http://www. georgiaencyclopedia.org/nge/Home.jsp).

iii   *He'd made it.* The sometimes snobbish but always colourful Benjamin Marston probably deserves a book of his own. Though later sections will draw heavily on Marston's own diaries and letters, the information in this section comes primarily from the writings of others, including the Rev. John L. Watson's "The Marston Family of Salem, Mass.," W.O. Raymond's "The Marston Diaries," Violet Mary-Ann Showers' "The Price of Loyalty: The Case of Benjamin Marston," and Maud Maxwell Vesey's "Benjamin Marston, Loyalist."

iv   *David George stared nervously out into the motley gathering.* From David George's account. The role of the Dunmore proclamation is detailed in James Walker's *The Black Loyalists: The Search for a Promised Land in Nova Scotia and Sierra Leone 1783–1870.* You can learn more about the importance of the Silver Bluff church in "The Priority of the Silver Bluff Church and Its Promoters" in *The Journal of Negro History* (Vol. 7, No. 2, April 1922).

v   *There really was nowhere left to escape this madness.* What little we know of the Durfees' brief stay in Dartmouth comes from Mary Archibald's account of Durfee's life in *Eleven Exiles.* In preparing this work, she had access to Joseph Durfee's correspondence from this period.

vi   *At last! After lingering for more than a week at the mouth of Boston Harbor . . .* This section combines what we know of Marston's time in Boston from his letters with the historical record and a little reasonable extrapolation. Given his own penchant for gossip, for example, it's almost certain Marston would have been aware of the stories circulating about General Howe's mistress and her role in the British reversals in Boston. We don't know whether Marston spent any time with his cousin Gideon White or John Prince but, given the size of the loyalist contingent in the garrison, it's almost certain he would have been aware of their presence and, given his later partnership with Prince in his first West Indian venture, it's likely he would have discussed the idea with them at some point.

CHAPTER 2

i *In all likelihood, the moment only began to take on its mythic import* . . . Gideon White's papers are available at the Public Archives of Nova Scotia. Local historian Mary Archibald's *Gideon White, Loyalist* offers a helpful overview of his life and times. Information in this section about the history of the Shelburne area prior to the arrival of the Loyalists comes primarily from Marion Robertson's *King's Bounty* and Christopher Moore's *The Loyalists.*

ii *Benjamin Marston stood slack-jawed on the wharf* . . . In addition to Marston's own diaries and the various third-person accounts of his adventures, I have drawn on various histories of Santa Cruz and St. Eustatius to flesh out Marston's account, especially in terms of the relations between the island and the new United States.

iii *Like David George, the slave preacher* . . . Boston King's life story was originally published in serialized form in *The Methodist Magazine* from March to June 1798. I've used a very helpful annotated version of his memoir prepared by the Antislavery Literature Project at Arizona State University and published through the EServer at Iowa State University to put flesh on the bones of King's life. I also, of course, looked at other texts, including *The Book of Negroes* and James Walker's entry in the *Dictionary of Canadian Biography.* And I consulted a variety of other Web and printed sources to get background information on the plantation where he grew up, the role smallpox played in the revolutionary war, etc. Even with all of that, it's not always easy to divine accurate details from King's often sketchy narrative. Although his memoir does not name Mr. Waters as the man to whom his master apprentices him, for example, I believe from the context that Mr. Waters, the cruel man whose horse Boston King borrowed to go see his parents, and the equally cruel man to whom he was apprenticed are one and the same, and therefore I have written the narrative that way.

iv *Finally, Joseph Durfee had something to show for his efforts on behalf of the cause!* The disputes among the British military command leading up to the siege of Charles Town are recounted in William Willcox's "The British Road to Yorktown: A Study in Divided Command," in the "Journal of Captain Peter Russell, December 25, 1779 to May 2, 1780," and in Paul David Nelson's "British Conduct of the American Revolutionary War: A Review of Interpretations."

v *New York in the summer of 1781, as Benjamin Marston quickly discovered . . .* While the spine of this section comes from information in Marston's diaries, many of the details of life in occupied New York are drawn from other sources, including *The Battle for New York* by Barnet Schecter, *The New York Loyalists* by Philip Ranlet, *Rivington's New York Newspaper: Excerpts from a Loyalist Press 1773–1783* by Kenneth Scott, "The Loyalist Experience: New York 1763–1789" by Rick Ashton, "Garrison Town: The British Occupation of New York City 1776–1783" by William A. Polf, *New York's Buried Past: A Guide to Excavated New York City's Revolutionary War Artifacts* by Robert Apuzzo, *New York City during the War for Independence* by Oscar Theodore Barck, *Loyalism in New York during the American Revolution* and *The American Revolution in New York: Its Political, Social and Economic Significance*, both by Alexander Flick, and *So Obstinately Loyal* by Susan Burgess Shenstone.

vi *The news that swept through the city . . .* Willcox's "The British Road to Yorktown: A Study in Divided Command" provides the backdrop for the story of the British defeat at Yorktown.

vii *In London in the late fall of 1781 . . .* The story of Guy Carleton's appointment is told in Paul Reynolds' *Guy Carleton: A Biography* and in A.L. Burt's "Guy Carleton, Lord Dorchester, 1724–1808." The background on George Germain can be found in George Guttridge's "Lord Germain in Office, 1775–1782."

CHAPTER 3

i *Guy Carleton's world had unravelled quickly . . .* In addition to Reynolds' biography of Carleton, I've drawn on a variety of sources, including

Barnet Schecter's *The Battle for New York* and Shenstone's *So Obstinately Loyal* to describe Carleton's early days in New York.

ii   *John Parr was feeling more than a little smug.* Parr is a polarizing figure in loyalist history. Though reviled by many Loyalists of the day, later historians have treated him more kindly, accepting the impossibility of the tasks he would face. The account in this section is based on a number of sources, including Neil MacKinnon's "A Dearth of Miracles: Governor John Parr and the Settling of the Loyalists on Nova Scotia" and *This Unfriendly Soil*, as well as James MacDonald's "Memoir of Governor Parr." Wentworth's unhappiness at being passed over for the job is described in Bryan C. Cuthbertson's *The Loyalist Governor.*

iii   *"My time," said Benjamin Marston in a fit of melancholy* . . . Although built around Marston's journal entry for November 1, 1782, this section draws on most of that year's entries, as well as an entry from January 1783 in which he complains about a group of rowdy soldiers who've been living in the same inn as him since summer.

iv   *John Parr had glimpsed his future, and he didn't like what he'd seen.* The story of Parr's handling of the arrival of the Carolina refugees is based on Neil MacKinnon's *This Unfriendly Soil*, while the background on Parr's early relations with the Port Roseway Associates comes primarily from Marion Robertson's *King's Bounty.*

v   *The New York members of the Port Roseway Associates were not amused.* Much of the information in the following sections come from the *Minutes of the Port Roseway Associates* as well as Marion Robertson's *King's Bounty.* Descriptions of the chaos during the preparations for departure come primarily from Schecter's *The Battle for New York* and Moore's *The Loyalists.*

vi   *George Washington was aghast.* The story of the meeting between Washington and Carleton is described in great detail in William Smith's journal. That journal has been the basis of a number of wonderfully vivid accounts by later writers, including Adam Hochschild in *Bury the Chains* and Simon Schama in *Rough Crossings.*

CHAPTER 4

i   *You couldn't blame them.* These accounts of the arrival of the newcom-
     ers come from a number of sources, including Marion Robertson's
     King's Bounty, Judith Van Buskirk's *Generous Enemies*, and W. Stewart
     Wallace's *The United Empire Loyalists: A Chronicle of the Great Migration.*

ii   *The settlers weren't the only ones with plenty to keep them occupied.* William
     Lawson's orders are reprinted in W.O. Raymond's "Benjamin Marston
     at Halifax, Shelburne and Miramichi."

iii *David George knew it was another sign that God would provide.* The story of
     how the British took David George and his fellow slaves hostage is
     told in Edward Cashin's *The King's Ranger.*

iv   *If the cheers the Loyalists offered in response to his toasts . . .* Parr's visit to
     Shelburne is documented by a number of works, including
     MacKinnon's *This Unfriendly Soil* and Marion Robertson's *King's Bounty*,
     as well as in Benjamin Marston's diaries.

v   *"We did carefully inspect the aforegoing vessels . . ."* Though the focus of
     this section is Boston and Violet King, information about the inspec-
     tion process and the other passengers aboard *L'Abondance* is derived
     from a variety of sources: Simon Schama's *Rough Crossing*, James
     Walker's *Black Loyalists*, Ellen Gibson Wilson's *The Loyal Blacks*, and
     the *Book of Negroes*.

vi   *Alexander Watson had one, too.* Most of what I know about Margaret
     Watson and her family comes from her loyalist claim and from infor-
     mation compiled by the Shelburne County Genealogy Society for a
     family history.

vii *He was doing his best to complete the evacuation of New York . . .* Much of
     this part of the evacuation is documented in Reynolds' biography of
     Carleton. The story of Carleton's dinner with William Smith is
     referred to in "New York City during the American Revolution,"
     which was published privately by the Mercantile Library Association
     of the City of New York.

viii *The feud between George Panton . . .* There are many sources for the
     Panton–Walter feud, including the 1891 book *The Church of England in
     Nova Scotia and the Tory Clergy of the Revolution* by Arthur Wentworth
     Eaton. Neil MacKinnon also writes about it in *This Unfriendly Soil.*

ix   *Benjamin Marston was not impressed.* Van Buskirk's personal history in this section is drawn from his loyalist claim.

x   *As he sat down at his desk in Halifax on Tuesday, December 16, 1783 . . .* While the centrepiece of this section is Parr's letter to Shelburne, much of the information on the state of Shelburne's development comes from Robertson's *King's Bounty* and Raymond's "Benjamin Marston at Halifax, Shelburne and Miramichi." The background story of the Robertson brothers' various printing ventures before and during the revolution is told in Douglas McMurtrie's *The Royalist Printers at Shelburne, NS.*

CHAPTER 5

i   *It was a welcome worthy of a governor.* Wentworth's visit to Shelburne is chronicled in Brian Cuthbertson's *The Loyalist Governor.*

ii   *Brigadier-General John Campbell was not seeking the answer . . .* Information about the Muster of 1784, as well as the development of Shelburne's courts—and the crime that went with it—comes primarily from Robertson's *King's Bounty* and MacKinnon's *This Unfriendly Soil.* The tale of how Edward Winslow attempted to enlist his infant son as an ensign in order to qualify for half pay is contained in *The Winslow Papers.*

iii   *By the beginning of the first snows of the second winter . . .* This state-of-Shelburne section draws heavily on Robertson's *King's Bounty* and Neil MacKinnon's *This Unfriendly Soil,* with additional material from a variety of sources including McMurtrie's *The Royalist Printers at Shelburne* and J.P. Edward's "The Shelburne that was and was not" and "Vicissitudes of a Loyalist City."

CHAPTER 6

i   *William Booth had decided not to accompany his boss . . .* Booth's "Journal on a Tour with Genl. Campbell in July & August 1785" can be found in the *Report of the Public Archives of Nova Scotia for 1933.* The story of Booth's experiences in Gibraltar are in Whitworth Porter's *History of the Royal Corps of Engineers,* Volume 1.

ii   *The first official handbills announcing a new bylaw . . .* The primary source for this section is Robertson's *King's Bounty,* but the unequal treatment of the blacks in Shelburne and Birchtown is also well documented in Walker's *The Black Loyalists* and Wilson's *The Loyal Blacks*.

iii *All things considered, Benjamin Marston thought . . .* This section combines background from Marston's diaries about the context for his appearance before the claims commission along with a copy of his statement of claim and publicly available biographical information on the commissioner, Jeremy Pemberton.

iv *Not everyone was leaving Shelburne.* The saga of the Great East Jersey Treasury Robbery is told in Sheila Skemp's biography *William Franklin: Son of a Patriot Servant of a King*, as well as in *Benjamin and William Franklin, Father and Son, Patriot and Loyalist*. Skinner's biography is fleshed out in Susan Burgess Shenstone's *So Obstinately Loyal*. The previous relationship between Skinner and Stephen Blucke is referred to by a number of sources, including Laird Niven in "Was this the Home of Stephen Blucke?"

v *"I was very sorry to hear about the man from England . . ."* Freeborn Garrettson's adventures in Nova Scotia are recounted in Samuel Rogal's *The Wesleyan Connection in Shelburne and Birchtown* while John Marrant's ministry is the subject of John Saillant's "Wipe Away All Tears from Their Eyes: John Marrant's Theology in the Black Atlantic, 1785–1808" and Joanna Brooks's "John Marrant's Journal: Providence and Prophecy in 18th Century Black Atlantic." Information on Boston King's appointment and his feelings about it can be found in his autobiography.

vi *"The inhabitants of Shelburne from the highest to the lowest . . ."* Though this essay was published anonymously, the evidence that the author was Fraser is compelling ("Fraser's 'A Sketch on Shelburnian Manners'—anno 1787" in the *Nova Scotia Historical Review*, Vol. 10, No. 2, 1990). Fraser also served for a time as a district judge in New Brunswick and later became an important merchant in Halifax. You can find more background on the man who commissioned the essay in Sara Beanlands' "The Rev. Dr. Andrew Brown: Nova Scotia's Elusive Historian."

CHAPTER 7

i   *William Booth was not feeling well.* The story of William Booth's unhappy sojourn in Shelburne is contained in his "Remarks and Rough Memorandums." I was lucky enough to have access to a well-annotated version prepared by the Shelburne County Archives and Genealogical Society.

ii   *The most exciting event in Shelburne in the fall of 1788 . . .* Although fleshed out with material from other published sources, the primary source for this section is William Dyott's diary of his days—and nights—spent with the prince.

iii *In 1785, Shelburne boasted three newspapers.* The demise of Shelburne's newspapers is documented in McMurtrie's *The Royalist Printer at Shelburne* while the saga of the Swords family is told in Polly Hoppin's "The Thomas Swords Family." Neil MacKinnon's "The Changing Attitudes of the Nova Scotian Loyalists Towards the United States, 1783–1791" provides the underpinning for the story of the return of many of the Loyalists to the United States. Margaret Blucke's decision to return to New York and Stephen Blucke's apparent relationship with Isabella is referenced in Niven's "Was this the Home of Stephen Blucke?"

iv   *Boston King slowly, awkwardly plowed through the waist-high snow . . .* Walker's *The Black Loyalists* provides an excellent overview of the famine and its impact on blacks. John Marrant's encounter on the road from Birchtown to Shelburne is described by a number of authors, including Saillant in *Wipe Away All Tears from Their Eyes* and Rogal in *The Wesleyan Connection in Shelburne and Birchtown.*

v   *Shelburne's Anglicans had much to celebrate.* The story of the reconciliation of Shelburne's Anglicans is well told in Otto Lohrenz's biographical essay "The Reverend John Hamilton Rowland of Revolutionary America and Early Shelburne."

CHAPTER 8

i   *"Governor," the young man said . . .* There are, of course, many richly detailed accounts of John Clarkson's expedition to Nova Scotia, the black Loyalists' journey to Sierra Leone, and their early days in

Africa, including in Simon Schama's *Rough Crossings* and Adam Hochschild's *Bury the Chains*. Wilson's *The Loyal Blacks* and Walker's *The Black Loyalists* also contain many helpful references to the events of those days. As well, many journal articles explore the issues surrounding the exodus, including Monday Abasiattai's "The Search for Independence: New World Blacks in Sierra Leone and Liberia, 1787–1847" and A.P. Kup's "John Clarkson and the Sierra Leone Company."

ii *John Parr hesitantly swung his legs out from the coverless bed* . . . John Parr suffered from gout; according to the reports of the day, it would soon lead to his death. I don't know for certain whether he was coping with gout as he considered how to deal with the conflicting instructions from his superiors in London; that much is literary licence, but the rest—including those "two-faced" instructions and Parr's appointment of "unfriendly" agents to compile the lists of those blacks who wanted to leave—are well documented.

iii *Dead! No one had expected that!* Wentworth's response to Parr's death comes from Cuthbertson's *The Loyal Governor.*

iv *Gideon White had been convinced he had weathered the worst Shelburne had to offer* . . . While Mary Archibald's *Gideon White: Loyalist* provides the personal narrative, the more general story of the decline of Shelburne after the departure of the black Loyalists is well documented in, among other sources, Robertson's *King's Bounty.*

BIBLIOGRAPHY

Abasiattai, Monday B. "The Search for Independence: New World Blacks in Sierra Leone and Liberia, 1787–1847." *Journal of Black Studies*, Vol. 23, No. 1 (1992).

Alden, John R. *A History of the American Revolution*. New York: Da Capo Press, 1969.

Apuzzo, Robert. *New York's Buried Past: A Guide to Excavated New York City's Revolutionary War Artifacts*. New York: R&L Publishing, 1992.

Archibald, Mary. *Gideon White: Loyalist*. Shelburne, NS: Shelburne Historical Society, 1975.

Archibald, Mary. *Rules and Orders of the Friendly Fire Club, Shelburne 1784*. Halifax: Petheric Press, 1982.

Archibald, Mary, Elizabeth deMolitor, and Cathy Holmes. *Loyalist Dress in Nova Scotia*. Shelburne, NS: Shelburne County Museum, 1982.

Ashton, Rick J. "The Loyalist Experience: New York 1763–1789." Unpublished Ph.D. thesis, Northwestern University, 1973.

Atkinson, Heather Doane, and Eleanor Robertson Smith. *Land of My Fathers*. Yarmouth, NS: Stoneycroft Publishing, 1989.

Barck, Oscar Theodore, Jr. *New York City during the War for Independence*. New York: Columbia University Press, 1931.

Beanlands, Sara. "The Rev. Dr. Andrew Brown: Nova Scotia's Elusive Historian." *Journal of the Nova Scotia Historical Society*, Vol. 9 (2006).

Blakeley, Phyllis R., and John N. Grant (eds). *Eleven Exiles: Accounts of Loyalists of the American Revolution*. Toronto: Dundurn Press, 1982.

Booth, William. "William Booth's Memorandums." Shelburne County Archives and Genealogical Society. Transcription of Capt. William Booth's Diary. Originals at Vaughan Memorial Library, Acadia University, Wolfville, NS.

Bradley, A.G. *Colonial Americans in Exile*. New York: E.P. Dutton & Co., 1932.

Brooks, Joanna. "John Marrant's Journal: Providence and Prophecy in 18th Century Black Atlantic." *The North Star: A Journal of African American Religious History*, Vol. 3, No. 1 (Fall 1999).

Brooks, Walter H. "The Priority of the Silver Bluff Church and Its Promoters." *The Journal of Negro History*, Vol. 7, No. 2 (April 1922).

317

Burt, A.L. "Guy Carleton, Lord Dorchester, 1724–1808 (Revised Version)." Ottawa: The Canadian Historical Association, 1960.

Buzek, Beatrice Ross. "By Fortune Wounded: Loyalist Women in Nova Scotia." *Nova Scotia Historical Review*, Vol. 7 (1987).

Cahill, Barry. "Stephen Blucke: The Perils of Being a White Negro in Loyalist Nova Scotia." *Nova Scotia Historical Review*, Vol. 11, No. 1 (1991).

Cashin, Edward J. *The King's Ranger*. New York: Fordham University Press, 1999.

Coldham, Peter Wilson. *American Loyalist Claims*. Washington, DC: National Genealogical Society, 1980.

Coldham, Peter Wilson. *American Migrations: 1765–1799*. Baltimore, MD: Genealogical Publishing Co. Inc., 2000.

Cook, Don. *The Long Fuse: How England Lost the American Colonies, 1760–1785*. New York: Atlantic Monthly Press, 1995.

Crary, Catherine Snell. "The Tory and the Spy: The Double Life of James Rivington." *The William and Mary Quarterly*, 3rd Series, Vol. 16, No. 1 (January 1959).

Cuthbertson, Brian C. *The Loyalist Governor*. Halifax, NS: Petheric Press, 1983.

Edwards, J.P. "The Shelburne that was and was not." *Dalhousie Review*, Vol. 1, No. 1 (1922).

Edwards, J.P. "Vicissitudes of a Loyalist City." *Dalhousie Review*, Vol. 1, No. 2 (1922).

Fenn, Elizabeth A. *The Great Smallpox Epidemic of 1775–82*. New York: Hill & Wang, 2001.

Flick, Alexander Clarence. *Loyalism in New York during the American Revolution*. Honolulu, HI: University Press of the Pacific, 2002.

Flick, Alexander Clarence (ed). *The American Revolution in New York: Its Political, Social and Economic Significance*. Albany, NY: University of the State of New York, 1926.

Fraser, James. "Fraser's 'A Sketch of Shelburnian Manners—Anno 1787.'" *Nova Scotia Historical Review*, Vol. 10, No. 2 (1990).

George, David. "An Account of Life of David George from S.L.A. Given by Himself." http://collections.ic.gc.ca/blackloyalists/documents/diaries/george_a_life.htm.

Guttridge, George H. "Lord Germain in Office, 1775–1782." *The American Historical Review*, Vol. 33, No. 1 (October 1927).

Harding, Anne Borden. "The Port Roseway Debacle: Some American Loyalists in Nova Scotia." *The New England Historical and Genealogical Register*, Vol. 117 (January 1963).

Hartzell, Joseph C. "Methodism and the Negro in the United States." *The Journal of Negro History*, Vol. 8, No. 3 (July 1923).

Harvey, Mary Mackay. "Gardens of Shelburne, Nova Scotia 1785–1820." *Bulletin of the Association for Preservation Technology*, Vol. 7, No. 2 (1975).

Hochschild, Adam. *Bury the Chains.* New York: First Mariner Books, 2005.

Hoerder, Dirk. *Crowd Action in Revolutionary Massachusetts, 1765–1780.* New York: Academic Press, 1977.

Hoppin, Polly. "The Thomas Swords Family." 1976. http://www.rootsweb.com/~nysarato/swords.html.

Ketchum, Richard M. *Divided Loyalties: How the American Revolution Came to New York.* New York: Henry Holt and Company, 2002.

Kup, A.P. "John Clarkson and the Sierra Leone Company." *The International Journal of African Historical Studies*, Vol. 5, No. 2 (1972).

Lindsay, Arnett G. "Diplomatic Relations between the United States and Great Britain Bearing on the Return of Negro Slaves, 1783–1828." *The Journal of Negro History*, Vol. 5, No. 4 (October 1920).

Lohrenz, Otto. "The Reverend John Hamilton Rowland of Revolutionary America and Early Shelburne." *Nova Scotia Historical Review*, Vol. 17, No. 1 (1987).

MacDonald, James S. "Memoir of Governor Parr." *Nova Scotia Historical Society*, Vol. 14 (1909).

MacKinnon, Neil. "The Changing Attitudes of the Nova Scotian Loyalists Towards the United States, 1783–1791." *Acadiensis*, Vol. 5, No. 1 (1973).

MacKinnon, Neil. "A Dearth of Miracles: Governor John Parr and the Settling of the Loyalists in Nova Scotia." *Nova Scotia Historical Review*, Vol. 15, No. 1 (1995).

MacKinnon, Neil. *This Unfriendly Soil.* Kingston, ON: McGill-Queen's University Press, 1986.

Mathews, Hazel C. *The Mark of Honour.* Toronto: University of Toronto Press, 1965.

McCullough, David. *1776.* Audiobook.

McMurtrie, Douglas C. *The Royalist Printers at Shelburne, NS.* Chicago: privately printed, 1933.

Mercantile Library Association of the City of New York. "New York City during the American Revolution." New York: privately printed, 1861.

Moore, Christopher. *The Loyalists: Revolution, Exile, Settlement.* Toronto: Macmillan of Canada, 1984.

Nelson, Paul David. "British Conduct of the American Revolutionary War: A Review of Interpretations." *The Journal of American History,* Vol. 65, No. 3 (December 1978).

Niven, Laird. *Birchtown Archaeological Survey (1993).* Lockeport, NS: Roseway Publishing, 1994.

Niven, Laird. "Was this the Home of Stephen Blucke?" Halifax, NS: Nova Scotia Museum, 2000.

Polf, William A. "Garrison Town: The British Occupation of New York City 1776–1783." Albany, NY: New York State American Revolution Bicentennial Commission, 1976.

Porter, Whitworth. *History of the Corps of Royal Engineers, Volume 1.* Chatham, UK: The Institution of Royal Engineers, 1889.

Raddall, Thomas H. *The Path of Destiny.* Toronto: Doubleday & Company, 1957.

Randall, Willard Sterne. *A Little Revenge: Benjamin Franklin at War with his Son.* New York: William Morrow, 1984.

Ranlet, Philip. *The New York Loyalists.* New York: University Press of America, 2002.

Raphael, Ray. *A People's History of the American Revolution.* New York: The New Press, 2001.

Raymond, W.O. "Benjamin Marston at Halifax, Shelburne and Miramichi." http://ultratext.hil.unb.ca/Texts/Marston/articles/Shelburne.html.

Raymond, W.O. "Benjamin Marston of Marblehead, Loyalist." http://ultratext.hil.unb.ca/Texts/Marston/articles/NBHS.html.

Raymond, W.O. (ed.) *The Winslow Papers a.d. 1776–1826.* Manotick, ON: Archive CD Books Canada, 2004. Originally published 1901.

Reynolds, Paul. *Guy Carleton: A Biography.* Toronto: Gage Publishing, 1980.

Robertson, Marion. *King's Bounty: A History of Early Shelburne.* Halifax, NS: Nova Scotia Museum, 1983.

Rogal, Samuel J. *The Wesleyan Connection in Shelburne and Birchtown.* Studies in the History of Missions, Volume 20. Queenston, ON: Edwin Mellen Press, 2000.

Ross, Beatrice Spence. *Adaptation in Exile: Loyalist Women in Nova Scotia.* Ph.D. thesis, Cornell University, 1981.

Russell, Peter. "The Siege of Charleston: Journal of Captain Peter Russell, December 25, 1779, to May 2, 1780." *The American Historical Review,* Vol. 4, No. 3 (April 1899).

Saillant, John. "Wipe Away All Tears from Their Eyes: John Marrant's Theology in the Black Atlantic, 1785–1808." The African Commune, africancommune.com, 2005.

Schama, Simon. *Rough Crossings.* New York: HarperCollins, 2006.

Schecter, Barnet. *The Battle for New York.* New York: Penguin Books, 2002.

Scott, Kenneth. *Rivington's New York Newspaper: Excerpts from a Loyalist Press 1773–1783.* New York: New York Historical Society, 1973.

Shenstone, Susan Burgess. *So Obstinately Loyal.* Montreal: McGill-Queen's University Press, 2000.

Showers, Violet Mary-Anne. "The Price of Loyalty: The Case of Benjamin Marston." Unpublished M.A. thesis, University of New Brunswick, 1982.

Skemp, Sheila L. *Benjamin and William Franklin, Father and Son, Patriot and Loyalist.* New York: Bedford St. Martin, 1994.

Skemp, Sheila L. *William Franklin: Son of a Patriot, Servant of a King.* New York: Oxford University Press, 1990.

Smith, Pauline B. *Ladder Laddies: The Shelburne Volunteer Firefighters.* Shelburne, NS: Shelburne Volunteer Fire Department, 1999.

Stewart, Walter. *True Blue.* Don Mills, ON: Collins, 1985.

Van Buskirk, Judith L. *Generous Enemies.* Philadelphia: University of Pennsylvania Press, 2002.

Van Tyne, Claude Halstead. *Loyalists in the American Revolution.* New York: Macmillan Company, 1902.

Vesey, Maud Maxwell. "Benjamin Marston, Loyalist." *The New England Quarterly,* Vol. 15.4 (December 1942).

Walker, James W. St. G. *The Black Loyalists: The Search for a Promised Land in Nova Scotia and Sierra Leone 1783–1870.* Toronto: University of Toronto Press, 1999.

Washington, George. "Letters of George Washington Bearing on the Negro." *The Journal of Negro History*, Vol. 2, No. 4 (October 1917).

Watson, John L. "The Marston Family of Salem, Mass." *The New England Historical and Genealogical Register*, Vol. 27.

Wetherell, Charles, and Robert W. Roetger. "Another look at the Loyalists of Shelburne, NS, 1783–1795." *Canadian Historical Review*, Vol. 70, No. 1 (1989).

Willcox, William B. "The British Road to Yorktown: A Study in Divided Command." *The American Historical Review*, Vol. 52, No. 1 (October 1946).

Wilson, Ellen Gibson. *The Loyal Blacks*. New York: G.P. Putnam, 1976.

Wright, Esther Clark. "The Evacuation of the Loyalists from New York in 1783." *Nova Scotia Historical Review*, Vol. 4, No. 1 (1984).

Wright, Esther Clark. *The Loyalists of New Brunswick*. Lancelot Press, 1955.

INDEX

Note: Page numbers followed by the letter n (e.g., 72n) refer to footnotes on those pages.